The Poetics of the Sensible

Explorations in Philosophy and Theology

Series Editors: Kevin Hart (University of Virginia, USA) and Jeffrey Bloechl (Boston College, USA)

This series promotes philosophical and theological works committed to drawing on both disciplines, without either holding them strictly apart or overlooking important differences between them. The series favors philosophical approaches covered under the umbrella of "continental European," by which is meant a general commitment to developments sharpened since the work of Kant, German idealism, and Nietzsche. It provides a space for theological approaches historically informed and actively engaged via modern thought and culture. The series will focus on Christian theology in the first instance, but not to the exclusion of work in dialogue with multiple religions. Expanding the historical and cultural origins of both continental European philosophy and Christian theology, the series will embrace a global outlook. The series thus provides a platform for work from Africa, Asia, Australia, North and South America. Featuring edited collections, single-authored works, and translations managed by an active and global editorial board, the series is one of the main destinations for scholarship in the continental philosophy of religion today.

Editorial Board

Sarah Coakley, University of Cambridge, UK
Werner Jeanrond, University of Oslo, Norway
Jean-Yves Lacoste, Paris
Adriaan Peperzak, Loyola University of Chicago, USA
Pheme Perkins, Boston College, USA
David Tracy, University of Chicago, USA
Claudia Welz, Aarhus University, Denmark
Olivier Boulnois, École Pratique des Hautes Études, France
Nythamar de Oliveira, Pontifical Catholic University of Rio Grande do Sul, Brazil
James Heisig, Nanzan Institute for Religion and Culture, Japan
Robyn Horner, Australian Catholic University, Australia
Leonard Katchekpele, University of Strasbourg, France
Judith Wolfe, Durham University, UK

Available Titles

By Faith Alone, by Lev Shestov and translated by Stephen P. Van Trees
The Book of Experience, by Emmanuel Falque and translated by George Hughes
Anthropomorphism in Christian Theology, by William C. Hackett

The Poetics of the Sensible

Stanislas Breton

Translated by Sarah Horton

BLOOMSBURY ACADEMIC
LONDON • NEW YORK • OXFORD • NEW DELHI • SYDNEY

BLOOMSBURY ACADEMIC

Bloomsbury Publishing Plc, 50 Bedford Square, London, WC1B 3DP, UK
Bloomsbury Publishing Inc, 1385 Broadway, New York, NY 10018, USA
Bloomsbury Publishing Ireland, 29 Earlsfort Terrace, Dublin 2, D02 AY28, Ireland

BLOOMSBURY, BLOOMSBURY ACADEMIC and the Diana logo
are trademarks of Bloomsbury Publishing Plc

First published in 1988 in France as *Poétique du Sensible* by Les Éditions du Cerf

First published in Great Britain 2024
This paperback edition published 2025

Copyright © Les Éditions du Cerf, 1988

English language translation © Sarah Horton 2024

Sarah Horton has asserted her right under the Copyright,
Designs and Patents Act, 1988, to be identified as Translator of this work.

Series design: Ben Anslow
Photography © Sashanna Hart

All rights reserved. No part of this publication may be: i) reproduced or transmitted in any form, electronic or mechanical, including photocopying, recording or by means of any information storage or retrieval system without prior permission in writing from the publishers; or ii) used or reproduced in any way for the training, development or operation of artificial intelligence (AI) technologies, including generative AI technologies. The rights holders expressly reserve this publication from the text and data mining exception as per Article 4(3) of the Digital Single Market Directive (EU) 2019/790.

Bloomsbury Publishing Inc does not have any control over, or responsibility for, any third-party websites referred to or in this book. All internet addresses given in this book were correct at the time of going to press. The author and publisher regret any inconvenience caused if addresses have changed or sites have ceased to exist, but can accept no responsibility for any such changes.

A catalogue record for this book is available from the British Library.

A catalog record for this book is available from Library of Congress.

ISBN: HB: 978-1-3503-8685-3
PB: 978-1-3503-8705-8
ePDF: 978-1-3503-8686-0
eBook: 978-1-3503-8687-7

Series: Explorations in Philosophy and Theology

Typeset by Integra Software Services Pvt. Ltd.

For product safety related questions contact productsafety@bloomsbury.com.

To find out more about our authors and books visit www.bloomsbury.com
and sign up for our newsletters.

For Annick

Contents

Preface: The Poetics of the Sensible		viii
Translator's Note		xxiv
Introduction		1
1	Sensible, Sense, Sensibility	3
2	The *Meta* Function	25
3	Mask and Metastasis	43
4	The Angel's Wing: The Feast of the Ascension and of Metaphor	53
5	The Metamorphoses of Fire	75
6	Flavors, Fragrances, Colors	87
7	The Abode	97
8	Figure, Image, Icon	107
Notes		136
Bibliography		147
Index		150

Preface: The Poetics of the Sensible

Jean Greisch

The text whose English translation one will read here originated in the last seminar that Stanislas Breton gave in the Department of Philosophy of the Catholic Institute of Paris in 1985. It was his Farewell to the last of the many generations of students who had taken his classes in Paris. This philosopher who tenaciously practiced the art of gardening knew that much care and lasting patience are necessary before one can gather a tree's ripe fruits.

I retain a particularly keen memory of the first meeting of the seminar, at the end of which a Japanese student was imploring the professor for a bibliography. In his inimitable gravelly voice, Breton answered him, "Ah, yes, of course, the secondary bibliography! Well, take a sunset at the seaside, a night sky strewn with stars in the desert, and a child's smile: this will amply suffice for you as far as bibliographical information is concerned!" The reader who will leaf through the pages of *Poetics of the Sensible*, a work that includes no footnotes, will easily be persuaded that this remark was more than a mere witticism.

Poetics of the Sensible or Poetics of the Imagination: A False Choice

Before approaching this work, it is useful to distinguish two axes of reflection that both take Husserl's phenomenology as their point of departure and that can be designated by the terms "poetics of the sensible" and "poetics of the imagination."

1. The keyword of the first axis is "perception." Putting himself in a precarious position against any reductive sensualism, Husserl took Kant's formula at its word, judging that the world's readability depends on the possibility of synthesizing the chaotic muddle of our sensations in order to transform them into contents of experience. The royal road of this synthesis is perception, which offers us the "presence in the flesh" (*leibhafte Gegebenheit*) of the thing itself, thus fulfilling phenomenology's fundamental watchword: "To the things themselves!"

As soon as 1935, the same rejection of sensualism found a remarkable development in Erwin Straus's *Vom Sinn der Sinne* [*On the Sense of the Senses*].[1]

"To sense," declared Straus, "is to not know wholly: it is to leave to the thing sensed its power and its mystery. It is to devolve; therefore it is to lack a point of view; either one perceives space to know its perspective, or one senses the place to feel [*éprouver*] its immanence and its opacity. Sensing is to knowing as the caress is to palpating, as breath—the suspension of the word and its physical carrier—is to the linguistic message, as the moment of attraction or fright is to the stasis of the 'I think' and the representation that results from it."[2] This declaration furnishes us with an excellent key for approaching Breton's *Poetics of the Sensible*.

On the same axis, Maurice Merleau-Ponty's *Phenomenology of Perception* and his posthumous writings gathered under the title *The Visible and the Invisible* must be mentioned. From them I extract a single citation, often commented upon: "Unto where does my perception extend? Unto the stars."[3] One can relate it to the magnificent "Ballad of Nadine" with which Breton concludes his *Poetics of the Sensible*, evoking the play of the world in the hand of a little girl seeking to embrace the constellation of Orion's shield.

That which organizes what Merleau-Ponty names a "synthesis of transition" is the proper body or the flesh, endowed with an expressive force that grounds and renders possible an elementary comprehension of the world. Only one who inhabits his body can also inhabit things, language, and, finally, the world itself.[4] When, in a famous passage of the First Letter to the Corinthians, Saint Paul describes the human body as a "temple of the Holy Spirit,"[5] he is not indulging in edifying rhetorical overkill but is appealing to the indisputable experience of the intimacy of the relation that we maintain with our bodies. The lived body, the *Leib* (the "flesh"), insofar as it is distinguished from the objective anatomical body (*Körper*), is not a mere instrument that can be manipulated from the exterior like a marionette.

The proper body, the flesh that we are and that is constitutive of our ipseity, and that which Merleau-Ponty names the "flesh of the world" are not distinct phenomena but rather two sides of the same coin. David Abram's work *The Spell of the Sensuous* shows that we are far from having exhausted the consequences of this approach.[6]

2. Before specifying in what sense this first axis justifies the name "poetics of the sensible," let us quickly turn to the second axis of reflection, which has as its keystone the duo of the imaginary and the imagination, to which one could add the term "imaginal," in the way Henry Corbin used it. In his work *Poetics of Imagining*,[7] Richard Kearney presents the main protagonists of such a reflection, from Husserl to certain postmodern philosophers, passing via Sartre, Bachelard, Merleau-Ponty, and Ricœur, to which one can add Kearney's own *Poétique du possible* [*Poetics of the Possible*].[8]

Even though we must not conflate these two axes, of which the first has as its center of gravity the habitability of the world and the second the distinction, or rather the joint, between the sense of the real and the sense of the possible,[9] it is not as if we were dealing with two parallel lines that would intersect only at infinity. We find an indication of this as soon as the first page of *Poetics of the Sensible*, where Breton evokes a "power of unreality that makes all things iridescent," lacking which the human would topple into unreality.

Metaphysics, Ontology, Staurology: Three Summits

A brief retrospective look at this philosopher's proteiform oeuvre and his intellectual itinerary confirms the importance of these overlaps.

Without retracing in detail the different stages of that itinerary, which he himself recapitulated in *De Rome à Paris* [*From Rome to Paris*],[10] we can compare it to the ascending of three summits that, in his mind, belonged to one and the same mountain range and that he climbed successively in *Du Principe* [*On the Principle*] (1971), *Être, Monde et Imaginaire* [*Being, World, and Imaginary*] (1976), and *Le Verbe et la Croix* [*The Word and the Cross*][11] (1981).

1. Dedicated to his "unknown parents and to the unknown God," *Du Principe* forms the summit of a speculative thought nourished by the great texts of the tradition, in particular by Neoplatonic henology, which invites us to distinguish the notion of the Cause that is reflected in the effects it produces and that of the Principle that in no way resembles what derives from it.

Breton distinguishes the notion of the Principle from that of the beginning and of the origin. Beginnings are multiple, just like ends; the Origin in the proper sense is declined in the singular, a singular of which Breton distinguishes two faces: the "first dawn of things" and the "first dawn of the magician" (the very one to which Abram's phrase "spell of the sensuous" applies), each one referring to different sensibilities.

Just as *starting* and *initiating* are not the same, "finishing" [*finir*] and "completing" do not amount to the same thing. For Breton, "archeology" and "eschatology" always walk hand in hand. If the *Alpha* has the splendor of the initial, so too the *Omega* cannot be reduced to a simple "endgame" [*fin de partie*].

To say and think the Principle, the philosopher invents a discourse that is neither that of science nor that of an originary word, be it mythic or religious. This discourse appeals to the "*meta* function," to which Chapter 2 of *Poetics of the Sensible* is devoted, but which in reality governs all the work's developments.

The phrase "the joy of seeing the same otherwise"[12] is well suited to the intrinsic link that connects *Du Principe* to *Poetics of the Sensible*. Nothing would be more wrong than placing the sensible and the intelligible in opposition. Retracing the innumerable versions of the myth of the cave that punctuate the history of Western philosophy, Hans Blumenberg suggests reading the myth of the cave as that of philosophy, full stop.[13] But the same author cautions us against the temptation of hiding behind the first phrase of Aristotle's *Metaphysics*, highlighting the privilege of vision and of hearing, outside of which we would supposedly be condemned to blind gropings that would never lead to a knowledge worthy of the name.

The well-understood idea of the Principle carries us beyond this sort of dichotomy by suggesting that what is last in a certain order can be first in another order and engender precisely that which conditions it.

In the sixth chapter of *Du Principe*, Breton formulates three postulates that illuminate in advance the metaphysical background of *Poetics of the Sensible*.

The first ("henological") stipulates that "every multiple, whatever it may be, is and is thinkable only as a function of the one," which excludes the notion of "dissemination" that we encounter under the pen of Jacques Derrida. The second ("ontogenetic") makes the multiple the result of an "originating mediation," such that "the being of things sways between a first dawn and an Ash Wednesday." The third ("epistrophic," forged from the Greek *épistrophè*, "return" or "conversion") transforms the labor of thinking into an unceasing conversion.

A world in which these three metaphysical postulates are no longer valid ceases to be a "universe" and becomes what the German philosopher Odo Marquard calls a "multiverse." In such a world, nothing "flows from the source" any longer; all is subject to a universal pulverizing whose possibility the Biblical Qohelet glimpsed. Everything goes on forever and ever, and there will never be anything new under the sun.

To better resist this temptation that he himself has experienced at times, Breton proposes to us a practical imperative: "Faced with all that happens, never be content with the mere fact; seek, below what happens, that by which it is what it is. Pure facticity is impossible to think; it is always to be constructed."[14] *Poetics of the Sensible* can be read as an attempt to verify the pertinence of this imperative even in the depths of fundamental sensing by wagering on the fact that "all that, with the distinction of the inaugural, bears the human fingerprint presupposes a sort of enchantment that, more than a simple lullaby, would be the cradle of a new world."[15]

More than to the eternal recurrence of the same, Breton shows himself to be sensitive [*sensible*] "to the irruption over the rock walls of an act of creation."[16] When, in the darkness of Lascaux, he contemplates the shadow of a hand, the breath of a soul, the unlimitedness of a space, he deciphers there the first traces of that "*meta* function" whose most remarkable unfoldings *Poetics of the Sensible* interrogates.

2. Breton often affirmed that one day or another every philosopher must write his *Theaetetus*, his *Parmenides*, and his *Sophist*, that is, propose a theory of knowledge, a metaphysics, and an ontology. The declaration of the Eleatic Stranger that Heidegger cites as an epigraph to *Being and Time* could also be placed in Breton's mouth: "So since we're quite puzzled about it all, it's for you to explain what exactly you want to indicate when you utter the word 'being.' Clearly you've known all along; until now we thought we did, but now we find ourselves puzzled."[17]

Present from his *Approches phénoménologiques de l'être* [*Phenomenological Approaches to Being*] onward, his ontological preoccupation found its completed expression in *Être, Monde et Imaginaire*, a complement and almost a twin work to *Du Principe*. If *Du Principe* is Breton's *Parmenides*, *Être, Monde et Imaginaire*, in which he develops his conception of the relations of being and of the world, is his *Sophist*.

From Aristotle to Brentano and Heidegger, philosophers have confronted the enigma of the multiple significations of being [*étant*], which, for Breton, means that they must avoid dissociating in being [*être*] the unity that orders and the fecundity that multiplies and must think rigor and movement simultaneously.

The chief originality of Breton's analytic of being is that it has the form of a diptych: *ontology* and *ontomythology*.

His first deduction of the senses of being, that of *ontology* properly so called, leans on wanting-to-say [*vouloir-dire*][18] and wanting-to-be and is expressed in propositional language. The proposition is the condition of possibility of any "judgment," that is, of a taking-position that expresses the able-to of a wanting-to-be. Its essence consists in positing what it proposes by composing it, either as a position of existence or as a position of determination. By making manifest the powers of being qua wanting-to-be, it sets us on the path of a definition of being.

"Insofar as we are, we are only by Being, and as beings, we feed on Being," declared Meister Eckhart, adding, "Thus every being eats God as Being, and every being thirsts for Being."[19] Ontology is first and fundamentally a matter of hunger and thirst for being and, conjointly, of hunger and thirst for meaning. Understood in this sense, being "is but the syncopated formula of a wanting-to-be," itself oriented toward a should-be. Where there is *Wollen* [want], there is also a *Sollen* [should].

But nothing guarantees for us that wanting-to-be and should-be exhaust all the significations of being. *Ontology* properly so called is focused on three senses of being that are so many powers: the power of *synthesis*, transcending any dreamt-of simplicity but also the absolutely diverse of dissemination; the power of *position* in the triple sense of the *exteriority* of all that is imposed on us without us, of active *production*, and of *existence*; the power of *self-affirmation*, of which the Spinozist *causa sui*, in which everything comes down to "an affirmation that gives itself, in the determinations that it posits and that it binds, the means of its effectuation," is the hyperbolical expression.

This analytic of the powers of being allows the distinguishing of three types of ontology: a formal ontology as the discipline of the possible in its purity, in other words a "white ontology" that has the means to charm all those who are haunted by the dream of the *mathesis universalis*; an ontology of the pure position for which the world and being itself is nothing other than the sum of all that is the case—an ontology of the solipsist affirmation of being similar to Fichte's *Tathandlung*.

Refusing the dichotomy of *logos* and *mythos*, Breton wagers on their necessary complementarity. The ontological discourse that is the "saying of a will whose powers the logos of being declares" is not the only possibility for speaking of being. The poets, like Hölderlin or Saint-John Perse, evoking a "very high gaze cast over the breadth of things and over the course of being, its measure," are equally capable of it, precisely because their language is not a simple gloss of philosophical ontologies. As Heidegger has emphasized many times, when the chorus of the *Antigone* evokes the most uncanny of beings [*êtres*] that is man, Sophocles proposes to us an "ontology," the one whose contours Breton seeks to outline by speaking of *ontomythology*.

Ontomythology proceeds to a triple reduction of logos, thought as order, as all, and as system, by highlighting the significations of being that drive mytho-poetic language. From the *propositional* language "that states by declaring," we cross over [*passons*] to the *prepositional* language "that illuminates by making manifest." The being [*être*] that first gives itself to be thought as a power of liaison, of position, and of affirmation is manifested in the ontomythological register, as light and glory, in an echo of the verse of the Psalm that medieval thinkers loved to quote: "In your Light we see the light."[20]

The fact that Breton's discourse on being qua being unfolds in the double register of ontology and ontomythology is not a flaw; quite the contrary. With regard to the thought of being also, man is a two-legged animal. It is by relying on the two legs of ontology and ontomythology that he advances in his understanding of being.

The very existence of this double register refers us to a beyond of this duality. Just as Plato, in a famous passage of the *Republic*, envisioned the possibility that the idea of the Good carries the thinker "beyond being" (*epekeina tès ousias*),[21] Breton, faithful to Neoplatonic henology, speaks of a "seed of non-being" that transcends the principle of reason that governs ontology just as much as the principle of gratuity that governs ontomythology. If being lends itself to this sort of transgression, it is because "the two figures that divide it into *logos* and *mythos* say to us, by their mutual limitation, something other than themselves."

"I need dreams to waken me to reality," admits Breton, proof that the thinker is also a dreamer. But nothing indicates that when he begins to dream he ceases to think. He simply thinks otherwise, by appealing to a particular imaginary that he designates by the term *imaginary nothing*. Prior to *logos* and *mythos*, there is the infinity of the seed of non-being that the imaginary-nothing strives to think. It alone permits thinking being-*logos* as the process of figuration and being-*mythos* as the play of overabundance.

Supposing that this ultimate source of being and the world is thinkable, is it for all that sayable, or does it transcend the resources of human language? For that it is necessary to envision a founding *word* more originary than that of *logos* and *mythos*. Breton designates it with the term *Fable*, which is not unreminiscent of the *Saying* (*Sage*) of which Heidegger speaks in *On the Way to Language*.

By speaking of the "Fable," Breton emphasizes a kinship with the notion of the "ineffable" of negative theologies: "the ineffable, by the Word, is made fable." The Fable enacts the imaginary as "that on the basis of which" forms can arise, but it can just as well take the path of overabundance and excess.

All these distinctions lead to an original conception of the relations between being and the world that Breton develops in the second part of the book. In view of *Poetics of the Sensible*, we will retain above all the thesis that from the outset the expressions of being-in and being-toward are equally necessary for understanding the ties that man weaves with his environment, even as he transcends it, because man, unlike animals, is open to the world as such.

3. More briefly, I will evoke the third summit that Breton, a philosopher and a priest belonging to the Congregation of the Passionists, never ceased to climb, within the framework of what he called his "trilogy of the Passion" that found its ultimate expression in 1981 in *The Word and the Cross*.

Not only is he one of the few philosophers who have dared to climb the naked summit of Golgotha, but, which merits notice, his audacious meditation on what he called the Pauline "staurological ternary," *Logos* ("Word"), *Moria* ("Folly"), *Dynamis* ("Power") appeals to the same fundamental polarity of "being-toward" and "being-in" that forms the guiding thread of *Poetics of the Sensible*. His reflections on "the exhilarating and redoubtable mission of recording, in its figures and its transfigurations, the power of the Cross," place the emphasis more strongly on "being-for," concerning which one can wonder, with Levinas, if it does not presuppose a thin-skinned sensitivity-vulnerability [*sensibilité-vulnerabilité*] irreducible to the gnoseological role of sensation.[22] Nothing, therefore, supports the hypothesis that in comparison with the austerity of *The Word and the Cross*, *Poetics of the Sensible* would be only a pleasant diversion.

"O My Poetic Soul": Fundamental Sensing and the Experience of the World

"*O my prophetic soul!*"[23] exclaims Hamlet when his father's ghost confirms to him what he has already guessed: that his father's assassin is his own uncle!

"*O my poetic soul*" would be an excellent epigraph for *Poetics of the Sensible*, which is anything but a treatise on aesthetics. There the philosopher goes to a "nonlocalizable place where the poetic is sensed in a sort of resonance or resounding." His investigation of the multiple ways that we feel the world in which we are, without being of it, could be placed under the aegis of an Aristotelian adage that finds a broad echo in medieval thinkers: "*anima est quodammodo omnia*," "the soul is, in a certain way, all things."[24]

What is proper to man is his capacity to "make fire from any wood,"[25] in other words to make use of all things with an eye to a certain end. This affirmation does not lead us back to a reductive utilitarianism. The use that we make of things has the merit of being an ontological detector that could be expressed in the following phrase: "Tell me how you make use of things, and I will tell you *who you are* and *what* the things are."

Placing the self at the center of the world (everything concerns *me*) and making man the center of the universe (anthropocentrism: everything exists only for man) are not at all the same thing! "What regards me," emphasizes Rémi Brague, "is vaster than what it falls to me to *do* because of having chosen it. My life concerns me above anything else, and perhaps even to the exclusion of anything else. I did not, however, choose it."[26]

Man is the universal animal in both senses of the word: all aspects of the universe meet in him; he has the capacity to open himself to the universe entire. This openness to the universal is not limited to the human soul alone. Anaxagoras had already noticed the deft use that man makes of his hands.[27] For Aristotle, the human hand is distinguished from animals' prehensile organs by the fact that it too is, in a certain way, capable of doing everything.[28] Not being specialized after the fashion of an instrument, it "knows how to do everything." "Instrument of instruments,"[29] it "is all these things because it is capable of grasping and holding them all."[30] Aristotle himself highlights the link between the hand, "instrument of instruments," and the soul, "form of forms."[31]

There is a profound relation between the hand, capable of taking hold of everything, and *phronésis*, capable of envisioning life in its totality: "*Phronésis* is [...] in the domain of *praxis* what the hand is in that of *poiésis*. It is something like the means of means."

A third of Aristotle's observations about the thinness and the texture of human skin brings us even closer to the sphere of the sensible: "Human skin is, as it were, the skin of skins."[32] "Man has the thinnest skin of all the animals, in relation to his size. For the same reason, he is the one whose flesh is softest and the only one who is ticklish."[33]

If man is, "among the animals, the most sensitive [*sensible*] *(aisthétileôtaton)* when it comes to the sensation that comes about by the intermediary of touch,"[34] human sensitivity is made manifest beginning with the haptic register of touch that many contemporary philosophers, such as Emmanuel Levinas, Jacques Derrida, Jean-Luc Nancy, Rémi Brague,[35] and obviously Breton also, have sought to rehabilitate. For Aristotle, an advanced sense of touch is a proof of intelligence: "Those who have hard skin have little talent when it comes to thought, whereas those who have soft skin are very talented."[36] The human pachyderm is stupider than the man who has "thin-skinned" nerves. This thesis finds a literary illustration in Ionesco's *Rhinoceros*. In this play, the rhinoceros symbolizes the contagious stupidity of the ideologies that spread everywhere, with the exception of Béranger, "the hypersensitive one"[37] whom one encounters in many of Ionesco's plays.

Poetics of the Sensible can be read as an attempt to explore the modalities of the *quodammodo* that are made manifest in the triple register of the psychic, of commerce with things, and of touch.

The whole investigation could be placed under the aegis of the famous lines of Friedrich Hölderlin's late poem "In lieblicher Bläue": "*Voll Verdienst, doch dichterisch/wohnet der Mensch auf dieser Erde*," also commented on by Heidegger.[38]

In Hölderlin's poem, *Dichterisch* [poetically] and *Wohnen* [inhabiting] form a hendiadys because the capacity of inhabiting, that is, of investing the world with human significations, is the expression of a primordial poetry that does not necessarily manifest itself in the form of the composition of poems.

Inhabiting and Traveling: A Fundamental Polarity

The distinction between being-in [*être-dans*] and being-toward that Breton has already employed to sketch out a thought of the world in *Être, Monde et Imaginaire* takes on a much more pronounced relief in *Poetics of the Sensible*. The concrete world with which we are daily in relation, the one that Heidegger designates by the term "being-in-the-world" [*être-au-monde*] (*In-der-Welt-sein*), is both a habitable space in Hölderlin's sense and a place of transit in which we ceaselessly move about.

Inhabiting and traveling are two equally originary possibilities, for nothing is more artificial than the opposition between sedentism and nomadism, that between Odysseus, who seeks at all cost to recover his palace at Ithaca, and Abraham, whose peregrinations lead him toward an unknown land. Contrary to what political populism suggests, nomads and migrants are also the inhabitants of a common world. Breton's phrase, "We have perpetually to give ourselves the world where we are,"[39] concerns everyone, the homeowners just like the homeless.

From archaic thought in Greece onward, the polarity of two conceptions of space is outlined, each one placed under the tutelage of a protecting divinity: Hestia who keeps the fire of the domestic hearth protects the values of property and patrimony; Hermes, the divine messenger, uncatchable and always in motion, is the protector of shepherds, of travelers, of thieves, of merchants, of diplomats, and of migrants of all sorts.[40] A lucid gaze on the conflicts that agitate the contemporary world shows us what happens when these two complementary functions drift apart.

We encounter a similar complementarity in Breton's definition of the poetics of the sensible that designates the double way we inhabit the sensible world. It forbids us from reducing being-in to a relation of container to content. We are not "in" the world in the way that sardines are squeezed against each other in a sardine can or that rabbits are confined in a hutch. Certainly, in certain limit-situations, for example, when we travel standing up in a crowded metro car during rush hour, or when we go into an HLM,[41] such comparisons spring to our minds.

But, fortunately, there are other experiences, those that are described and analyzed in *Poetics of the Sensible*, that are more like what is implied in the above-cited lines from Hölderlin.

The "Meta Function" or the Tiger in the Philosopher's Motor

It is on these experiences that Breton sheds light in his *Poetics of the Sensible*, by appealing to what he designates with the term "meta function." This term that permits joining, instead of opposing, the "menic function" of being-in and the ekstatic-exodic function of being-toward is the organizing principle of all of *Poetics of the Sensible*, which explicates their different powers.

In a talk that Breton gave in 1981 before the Société de Philosophie de Montréal,[42] he asked whether there could not be a way, more adapted to our time, of restoring to the old doctrine of analogy a broader basis and a slightly less problematic efficacy. His response is contained in the notion of the "meta function," a notion that one also encounters a bit later under the pen of Paul Ricœur.[43]

In this regard, Ricœur distinguishes two strategies, that of *hierarchization*, inspired by the Platonic theory of great kinds, dominated by the polarity of the Same and the Other, and the strategy of *differentiation* that guides Aristotle's reflection on the multiple significations of being [*étant*]. One can speak of the "meta function" each time one employs one or the other of these complementary strategies.

As Breton conceives of it, metaphysical thought deploys the *meta* function in the uni-diversity of its powers. The prefix "*meta*" that one finds in a great number of scholarly terms as diverse as "metalanguage, metatheory, metapsychology, metaethics, metaphorology," etc., brings to bear a whole hermeneutic of transcendence that, for my part, I have proposed to bring back to the quadripartition of the concepts of "transascendance" (Levinas), "transdescendance" (Merleau-Ponty), "transpassibility," and "transpossibility" (Henry Maldiney, Claude Romano).[44]

Poetics of the Sensible distributes the "meta function" across two ternaries, of which the first relates to being-toward and the second to being-in.

Being-toward invites us to approach the world as a field of experience, by rehabilitating the first etymological signification of the term, which modern experimental science has obscured little by little. As Gadamer emphasized, we have not given sufficient attention to the fact that the concept of experience is paradoxically "one of the most obscure [concepts] we have."[45] Hence the interest of a reflection on the multiple senses that the term "experience" can take on, going back to the foundational experiences that gave this word birth.

The disconcerting plurivocity of the Indo-European root "*per-*" that still resonates in the terms *empereia* in Greek, *experiri* in Latin, *Erfahrung* in German, *expérience* in French, *experience* in English, etc.,[46] connotes the enemy and peril (*periculum*) just as much as the traversal or the crossing [*passage*], identified with an authentic breakthrough. Whatever the concrete experiences to which these words apply may be, they gravitate around a single center of sense: the idea of a perilous traversal, that is, of a highly risky "experience," dangerous by definition. In German, the same root brings together the term *Erfahrung*, connoting itinerary and traversal, and the term *Gefahr*. connoting danger, peril.

Children of a scientific and technological civilization, today we spontaneously associate the notion of experience and the idea of experimentation.[47] If we retrace the history of the concept of experience, we discover at the origin a wholly other use that places us almost at the antipodes of this scientific definition. The German language still has a word for saying this originary sense: experience (*Erfahrung*) is first a *Widerfahrnis*, something that befalls us, that catches us unexpectedly, off guard.

The Powers of Being-Toward

Taken in this originary sense, experience lets itself be elucidated in light of the three uses of the "meta" prefix, expressing a universal demand for movement and overtaking that Breton designates by means of the terminological ternary "meta-stasis," "meta-phor," and "meta-morphosis."[48]

By relating each of these terms to a sensible schema, he confirms the hermeneutical fecundity of his poetics.

1. The first term, a sinister omen in the mouths of doctors, designates a basic instability that clears the path for a future alteration[49] that Breton schematizes with the figure of the *mask*.

2. The second term echoes the numerous debates in the beginning of the 1970s concerning the status of metaphor and its relation to philosophy, as Jacques Derrida's "White Mythology"[50] and Paul Ricœur's *The Rule of Metaphor*[51] testify, to which we should add Hans Blumenberg's impressive *Metaphorology*,[52] which is being rediscovered only today.

Metaphorizing well, said Aristotle, is the art of seeing the like through the unlike, to which one could add, in reference to Breton's *Poetics of the Sensible* and Ricœur's *The Rule of Metaphor*, that it is also the art of rendering the world habitable by impregnating it with new senses.

Of all these theoreticians of metaphor, it is doubtless Ricœur who is closest to the idea that Breton has of it, but with the exception of one crucial nuance that takes shape from the end of the chapter devoted to the "meta function" onward. What is said here about the importance that the Song of Songs takes on in Breton's eyes is confirmed by the fact that he associates metaphor with the schema of the angel's wing.

What does this mean? The passage from one order to another, in other words the "transfer of sense" from the literal to the figurative that metaphor brings about, does not play out only on the horizontal plane of expansion but also on the vertical axis of elevation or "sublimation."

In his contribution to the "Paul Ricœur Décade" at Cerisy-la-Salle, Breton distinguished the *metaphorical* and the *metaphoral*. This distinction induced a dialogue between the two philosophers, over the course of which Breton feigned surprise that the young man of the Song compares his beloved to a gazelle when he could just as well have compared her to an elephant. This remark, which made Ricœur roar with laugher, allowed me to take one of the few photos in which one sees a smiling Ricœur.

One will also note that in the last study of *The Rule of Metaphor*, Ricœur orders metaphor toward the habitability of the world, whereas for Breton it is one of the three fundamental expressions of being-toward.

3. There remains, finally, the "lability of metamorphoses"[53] that Breton, in this regard rather close to Gaston Bachelard's *Psychoanalysis of Fire*, associates with the schema of *fire*. An assiduous reader of Meister Eckhart, he kept in his memory the Rhine master's texts, in which Eckhart asks why the logs that burn in the fireplace make so much noise. It is because they protest and complain about the changes that fire makes them undergo, answers Meister Eckhart, a remark that applies equally to the protests we raise against the changes that life imposes on us.

Another text, much less well known, accompanies Breton's meditation on fire's power of transformation and purification: it is the "flowers of fire" of the *Chaldean Oracles* that the Neoplatonists interpreted as a symbol of the flower of the soul. Breton, who regularly met with his Neoplatonist friends Jean Trouillard and Henri Duméry before the fireplace of the Provincial House of the Passionists at Clamart, knew to what extent these flowers of fire set ablaze his own philosopher-poet's soul.

The Powers of Being-In

The last three chapters of *Poetics of the Sensible* outline three other potentialities of the "meta function" that concern, this time, the register of being-in.

1. In this regard, one will first note that Breton does not cede to the temptation of reducing all forms of being-in to the phenomenon of habitation alone. Grasped again at an elementary level that makes the experience we have of the proper body intervene directly, being-in is manifested in what Heidegger designates as *Befindlichkeit* ("affectivity") or *Stimmung* (affective tonality or mood).

At each instant of our existence, we are plunged into an atmosphere that we do not control. We sense ourselves as well or ill in our skin.[54] Certain ambiances make us ill at ease; they are unbreathable, whereas others plunge us into elation.

With great subtlety, Breton gathers together three sensible experiences, that of taste, that of fragrances, and that of color, which have in common that they again call into question the primacy of the visual sense that imposes on us its "*noli me tangere.*" Because "the flesh is spirit,"[55] the medieval thinkers were not wrong to emphasize that apart from the flavor of being and of the world, wisdom itself would be insipid. The same is true of odors and fragrances.

French cinephiles all remember Arletty's famous cult phrase in Marcel Carné's movie *Hôtel du Nord*. To her lover, Monsieur Edmond, weary of his Parisian life, who confides to her that he would like a change of atmosphere, Madame Raymonde, a Parisian prostitute, answers, "Atmosphere, atmosphere! Do I look like some kind of atmosphere?"

A habitable world is first a "breathable" world, where one can breathe freely. This is why one can wonder, as I did in *Le cogito herméneutique* [*The Hermeneutic Cogito*], if the three powers of metastasis, metaphor, and metamorphosis could not be completed by a fourth, which I propose to call "meta-bolism" and whose sensible schema would be air.[56] In doing so I simply follow a suggestion of Breton himself, who in his "Reflections on the Meta Function" mentioned four sensible schemas: the *mask*, *Jacob's ladder*, *fire*, and *air*.

Nothing better illustrates the importance of these subtle exchanges between inside and outside (exchanges that a thought concerned above all with putting the "subject" in relation to "objects" always risks forgetting or failing to recognize) than the first verse of the poem that opens the second part of Rainer Maria Rilke's *Sonnets to Orpheus*:

Atmen, du unsichtbares Gedicht!
Immerfort um das eigne
Sein rein eingetauschter Weltraum. Gegengewicht
In dem ich mich rhythmisch ereigne.
[*Breath, you invisible poem!*
Worldspace turning ceaselessly around

*one's own being. Counterweight through which
I rhythmically encounter my self.*][57]

2. The notion of ambiance is more than a mere prelude to the brief but powerful analysis that Breton proposes of the "abode," once again taking care to not reduce it to the phenomenon of habitation. "Abiding" means much more than possessing a home or having an "at-home" or a "hearth."[58] The fact that, on this point, there is a great affinity between Breton and Levinas[59] is not a coincidence, for both refuse to reduce sensibility to an inferior theoretical knowledge, such that one could wonder if "the latent birth of the world" does not "arise from the abode."[60]

Of all the experiences described in this chapter, it is doubtless that of color that would deserve to be extended, for example, in the company of Goethe's *Theory of Colours* and its reprise in Wittgenstein's *Remarks on Colour*, not to mention James Turrell's perceptual installations.[61]

3. The last chapter of *Poetics of the Sensible*, which gravitates around the notions of "figure," "image," and "icon," gives readers cause for surprise, in particular if one compares it to the epiphany of the face, in Levinas the manifestation of an irreducible exteriority, and to the distinction between the idol and the icon in Jean-Luc Marion.

In his work *Devant l'image* [*In Front of the Image*], Georges Didi-Huberman invites us to critique our certainties in front of the image by confronting us with the simple question of knowing how we gaze.[62] His conviction that there is no untamed eye, since we embrace images not only with our eyes but also with our words, our procedures of knowledge, and our categories of thought, invites us to replace the customary notion of the visible with a renewed notion of the *visual*, which is perhaps also Breton's intention in the pages that he devotes to the image.

The comparison of the two authors is again reinforced, thanks to Didi-Huberman's thesis that what we see lives and has value only by virtue of what gazes at us.[63] In a work that is presented as a "philosophical fable of visual experience," he compares two gazes, that of *believing vision*, which the verse of John's Gospel "He saw, and he believed"[64] illustrates, and *tautological vision*, for which the visible suffices to itself.

It is clearly evident that Breton's *Poetics of the Sensible* has its source in believing vision. But just like Didi-Huberman, he shows himself to be equally concerned with better understanding why what we see *in front* always gazes at us *inside*.

His meditation, which shuttles between the thinking Buddha of Kyoto and Rodin's Thinker, ends in another reading of the opposition between the idol, supposed to absorb and trap the gaze, and the icon that carries the gaze beyond the icon itself, and it invites us to a renewed reflection on Biblical iconoclasm. Even as he cautions us against the idolatrous temptation that, as Marion affirms, is equally manifest in the field of thought, and not only in that of religion, Breton takes seriously the affirmation of Genesis according to which man and woman are created in the image and likeness of God.

At this point a great debate opens between the interpretation that Breton proposes of the phenomenon of the face and Levinas's analysis of the epiphany of the face. The differences are blindingly obvious: one hardly sees Levinas making the face a modality of being-in. Is this to say that the difference of emphasis comes down to the opposition between a poetics of the sensible and an ethics of responsibility? This is not certain, as the allusion, at the end of *Poetics of the Sensible*, to "the true question to which an authentic poetics of the sensible responds or should respond"[65] shows. Breton's response accords with the one he develops at greater length in a chapter of *The Word and the Cross*. Those who show themselves to be sensitive [*sensible*] to the iron voice of verses 35-36 of chapter 25 of Matthew's Gospel, "For I was hungry and you gave me food, I was thirsty and you gave me drink, I was a stranger and you welcomed me, naked and you clothed me, sick and you visited me, a prisoner and you came to see me," cannot be content to put a poetics of sensibility and an ethics of responsibility in competition with each other.

Translator's Note

Sarah Horton

For the most part I have commented in the endnotes on any translation decisions that require explanation, but there are a few that it is best to discuss at the outset. The first is one of the book's central terms: *sensible*. As Breton generally uses it, this word means "capable of being perceived by the senses." Because this use of the English "sensible" is well attested in philosophy, I have simply rendered *sensible* as "sensible." The French term can also mean "sensitive," however, and when Breton employs it with this meaning, I have placed the French in brackets. Unlike the English word, *sensible* never means "sensible" in the sense of "rational," so in this translation I have never used "sensible" in that way.

The related verb *sentir* can mean "to sense," "to feel," or "to smell." Because of its connection to *sensible*, I have usually translated it as "to sense" and have included the French in brackets when context requires a different translation. *Ressentir* I have translated as "to feel"; unfortunately, there is no way to make its etymological connection to *sentir* and *sensible* explicit in English. A third word that is related in meaning but not by etymology is *éprouver*, whose relevant meanings are "to feel" and "to experience." For the most part I have used the latter translation, and when context demands the former, I have placed the French in brackets. Thus whenever the verb "feel" appears and is not followed by some form of *éprouver* in brackets, it translates *ressentir*, and the reader should bear in mind the French term's relation to *sentir* and *sensible*.

Two other key terms that deserve mention here are *demeure* and *demeurer*. *Demeurer* can mean "to live [somewhere]," "to reside," "to dwell," "to abide," "to stay," or "to remain," and all these meanings are relevant. I selected "to abide" as the English translation that best indicates both residing and remaining, and when *demeurer* appears as a noun rather than a verb, I have translated it as "abiding." Accordingly, I render *demeure* as "abode."

Finally, I must state my gratitude to several people who assisted me in this work. I thank Dr. Jeffrey Bloechl for arranging for me to translate *Poétique du sensible*; Dr. Catherine Trammell and Dr. Kevin Newmark for advising me about the translation of certain phrases; and my mother, Joanna Horton, for carefully proofreading every page of this translation. Any errors or infelicities that remain are of course mine alone.

Introduction

As an epigraph to this work, I would gladly write the ending of Plato's *Parmenides*: "'As it seems, whether one is or is not, it and the others both are all and are nothing, and both appear all things in all ways and appear nothing, both in relation to themselves and in relation to each other.'—'Very true.'"[1]

One can smile at these laborious exercises where sophistry lurks. Could the philosopher have, as the saying goes, "taken us for a ride"? It matters little to me what the very serious logician who knits his brow thinks of this today. The climax of the text tells us something that we can no longer forget: there is in the human, and in order for him to be human, a power of unreality that makes all things iridescent and that sets on each one of them this East point[2] where the angel's wing crosses paths with the will to knowledge in a single seed. In any case, the weight of being that we accord to what is seems to require a certain contact with nothing. This new version of the theologian's *ex nihilo* will guide me in this search that I entitle "poetics of the sensible." What I thus designate heralds neither a system of the fine arts nor a treaty on aesthetics. Beneath the specifications that particularize it and reserve it to artists whose titles are more or less regulated, the poetic would be this "beneath," this "neuter" where the Benjamin Bunnies that we all are drink the morning dew. The sensible, also a neuter, is this non-localizable place where the poetic is sensed in a sort of resonance or resounding. Monsieur de la Palice[3] would add that there is no sensible save as a function of sense and sensing. It would be difficult, at first, to not agree. Is it necessary for all that to embark on a discourse on sensations or on sensation and devote to each sense an essay that would show in what manner, in what *sense*, it modulates or inflects the sensible and the poetics of the sensible? I lack the universal competence that would permit me the audacity to do so; and what is more, this fragmentation depends on a fundamental sensing that it would be useful, to say the least, to explain. I will have occasion to insist on this nodal point where the threads of our powers, whose originality and common intersection it is important that we not forget, are born and flow back again.

It is, however, a fact that most often an immemorial and practically uncontested privilege accords a primacy of honor and jurisdiction to the eye and to hearing, leaving the heat of contacts, the seduction of fragrances, and arousing flavor in the shadow and thickness of the biological. Why this exceptional treatment? What turning of the poetical comes to light there? What relation does it establish between us and a world that we must perpetually remodel? The very duality of "seeing" and "hearing" already raises a problem. Rarely have they been simply juxtaposed. Sight has taken first place in the Western tradition. For the theologian of old, faith's listening prepares and promises a blessed vision that realizes its hope. Perhaps I myself have ceded to the temptation of supremacy by the preferential treatment I have reserved for the icon as well as for the face. The theory of them that I timidly propose remedies this partiality in some ways. It is not at all sure that I avoid its disadvantages. I leave to more independent judges the care of deciding this.

This rapid overview of the questions anticipates the content of my work. It does not specify its pathway. In an exercise of this sort, one has, perhaps, the right to suppose oneself a son of the free spirit. I love the school of nature [*l'école buissonnière*],[4] but I supervise it out of the corner of my eye. I arrange as best I can the joy of the route and the rigor of discourse. If there are still young readers for this austere writing, I wish them a good journey in the beatitude of fervor.

1

Sensible, Sense, Sensibility

I open my window on this vast domain that surrounds me, here in this month of September when the fall of the leaves accelerates. I have some reason to be in accord with this fall of the day in which my poor flesh is complicit, enchained also in the same whirlwind. Could the world therefore be "everything that falls" and that "goes away"? And could the being of what is be this irrepressible transit in which, according to a medieval theologian, relation itself consists? One speaks, it is true, of the system of relations that binds the diversity of things into one universe and confers on them, beyond their fragile existence, the solidity of a *Logos* or of an eternal Word. But what I experience or feel, in a sensibility that hears the sentence of death, is closer to the relation-transit than to this accord of *interity*[1] that superposes structures, however variable they may be for our approximate knowing, on the contingencies of becoming that are their phenomenon or phenotype. We willingly speak of the "world," of the "sensible," and of the "sensible world." Must we distinguish several worlds and, within sensibility itself, several levels?

The Sensible World

I take up again that celebrated expression that itself refers, as if to its complement, to the no less famous phrase "intelligible world." At once, because I am an ancient people and a heavy memory, I join with the chorus of objectors. In me and by me as the place of their transit, they denounce an intolerable dichotomy, a dualism of separated, even Manichean, substances that are supposedly connected from the outside by a median or a mediator with multiple names but more or less Platonic or Christian resonances. It is thus, and nothing can change it: the criticism, by spreading, becomes the indispensable Vulgate that each one, not to be vulgar, laps right up. And here I am in agreement, so evident does the thing become, in order to not cause pain to anyone and least of all to myself. I will not insist, therefore, on a criticism that I spontaneously repeat, not as a hypothesis to verify but as a hypostasis to retain, a solidity of the establishment, academic or not.

1. I love, however, to remember, though this reminder is a bit worn with use, that ladder Jacob saw in a dream and on which angels ascended and descended. Doubtless the world is not a ladder, be it more or less mobile, on which we arrange the hierarchy of our preferences and our values. Still it would be prudent to explain ourselves on this subject, especially when we share, as is fitting, a vision of the world where cosmogenesis and evolution hold such a large place, contested though it is by serious recalcitrants. The essential lies not there but in this mobility that bears us from one point to another, whether by ascending or descending, not for attributions of excellence or superiority but for the joy of seeing the same otherwise, supposing that this indefinite pronoun is clear enough to not motivate indiscreet reticences. I am not particularly attached to the qualifiers *sensible* and intelligible, even while having a weakness for the former. At first glance, they at least have the advantage of suggesting the poetic possibility of varying the approach within an indicator language that is prone to saying the same thing in different modes, without for all that threatening us with schizophrenia or fatal fragmentations.

2. Saying that the sensible world is the one I sense [*sens*] and feel [*ressens*] is certainly not very instructive, since what I thereby designate appears so vague, and unendurably so. Let us remove the epithet. And let us retain the substantive preceded by the definite article. Does this removal finally deliver to us this absolute concreteness or this absolute singular that we justly call "the world"? The Gospel informs us that "we are not of the world," even as we are "in [*dans*] the world."[2] And it is common, or at least it was, to speak of "being-in-the-world [*être-au-monde*]"[3] as if these particles raised no question.

I owe a sincere gratitude to those supposedly drab philosophers who at least taught me to be suspicious of the definite article and its variants, the better to reflect on them. Too lightly do we say "being," "metaphysics," "history," etc.[4] To correctly use "the," etc.,[5] I must indeed put to work a rather complex notional framework, which the logician untangles as best he can. What we will later call more or less scholarly names feature in it: identity, diversity, existence, unicity, description, relative description, etc. Apparently, there is nothing enigmatic in the banal statement: "The automobile of Claude is a Renault." The thing thus described ("the x such that $f(x)$") contains what the Americans call "an ontological assumption": it exists and it is unique, for every x to which I attribute the property f is identical to the thing thus described. And if I add that it is a Renault, the specification that this property indicates implies *that there is* an automobile of Claude. But when I speak of *the* world, what am I saying, *exactly*? Would it not be impossible to be exact? Isolated, the expression "the world" does not state everything it presupposes. I must translate it by the advanced formula "the x such that x is world." Before even stating with regard to that x that is world and, with indicative propositions, such or such ulterior determination, I assume that *there is a world* and that it is *unique*. And yet, though these presuppositions of existence and of unicity seem self-evident when they concern a *thing* that falls within the sphere of our activity or our perception, that we have before our gaze or at hand and which we could *have at our disposal*, by going all round it, as it were, nothing of the sort is possible when it comes to the world. It cannot, therefore, be a question, strictly speaking, of a *unique existent*. Perhaps we could timidly advance that *there is* a world in the sense of a milieu of the apparition, genesis, and existence of everything that is, or even in the sense of a pre-given "in which we live and move and have our being"[6]—a pre-given that we signify as best we can in a language of "relative description" and by using linguistic tools whose inadequacy we feel [*éprouvons*] too much to delude ourselves about their validity. We will speak, therefore, of *a* world and of *the* world in the mode of *as*: as if there were a unique existent, and to signify thereby the singularity of an irreplaceable function that could not be represented in terms of a subject or an individual variable, since it is precisely that by which and in which *there will be* individuals and individual variables.

3. It does not, however, suffice to evoke this milieu of apparition to be sure of what we are saying. In this time of ecology, pretty well ubiquitous, sacred duty for some amounts to the defense of the environment. Yet the environment (*Umwelt* in German), even if it is indefinitely extensible to the point of covering planet Earth, does not encompass what the term "world" intimates. The problem, rarely approached even though it is the most serious one, concerns precisely their difference and the passage from one to the other: the passage from the *Umwelt* to the *Welt*, if one permits me a jargon that, for once, has the merit of precision. The functions surely resemble each other to such an extent that I wonder if credit for this new language does not go first to the theoretical biology that substituted it for the vague terminology of the milieu or of conditions of existence. The initial limitations that affected a discipline that is concerned above all with animal life have progressively been relaxed. People have spoken of a "human environment." But the anthropological itself is inscribed in a vaster space that could not be defined by designations borrowed from the specific fields of our different bodies of knowledge. One thus understands the malaise of the philosopher who means to preserve an irreducible without being able to fix it within a discourse

of exactitude and rigor. It is because the indeterminacy of the world recalls, to the point of being easily mistaken for it, the indeterminacy of being. But this liaison, far from being dangerous, is the best chance to say, about the world, a word that is not purely conventional. I will try to make it explicit in a sequence of propositions that suggest at the very least, for want of a demonstration, the plausibility of the passage:

— the environment, in which the living thing moves and exists, be it vegetable, animal, or human, can be defined as a field of positive or negative *stimuli* to which a definite need responds in the mode of a reaction, specific to each level, be it a need for assimilation or defense, conquest or flight;
— the determination of the stimulant, correlative to each species, thus determines the qualitative look and the extensive curvature of each environment. The *surroundings* that the very term "environment" irresistibly evokes mark a limit and a frontier. In a geographically common space, the biological differences of species cut out an original sector, itself indissociable from an essential bi-polarity: the environment is the place, the *there* where the living thing abides and toward which it moves; correspondingly, the living thing, henceforth no longer thought as an object or an organic substance but as a system of relations, is that which abides in its place and moves toward it. In a prepositional style, inevitable in this sort of description, we will sum up the function of the environment with the two expressions *being-in, being-toward*. The complementary of these two modes of being constitutes what I call *inhabiting*;
— consequently, if there must be a passage from the environment to the world, it can only be by a transgression of the stimulant thus understood: the transmuting transition amounts to a demise. The death of the regional stimulant, which is as limited in "comprehension" as in "extension," restores its stimulating virtue only by unlimiting it. And yet this unlimitation is itself the other side of a creative innovation that substitutes for the narrowness of *what-is-for-the-needs* of the living thing the unconditional extension of *what is* purely and simply. The suppression of *being-for* coincides with the absolute emergence of the *being-of-what-is*. The indeterminacy of being, which has so often been lamented, becomes thereby the condition of possibility of another play space. And the world assumes the functions of the environment only by subsuming the regionalism of vital stimulations under the amplitude of *what is*.

Another spirit of which "we do not know where it comes from or where it goes"[7] henceforth dominates, without destroying, the former state-of-things whose multiple determinations the human itself retains. Another stimulant, as imperious as the first ones, opens the original enclosure; and every effort to return to it, as to the ultimate determination, can only collide with this other that imposes on it its overdetermination. One would understand nothing of the gravity of our debates if one contented oneself with indefinitely repeating the charges of materialism and idealism. The perspectives must necessarily be inverted depending on whether one proceeds from the environment to the world or from the world to the environment. The genesis that our bodies of knowledge retrace goes, as is said, from bottom to top; the explanation they propose of the superior by the inferior is in no way scandalous: it is strictly what it must be when one grants a certain sense of evolution. But it is always possible to reverse the movement: what is last in a certain order can be first in another order and engender precisely that which conditions it. Certain philosophies have had a keen sense of that revolution that makes the environment revolve around the world, contrary to certain proofs of common sense. I am no prophet. But I judge probable, because it is necessary, a thought to come that will have the courage to confront the relation between these two geneses, without useless compromises, in the lucid consciousness of that which we are given to think by the rupture that causes there to be a world and by the continuity that integrates anew, in a hitherto unseen mode, the functions of the ancient abode. Our sciences themselves live from this rupture and this exodus. They claim to say what is and the world of what is; their efficacy is measured by this claim. And if they have their limits, they are always thought and provisional limits that have nothing to do with the constraints of an environment in the narrow meaning we have given that word. If one objects that authentic knowledge has no use for the world, for being qua being, and for the being of what is, or quite simply for what is, I will concede without restriction that this, indeed, is in no way scientific. For that by which science is what it is escapes its own grasp: it lives only on what it presupposes, but it exists only on the condition of forgetting it.

4. The functions vested in the world are indeed, as I have said, the very functions of the environment. We can therefore take up again, to define the new *inhabiting*, the two expressions *being-in* and *being-toward*, still connoting with these prepositional formulae the mutation that they commemorate and

the hitherto unseen complement to which they call. We have often recalled that a language, whatever it may be, and even if it is lexically rather poor, is a conception or, better yet, a constitution of the world. But before being a representation of what *there is* in the world, it specifies a certain manner of inhabiting it: it particularizes, by modalizing them, our being-in-the-world and our being-toward-the-world. And what we affirm of a language is just as true of religious forms, socioeconomic and political configurations, artist's creations, etc. It remains, consequently, for us to specify the originality of these two modes of being.

Being-in accentuates what I will call, to be brief, the *menic* function. I am borrowing the adjective from the Greek *Menein*, which, as we know, appears frequently in Saint John's Gospel. This intransitive verb marks rest, fixed and stable being, the abode, and abiding. As a prolongation of these indications, it evokes the home and, more generally, the place where "it is good to find oneself," according to the Gospel word: "Where your treasure is, there your heart will be also."[8] I note at once that this verb has no object. Beneath the intentional action that does something, it suggests an *acting* that does nothing, a profound acting that consists in *holding oneself there*, a substantial acting that underlies our transitive and transforming activities and brings them back to their center to rid them of their idolatrous importance. And thereby it maintains them in the smiling distance of a certain irony. India, in particular, has taught us the secret of this *acting*, whose radiance is sensed in the divine calm of its sculptural figures. At my own peril, I have formerly related it to the mathematician's neutral element, an element that, added to any other element, in no way alters it and that seems to be *there* only to permit what is not it to be what it is. Philosophy itself has had the presentiment of this when, for example, in this or that Aristotelian text, it is said that "being," added to any predicative expression, leaves intact its content. It is not rash, so it seems to me, and this hypothesis would perhaps be fruitful for research, to make out, in the background of the categorial notion of substance, the shadow of this "being-in." Yesterday's and today's critique most often sees in it only the "underlying thing," the inert "substratum" to which the adjectival multiplicity of the various attributes is supposedly pinned, in liaison with the grammatical form of the substantive. The most benevolent would at times concede that it heralds, with an impotent forefinger, our scientific principles of conservation. These interpretations are surely right to some extent. I fear, however, that they omit what is principal. Substance, indeed, is not first a thing that would be underneath another or a permanence that would thwart the instability of becoming. It is defined by a "being-in," specified as the "being-in-itself" that stands out, by contrast, against the "being-in-an-other" that it would be specious to consider as a simple "accident," as ephemeral as a ripple on the surface of water. These two values of "being-in" have been the occasion, I admit, of questionable conceptualizations that drew inspiration, one moment from a certain type of causality, the next moment from the architectural metaphor of foundation [*fondement*].[9] One would be wrong, abandoning the essential for the formulae that distort it, to forget that which was its origin. Neither is the self a subject whose transformations grammar, logic, cosmology, psychology, and law have successively commanded. It is above all that *place* or that *there* where one abides. And if one fears to thus fall again into the naivety of a spatial imagination that satisfies itself cheaply with a language as infirm as that of the container and the content, I will modestly admit that nobody is exempt from this danger. Like walking, discursivity, written or spoken, is a fall that must be continually caught. There is no infallible remedy for these weights that are part of our condition. We speak as best we can, and we must speak. This necessity that constrains us also offers us the free possibility of correcting without ceasing, or of catching, that throw of the die or that audacity that every word and every proposition represents, exactly to the degree that, without imposing or being able to perfectly justify it, it proposes the risk of a novelty that is never a pure reflection. I will therefore maintain the language of "being-in" because it overflows, in what it designates, the narrowness of the significations that the vicissitudes of history have stuck to it. I must, however, add a clarification. In its inevitable abstraction, "being-in" is susceptible to a double unfolding. Banally, one will say that one finds oneself *well* or *ill* [*se trouve* bien *ou* mal][10] in this or that system of thought, of economics, of religion, or more generally of culture. It is not that we must reify, beneath these specifications, an indifference point that would be the equivalent of a third factor that would transcend its determinations. But if we cannot isolate the function from its organic figures, we can at the very least envision a certain play, or a certain impatience, that does not permit it any definitive stabilization in the concrete environments that it gives itself. No religious form saturates the original possibility of abiding. No home is perfectly adequate to the aspiration that it should fulfill. That is why the believer, to the degree that his faith contains an inalienable margin of interrogation, is always tempted to look beyond its frontiers. And what we say of faith applies, despite the material diversity of cases, to every abode, whatever it be. I will be spared from multiplying examples. Our era is characterized in part by the necessity of a place to rest and by the impossibility of satisfying ourselves with the established abodes.

5. The second moment of *inhabiting*, which I designate by the relative description "being-toward-the-world," is based precisely on the *menic* function insofar as this function does not predetermine any localization that could be equal to it. We have perpetually to give ourselves the world where we are. Religions, it is true, accentuate the stability of rest. They dread, instinctively, like a death threat, the mutations that the difference of the times calls for. Heresy is always the temerity of a disorientation. But sooner or later, one is reconciled to change. One then arranges "being" and "becoming" in the postulate of a continuity that recalls, by its compromises, the median resultant where contrary forces reach equilibrium. The development operates, so it is said, "in the same sense and according to the same doctrine." Identity also inflects abiding in the direction of a permanence, which is only its schematization. The sciences and the arts have, in contrast, broken more decidedly with what we called the environment. They know better, perhaps, that the world where we are is also the one where we move to give it the transitory shape that is the *transitive* place of our passage. One abides only in passing. The Jewish people admirably illustrate this paradox that one never resolves perfectly, whether one is an artist or a savant. But in any case, whether the accent is shifted to one side or the other, it is impossible to divide what unites, by an unbreakable bond, our prepositional being. We have definitively left the country of our nature, however heavy our biological predestinations may be. And we can be *there* only by going toward the home that we will have invented. Our condition is our destiny. And this destiny is but the never-finished realization of this first opening that was, in the lightning-flash of the world, our first transit.

The Verb "To Sense"

Speaking of the world in the prepositional style that I have adopted, it is legitimate to wonder what the adjective "sensible," by which I have defined it, signifies. And yet the very manner in which I introduced the term "world," by invoking the function of being qua being, seems to belie the suitability of this qualifier. Have I not described an abstraction, an intelligible world in the most suspect meaning of this word that for many awakens the specter of the afterworlds? It is therefore important to explain myself in more depth; and I could do so no better than by reflecting on the verb "to sense."

1. In its most obvious signification, this verb responds, by signifying them, to the various sensory activities that we undertake at every moment. A long

tradition entrusted them to the classic five senses, called external to properly mark their orientation toward the outside. This pentadic nomenclature can appear summary and artificial, even though the deduction of it that certain medievals attempted deserves more than a smile. The number is debatable, and it matters little to me. I will retain, in contrast, the characteristic of exteriority. In memory of the heliotrope, the magnificent flower that made certain philosophers dream who were devoted both to prayer and to the sun, I will substitute for the expression "exteriority" the designation, more expressive though more scholarly, "exotropism." This "being-toward-the-outside," which is the unfolding of sense and sensing, is not to be confused, however, with intentionality understood as consciousness of an object. One can sense *something* without at once conferring on it the form of an ob-ject endowed with a more or less precise configuration and, what is more, localizable in space-time. As has often been remarked, the sense of smell, like odors and fragrances, diffuses an atmosphere more than it delineates a determinate sensible thing. The common expressions "it smells [*sent*] bad," or more simply yet, "it smells," and "it smells good," highlight an ambivalence of sensing but also and especially, by the neutrality of the *it*, the indeterminacy of the thing sensed. In the case of the most representative senses, like sight and hearing, the object perceived is itself surrounded by a more or less vague margin or background that unlimits the perception of it. More profoundly still, and beneath sensory operation, that which we call *sense*, before applying itself, benefits from a sort of potentiality [*puissance*], from an "I can [*Je puis*]" that exceeds and anticipates its multiple actualizations. Every act of sensing is thus borne, ahead of as behind itself, by a real thing that is distinct from it. This unlimitedness, whether we think it as the power [*puissance*] of sensing or the power of being sensed, constitutes a milieu or an environment in which it rests. Because it has no frontiers, it is explicable that a certain infinity has been attributed to it. It is therefore permissible, and more than permissible, to speak, on this subject, of a *being-in* that grounds *being-toward*, when it is a matter of a sensory activity. I will liken this *being-in* to a neuter, to an intransitive acting that is not yet an action. Thereby it is explained why a prescientific language does not hesitate to say that "the eye bathes in light," or that it is "connatural" with light, or even that it abides in light. And this invites us to a new deepening. Prior to all sensing, I posit the intransitive *to sense oneself* that would be the true radical of the verb *to sense*, its middle voice that is irreducible to the distinctions between active and passive, as to the distinctions between subject and object.[11]

2. These summary explanations doubtless do not suffice to clarify the enigma of the sensible in the expression "sensible world." But they set us on the path.

One might accuse them of disregarding any genetic preoccupation and of being situated, in consequence, outside any authentic knowledge. And yet the knowledge that wonders about sense and the sensible cannot but root them in their true soil, which is that of life and the living thing. The evolution of which they are the result is therefore of a strictly biological order. Consequently the only questions that are posed concern their condition as organs or instruments in the service of the living thing. This latter can live and survive in its environment only on the condition of rendering it habitable by the assimilation of that which suits it and by an effective protection against the dangers that threaten it. It is this double necessity that, at the end of a long process of fumbling and finding balance, gave birth to the senses and to sensory activity, of which we must, in consequence, distinguish the two great forms, which have been named "senses of need" and "senses of defense," respectively.

This conception, the principle of which is, on the whole, extremely classical, for we have long known that the senses are in the service of life, is perfectly acceptable. The only question that remains in suspense would be this one: what does the living thing become when it passes from the environment to the world, in short, when it takes on the ontological and cosmological inflection that I have described? The service of life remains intact but is diversified like life itself. However numerous the stages of a genesis may be, one cannot reduce to what came before the innovation that, in the final analysis, glorifies their fecundity. The rupture that was produced in the course of a genesis is henceforth inscribed in the very fabric of the living thing. And it would be artificial, to put it mildly, to divide this fabric into two parts, one that would be the share of a biological nature, the other that would be, as it were, its superstructure. Such a vivisection, which still underlies the distinction between nature and culture, feels the effects of an old dualism that one would have thought obsolete. This water divide that, in the traditional definition of the human, joined a differential of reason to an animal generality, already obeyed the same illusion, an illusion that, moreover, one finds in the metaphor of the infra- and the superstructure. What the mutation that I have already commented on signifies is precisely the impossibility of such a partition. We will no longer say: the cultural *modifies* the natural, or even: the artificial *accommodates* [*compose avec*] the biological. For it is a matter neither of a simple modification, since the mode is of the very order of "substance," nor of a compounding [*composition*] of two elements from which a third, hylomorphic entity would emerge. We must understand that the mutation that made the environment a world is more radical than the assumption of the old under a new sense or of factual conditions under an interpretation from which they would emerge transfigured. These exegeses, however subtle they may be, have only one defect, but it is prohibitive: they project into a past that one would suppose to be still intact a subsuming form that would take charge of it *such as it has remained*. It is this sophism that I refuse and this dichotomy that I denounce. Once again making my apologies for a jargon whose precisions redeem its unwieldiness, I prefer the following formula: the essence of the human is in no way human, meaning that it is not resolved into either an anthropological property or a merely biological definition; it is that by which the human accesses its proper difference by the advent of a mutation that is at the same time ontological and cosmological, and cosmological because it is ontological.

3. The consequences of this new definition are too serious to be left in the penumbra of the implicit. I will spell out those that are most important for my subject:

— the senses are in the service of life, but of life in its human difference that unfolds in a world properly so called. It will therefore always be a question of eating, drinking, sleeping, inhabiting, etc. But these verbs have a double reference: on the one hand to the acting insistence that gives itself its food, its sleep, its drink, and its home, on the other hand to the cosmological landscape in which these activities are henceforth inscribed. At the risk of astonishing, I will add: the sciences and the arts, philosophies and religions themselves must, each one in its own manner, satisfy these elementary functions that we judge to be prosaic because we constantly think them in a register that is no longer their own;

— the senses, as sensing powers, do not have only an object or a domain (the visible, the audible, etc.). Their *exotropism* necessarily brings them back and draws them beyond a biological milieu in the strict sense. Because they are exercised in relation to a world, they are essentially ontological and cosmological. The verbs *to see, to hear, to touch*, etc., are not addressed first to a sensible world only to be transposed later onto an intelligible world of understanding or reason. The acting that they signify is not dual-natured. It simply comprises a plasticity that is more and better than a metaphor in the most common meaning of the word; and this acting belongs always, by right, to the dimensions of the world;

— prior (an anteriority of nature, not of time) to every act of sensing, I posit, because it takes root there, a pre-sensing that is the intransitive *to sense oneself*. Each of our sensory powers senses itself as connatural with the world in which it moves. This connaturality is its own manner of inhabiting the world, according to the double modality of *being-in* and *being-towards*. But beneath these specific determinations, I posit, in correlation with the world, a fundamental, undifferentiated sensibility that makes us experience it *globally* according to the two modalities that I have just mentioned;

— the distinction that I have gathered in passing between the senses of need and the senses of defense can be maintained, on the condition, however, of being thought within the horizon of the mutation that it must incorporate. In my view, another distinction, which does not exactly overlie the first one, validates the difference, more topical for us, between the senses that accentuate *being-in* and the senses that valorize *being-toward*. This typology highlights a dominant chord. One will remember that a dominant chord includes precisely that which it does not highlight;

— an ever-tenacious dichotomy opposes the so-called cultural senses (sight, hearing) to the heavier senses, which are more bound, by the weight of the flesh, in the thickness of the biological (touch, but still more taste and smell). The former, on account of their immateriality and the greater distance that they maintain with regard to their object, seem more apt for the rigors of knowledge and the forms of art. The latter, on account of their immersion in matter, would supposedly be more refractory to the transfigurations that could discipline them. This typological duality is probably not gratuitous. It is based on the massive fact, at least in the West, of a primacy of the optical and the auditory. This primacy is itself based on their representative capacity, on their precision with respect to perceived forms, on their power of protection and defense whose efficacy is measured by their perception of what is distant, a perception that defers the imminence of danger by anticipating it. The aforementioned division intersects the more modern distinction between the senses of need and the senses of defense. It would be ungracious to take no account of this. Nonetheless, when carried to an extreme it seems to me to compromise, by so sharply cut a separation, the original mutation that affects, all at once, the whole scale of sensibility. In this regard, the "cultural," if one insists on the word, permeates the latter of these sensory apparatuses just as much as the former. And the difference arises less from their greater or lesser spirituality than from the originality of their relation to the world they permit us to inhabit. The carnal heaviness that characterizes touch, smell, and taste is sometimes interpreted according to the equivocal language of participation. But it is better understood if, far from condemning us to a sort of divorce or schizophrenia in a hierarchy whose lowest degrees they would occupy, their specificity fulfills the inalienable function that consists in anchoring us in the soil of our world and in attaching us to it by the intransitive acting of abiding. This quasi-feminine role—I will not, however, insist on this qualifier—is always presupposed by the complementary activity of the more clearly intentional senses like sight and hearing that I have characterized by the predominance of being-toward. They are par excellence the senses of movement, of the future [*avenir*] and of occurring [*ad-venir*], of our experience of the world insofar as this experience is closer to the voyage that disorients[12] us than to the simple report of perception or verification. To take up again the analogy that has already served us, the two groups, which share our fundamental sensibility, mutually sustain each other as the *thesis* and *arsis* in the continuity of a single march. Once again, we inhabit the world only by traversing it without ceasing; we abide there only on the condition of a perpetual exodus. If one will permit me this playful expression, we set foot only to lift it at once. There is no question of breaking this rhythm of our sensibility at the expense of one or the other of its times. Anticipating my later explanations, I will add that a work of art, a poem, whatever its modality of expression may be, touches us all the more and seems to us all the more successful the more it unites this double quality of an exodus that disorients us and a deep-rootedness that invites us to abide there.

The Sensible and the Poetic

The question henceforth becomes more urgent: what does the *poetic* add to the generic condition of the sensible and of what we have called *fundamental sensibility*?

1. At this very ethereal level at which we are temporarily holding ourselves, the poetic could not be the prerogative of a discipline or of some artistic specialty. It is identified with the possibility of our existence. The life of a man, however quotidian one supposes him to be, is worth living to the degree that it conjoins, in an actually experienced harmony, the *being-in* and *being-toward* of our condition as inhabitants of this world. The figure of the despairing one best reveals the limpid necessity of this. Despair rises to the surface when the two *elements* (in the profoundest meaning of this word) dissociate and thereby break the unity of a being [*être*][13] that exists and lives only in and by that unity.

Alighting nowhere, the despairing one no longer has anything with which to support his movement. He is therefore destined to the unbearable alternative: either he braces himself in "the fixed will of a fixed state," which, lower than the condition of the oyster whose shell subsists only in the beating of the swell, would be the very definition of matter, as proposed by a certain philosophy, or else he twists and turns in a frantic movement, unable to give himself the support of his own surpassing. It is a double impossibility that could not justify a choice. There remains, henceforth, only the last resort of a lucidity that duly records, in a *de-cision*, the intolerable divorce and completes in *sui-cide* the cut that already, virtually, exiled one from the world. The tragedy of certain youths who have, as the saying goes, done away with themselves is all the more telling a lesson, for the very age of their definitive departure seemed to promise the necessity of another solution. I would not have written a poetics of the sensible if I did not still have before my eyes the irreversible gesture of an adolescent who hailed with a final "Good day," in the white powder of cyanide, the arid society of which he was taking leave. The asphyxia of which he died was but the sensible sign of the unbreathability that was for him the torment of a too-long patience. The forward flight in the succession of days could not spare him, even by a heroic oblivion, from the place where our hearts rest. With an intrepid logic, he drew the conclusion from these premises. His last hour was also the hour of his first thought. In the evidence of a lightning-flash, he saw that the "I am" would collapse when one gazes steadily upon it, in an impossibility of being, by the disjunction of the double prepositional index that assures *existing*. At the horizon of my memory, from now on there will be this sorrowing shadow on the lookout. If our young pilgrims, of an Eastern absoluteness, today depart on the roads of another world, would it not be in order to find again the substantial link whose founding urgency they sense with a fundamental sensibility? Be that as it may, an introduction to poetry, if it wants to be taken seriously in our day, should begin with a meditation on suicide. Would it be foolhardy, I will add, to suspect at the origin of the Trinitarian dogma itself the piercing apperception of a necessity: the *being-toward* that distinguishes the three persons and the unity of the circumincession that causes them to be reciprocally one *in* another are the indispensable condition for there to be something rather than nothing. I foresee a chapter of theology entitled: the Holy Trinity and the temptation of suicide.

2. But if it falls to each one to practice, according to the unfolding that is the very acting of his life, the poetics of the sensible, history teaches us that we have never been content with this quotidian exercise. Just as a rudimentary practice has, over the course of the centuries, increased in knowledge and techniques

that exceeded everyday know-how, so too has the poetics of the quotidian taken on social forms (think of masques or carnivals) that have lost the ingenuity of the ordinary. If the *poetic* is the unity, in a fundamental sensing, of the two prepositional elements of the sensible world, *poetry* would be that thematic exercise, in an objectification that manifests it in broad daylight, of this always-presupposed unity. Thus understood, it encompasses not only the linguistic arts but also everything covered by the vague term *expression*, which we will be careful not to interpret in too narrow a sense. Expression, in the meaning I give it here, does not project into spatiotemporal exteriority a subjectivity or a punctual interiority previously lived in the mode of the ineffable. It prolongs, by supplying it with new means, a less contrived experience that is woven in the banality of work and of days. But why, one will ask, feigning the naivety of a question that is not naïve, was it necessary to leave that *state* that we judge to be primitive in view of what happened after? The question itself seems to posit at the origin a sort of paradisiacal life where the harmony of our two components was already given according to the theological model of a perfect consonance of man with himself, with others, and with God. I do not ask for so much, and in truth, I can do without paradise. The continuity between the two phases that I have distinguished must be sought in the very mutation that made it so that a world is, breaking with the biological narrownesses of the environment. And yet if the environment is already ready-made, if it is predestined for the living thing that is destined for it, the world in the strongest sense of the word emerges, in the light of being qua being, only in the form of a universal milieu that we have to give ourselves and for which we are responsible. To be correctly understood, the *being of what is* must therefore be dissociated from the fallacious representations that habitually accompany it. One cannot identify it with an inert light illuminating *from the outside* the things to which, *from the outside*, it would come. The image, always taken up again, is certainly significant. It translates rather well, by its unlimitation, the substitution of a universe for a regional enclosure and the expansion of the initial *stimulus* or stimulant to the universality of what is. This corrective, nonetheless, remains insufficient. It leaves unchanged the first situation, namely, that of a milieu or a prefabricated container into which the living thing is introduced. It is precisely this pre-existence that calls into question the advent of a world properly so called. The *being of what is is the active light* that makes precisely that which it illuminates. *Being qua being* thus becomes the having-to-be and the have-to-do that, by its freedom, produces the very thing of which I will say, by way of a trace: *it is what is*. In the expression *being qua being*, it is therefore necessary to conjugate the universality that universalizes the environment into a universe, the dynamism that constitutes that universe as the mediation of a freedom, and the giving joy that awakens that which, in the environment, remained [*demeurait*], by its annexation to the powerful organism, the slave of need to the dignity and the freedom of what is. One has the right to judge exorbitant such a conception that makes the "mystical body of spirits" the inaugural authority of the world. It is stigmatized with the name of idealism. I for my part deem it the only courageous conception and the only coherent one, for its refusal of the "half-heartedness" that juxtaposes, after a fashion, a natural origin and that which does not belong to nature. By its audacity, it invites us to better grasp the relation of the two geneses of which I spoke earlier. And thereby it invites us to think, with difficulty, that which, in a hackneyed terminology, is conventionally called "the human condition." It is not at all sure that poets themselves are so much strangers to it that one cannot discern in their work at least the appearance of a complicity. I allude to the "magical idealism" that has been discussed at such great length, but aside from this illustrious precedent, the very practice of language, in its poetic essence, constantly returns to that first *fiat* by which the world itself came about. If one insists on taking the poetic word seriously and on not exiling it, for weekend entertainment, to our cultural byways, it would be urgent to reconnect it to the carrier wave that in the beginning made the being of what is, I mean the world, the place of our abode and of our perpetual soaring. And if one objects to me that such a monstrous idealism arises from paranoia, I can but reply: blessed are the mad, for theirs is the kingdom. This madness of the beginning that favored us with a world is carried on in a continued creation that demands the indefinite givenness of a first creation. In this sense, humans' most humble gesture is inscribed within the axis of this radical genesis. And the poets have but one merit: actualizing, in an evocative recollection that rouses us from our sleep, that lightning-flash of the beginning that made the world in which we are and toward which we move. It is in this that they take up again, by giving it its full resonance, the quotidian poetics of the least among their brothers.

3. If the poetry of poets, when one thinks it radically, sends us back to the birth of the world, why would this not also be true of any other activity, of science, for example, or of religion? After having inordinately extended the poetic and its field of expression, do we not risk diluting it in the insignificance of a transcendental vagueness? Since it is everywhere, it is to be feared that it is nowhere or that it is conflated with reality itself. Rejoining the degree zero of difference, why should we concern ourselves with it to the point of making it a particular problem?

These worries, as legitimate as they may be, mix several questions that it is appropriate to distinguish. The first concerns the extension of poetry to all the arts of expression. The second, more serious, touches on the relation of the poetic to disciplines other than poetry in its enlarged signification. By calling *poetry* the thematization of the poetic, I do not mean to simply co-opt a Greek designation or to reunite under the umbrella of *language* disciplines as varied as painting, music, writing, etc. Indeed, it seems to me improper to thus level out differences. Strictly speaking, we must reserve the term *language*, oral or written, for a certain type of expression. Or else, if one classes language in the genus of *signs*, it is important to respect the semiotic specificity of each of its expatriates and to not impose on them the pretention and the precision of a wanting-to-say [*vouloir-dire*].[14] If each of the arts of expression indeed *proposes* something to us, it is never in the form of a propositional equivalent. But what unites them in their irreducibility is precisely the *proposition* of a world that they permit us to inhabit in the double mode of being-in and being-toward. I will have to explain myself at length on this last point. It suffices, for me, to let it be glimpsed, by this common feature, that *poetry*, in the multiplicity of its kinds, has a veritable *productive power* [*pouvoir réalisateur*]. Without carrying the analogy to an extreme, we could bring poetry closer to the sacraments about which a celebrated formula dogmatically states "that they cause precisely that which they signify." It is thereby, moreover, that poetry remedies the sign's inevitable abstraction, which is always at a distance from that which it signifies. Poetry, as the art of the poetic, thus reiterates the originary poetry that made the world our only and authentic environment. But this *fiat* of the origin, because it could only be a beginning, necessarily calls for a repetition that, without reduplicating it, radiates indefinitely the power of the first lightning-flash.

4. Would poetry therefore be the only authority entitled to speak of the poetic? What do we make of science and religion? As one suspects, it is not a question of refusing the religious and the scientific the right to poetry. I speak of these disciplines according to the austerity of their essences. And yet if they both also compose—and how could they not?—the *being-in* and *being-toward* that define *inhabiting*, they never do so save in the indirect or oblique mode. The various bodies of knowledge deal with *what is* with an eye to explaining it and retracing its genesis. They restore processes about which they inform us through indicative propositions of which we demand exactitude and rigor in order that they be established. The asceticism of their procedure is the best guarantee of their efficacy. But though they provide us with the means to be ever more at home [*être toujours mieux*] in the world where we abide, they do not as such have to modulate this

abiding. Their very dynamism ceaselessly pushes them beyond their provisional achievements. They thus exercise that *being-toward* that gives itself indefinitely in new conquests in which the face of the world, the soil of belief that nourishes their thrust, is recreated. In consequence, they will not be asked to wonder about that initial freedom that made it so that the world was. Nor will they be asked to concern themselves with that being qua being whose necessity I have stated but which, in the apparent void of its abstraction, could only paralyze their search. The limits that the probity of an approach prescribes to them thus entail a necessary forgetting. This forgetting from which they live is just as much a providential boon for us all. It would be ridiculous to hold this against them or to blame them for the multiple dysfunctions from which our societies suffer. But if these considerations are fundamentally just when we consider knowledge in itself, in its proud autonomy, allergic to any foreign interference, they remain biased when we envision it in its social existence, in the political context that integrates it into the becoming and the destiny of the city. Nonetheless, this reintegration of knowledge into the broader context in which it takes on its full scope does not modify the apoetic condition of its work. And if politics in its turn has its say, in order to adapt the means to ends that tend to render this poor world less uninhabitable, it too is powerless to make our desert bloom. The ever-difficult relations between politics and poetry testify rather to this congenital inability. The Platonic precedent is in this regard exemplary. The problem it poses has not been resolved. And if the poet, today more than ever, has such trouble being in our world, it is not only because his presence would be as gratuitous as it is ineffective. It is because he collides with the inevitable forgetting that has covered over a world whose origin he recalls without ceasing. Always *de trop* in a universe that is satisfied with what is, this man of the original rupture can say the being of what is only by returning to the *ex nihilo* that he celebrates by his death even more than by his life.

5. Does the Christian religion, in our Western countries, reserve for him a better fate? The history of the arts attests to a benevolence that was, at times, generously recompensed. In the service of faith, the artisans of the poetic rendered to the Lord of glory or of the Cross an homage that, even if it was solicited for the benefit of a Church triumphant, accorded with a cordial spontaneity. The artist truly worked in order that the faith of believers might inhabit our world. His creations did not only inspire piety by illustrating a dogmatics. They were inscribed within a "cosmic liturgy," in which the song of a celebrating universe, by the play of shadow, silence, and light, enveloped in its glorious cloud the presence of the Most High. The house of God replaced the tent and the temple of old. And it was good to abide there.

Poetry was thus in accord with what doubtless was, as I implied above, the most constant passion of the religious function: rooting man's heart in a depth, in a *being-there*, that would coincide with the very being qua being of what is. This accord, on a fundamental point, between the two authorities, outside any trick of diplomacy, far from alienating the artist, allowed him to affirm, in works in which he could recognize himself, the noblest half of his medieval soul. If I evoke the Middle Ages, it is not only because, even today, the ancient people that I shelter in myself, in the nostalgia of a new abode, is found without effort in those monuments of the past that bear the name of Our Lady. It is also and above all because that era was particularly sensitive [*sensible*] to the problem and the mystery of abiding. Monasteries, Roman and Gothic churches, and even the *summas* of theology—all seems ordered toward [*ordonné à*] the Real Presence of God with us and among us. The Virgin Mother is the first model of those tabernacles that seem to reproduce, by inverting it, Emmanuel's cradle. The Son of Man had no place to lay [*reposer*] his head; and when, at the moment of death, he bows it to finally rest [*reposer*], it is his pierced heart that offers him a final monstrance altar [*reposoir*].[15] The cathedral puts an end to a destiny of wandering. It schematizes the immobile and reciprocal movement that theologians called "circumincession." God in man and man in God, this double passage that reproduces the Trinitarian relations and the enigma of the Incarnation defines the sense and the human-divine consistency of the Home-God.

The *substance* on which philosophy discourses is no doubt a category of thought, which has been believed to have then ruled the intelligence of faith. Projected into a place which is that of the encounter, it becomes something wholly other than an abstraction. Architecture as the dominant form of artistic creation "symbolizes" (on the condition of giving this word its fullness of old) its essential signification. It tells, in its manner, of a "being in itself" that animates the heaviness of stone. And this is why the figures that the painter or the sculptor draws are less the accidents than the magnificent modes of its breadth. The history that they tell seems to find peace in this monumental rest that completes time in space and that bears space itself back toward its indivisible origin. A microcosm of the universe, of which it recapitulates, in the flowering of its rose windows, the unity of light in the diversity of its colors, the abode of faith fulfills on our earth the *menic* function of all religion. When one returns, today, toward these memorials, become museums, one sometimes experiences the sweet melancholy of the questioning of the prophet: Son of man, do you believe these bones can live again?[16] Could the cradle of old be a tomb whose stone crumbles away to remind us that it remains dust and that to dust it will return?

The Marian ship that sets forth on the Seine bears away in its nostalgia the poetry of another age. Could the artist who made it his heart's treasure be definitively bygone? If the poetic is indeed what I have said, it is impossible that he not be reborn with another face. The artist and the poet do not have to share the temptation of religious men: converting into permanence the necessity of abiding. Yet, and it is here that the gap between religion and poetry is marked, the poet exercises the function that I call *menic* only by opening it to the perpetual transit of *being-toward*. And if one insists on illustrating this difficult equilibrium between the two components of inhabiting, Trinitarian theology would provide a memorable example. For it must join together the being in itself of substantial unity or of abiding and the being-toward that distinguishes the persons by the eternal movement of their reciprocal reference. It is a difficult solution, and the theologian is not ignorant of its aporias. I have turned to it only to suggest a possible application.

6. It is therefore not my intention to divide the history of art into two great eras, each of which would monopolize one of the sides of the poetic and inhabit it. It would be ridiculous to split "poets," in the broad meaning that I have adopted, into two hostile races, of which one would supposedly have espoused the *being-in* of abiding and the other the exodus of *being-toward*. This quarrel between the Roman vault and the Gothic spire can amuse the fancy. It is no less, for all that, a parochial quarrel.[17] But though these simplifications denounce, of themselves, their outrageousness, it would be a great pity to retain nothing from them. In the hypertrophy that caricatures them, a truth that we must take advantage of is concealed. If one accepts what was proposed above concerning the sensible world, the manners of inhabiting it, and their relation to the poetic, and without imposing the drastic choice between substance and relation, one will not be surprised that one can inflect, according to this or that vection, the elements of a fundamental indivisible. In consequence, I will suggest, by way of hypothesis and guiding thread, the possibility of a theory of poetics inspired by a distinction that does not imply any vivisection.

7. The hypothesis itself presupposes the speculative context against which it stands out. To complete this first development, I think it is useful to recap, in a few propositions, its essential lines:

— the expression "poetics of the sensible" risks arousing suspicion of a pseudo-Platonic dualism. The only means of escaping this is a return to a thought of the world, itself based on a thought of the environment;

— the environment, at the most basic level of its biological expression, is characterized by its contents (positive and negative *stimuli*, to which assimilation and defense correspond) and by its functions (milieu in which the animal and, more generally, the living thing finds itself in order to there abide and move);
— in the terms of old, the appellations *being-in, being-toward* are suggested for its functions;
— the passage from the environment to the world implies a mutation on the plane of extension (passage to a universe) as much as on the plane of comprehension (*stimulus* of a new kind);
— the expansion of the environment into a world requires, in consequence, the demise of the old stimulant. This death substitutes for the narrowness of biological interest the comprehensive and extensive breadth of "being qua being of what is." The relation of being qua being and the world qua world is a necessary and reciprocal relation;
— this radical difference in the substance of the contents does not, however, annul the functional kinship of the environment and the world. I maintain, to name the new functions, the language of being-in and being-toward, on the condition of incorporating into them an irreversible mutation. *Being-in* and *being-toward* are the two essential components of that which the verb "inhabit" designates;
— *being-in*, or the *menic* function, has a certain affinity with the mathematician's neutral element. The fundamental [*fondamental*] acting that it specifies in no way changes "that to which it is added." Not making up the numbers with that very thing that it grounds [*fonde*], it is always presupposed by the complementary factor that, in its transitivity of *being-toward*, makes the world the springboard of a perpetual disorientation;
— the sensibility that "the sensible world" evokes refers, beyond the classifications of sensory powers, to a fundamental sensing of the world that exercises, in the pre-intentional mode, its two values of *being-in* and *being-toward*. The traditional division between sense and intelligence is unaware or ignorant of this radical sensibility that, what is more, permits a regrouping of the senses in accordance with the two components of inhabiting;
— I understand by "poetics of the sensible," in its generic meaning, a manner of inhabiting the sensible world that harmonizes its complementary factors of *being-in* and *being-toward*;

— this capacity presupposes no particular gift. Nonetheless, those whom I call "poets," in the Greek and transcendental meaning of the word, have the power of thematizing, by a transforming action, this poetic emerging of the sensible. When they are what they must be, they awaken in us that first lightning-flash, of rupture and of grace, that made an environment into the world where we have always been and toward which we move without end. An authentic poetry is precisely this marvel that actualizes a first lightning-flash and an original awakening;
— the sciences and religions have wholly different aims. The former forget being and the world in order to devote themselves to the exploration of what is. The latter, although they accept the artist's auxiliary service, are above all preoccupied with attaching the human to the security of an abode. By their insistence on the *menic* function, they risk suffocating or attenuating that *being-toward* or power of elsewhere that I depict by the poet's wings. As for philosophy, which seeks a difficult way between the two sources that inspire it (religion and knowledge), its art consists less in applying being and the origin in the shuddering of images and colors than in their projection in the logic of a discourse;
— although the poet, as I have defined him, must unite in a single surge the two sides of the poetic, it is not rash to presume that the dream of unity exceeds the limits of his power;
— by way of a regulative hypothesis, I distinguish, beneath a strict alternative, the poets of *being-toward* and the poets of *being-in*. This distinction does not aspire to the rigor of a judgment of Solomon or of an accurate division of the poetic noon.

To those who would ask me to verify the hypothesis, I can but answer, "Come and see." I do not reason from the possible to the real, nor from the real, even supposing we can speak of it, to the necessity of one or the other of the dominant chords that have been considered. I leave to each one the freedom of his path. What matters, after all, in these times of famine, is that, as best as we can and in spite of our weaknesses, the poet retains his right to pitch his tent among us.

2

The *Meta* Function

The works that sustain the discourse I am risking belong above all to the domain of literature. In so vast a field, I have cut out for myself the little garden where I love to tarry: books of the Bible, poems from yesterday or today, works said to be classic. I have nothing unknown to present.

I love to pass, to vary the delights, from one branch to another: from writing to painting or sculpture, in the naïve conviction that a single tree bears all these fruits. I mark out in this miscellany the movements that lead me elsewhere. And since it is a question of what I called *being-there*, I will attempt to take hold again of what hides beneath this prepositional language. It would perhaps be simplest to begin by what will appear to be an enigma: the *Meta* function.

On Transport

1. Today, the public transport in Athens is still called *Metaphorai*. A simple displacement from one place to another place. The legislation that governs them could be called *phoronomy*.

The mode of translocation matters little. What is most surprising is doubtless that one of the key words of our vocabulary is precisely the word *metaphor*. The banality of the designation does not clash with the unforeseeable extensions of its signified. Being displaced indefinitely has become essential to that which the change of place names. And that which it names is not only transit, in all directions; it is also and especially the power of *transiting*. It is this *I can* that is here the fundamental verb. It is in league with the possible, which is more and better than the absence of contradiction. The possible opens the road of other worlds. The mathematician, when it strikes his fancy, dreams of a universe with one, two, three, and n dimensions. It is always a displacement that he brings about. And even if he accepts that in the end there is only one real world, the manners of displacing himself in it conserve for him the joy of an innumerable plural.

2. What *metaphor* suggests, at the most basic level of its signification, is therefore freedom of movement, or more exactly the set of its degrees of freedom. And if I speak exactly [*de point*], it is first by implying the necessity of going farther, of "starting a new line," as the saying goes, and of doing so by the "fluxion of the point [*point*]." Well before people learnedly discoursed on the finite and the infinite, we had the premonition of them in a *transgression* that bears us beyond.

We no longer have, it is true, in our public transport, the least suspicion of what freedom of movement can be. To experience it we need an evasion or a break-in, as if it were necessary to pierce a rampart wall to breathe our connatural air. Blessed are we that we can thus leave our at-home [*chez soi*].[1] There are countries where, recently still, that gaze beyond could be only an impotent nostalgia. One is truly at home only to the degree that our home is bordered by an alterity that signals to us. This is a banal remark, but one with a great import that confirms for me what I was saying about the necessary complementarity of *being-in* and *being-toward* [*être-vers*]. If I did not fear that it would be a crude pun, I would dare to speak of versification [*versification*]. The "verse" [*vers*] with its rhythm, even its rhyme, be it as poor as that of doggerel, is already a displacement. It illustrates that freedom we associate with festivals, be they as quotidian as an encounter at the corner café. On the condition, of course, that the café be a free space, I mean not under surveillance.

3. Writing, for the one who writes, first presents itself, in its most modest manifestation, as a power of displacement—metaphor, the Greek of today and yesterday would say. Writing is made of points, of lines, of punctuation. Even before writing anything or giving this verb an object, we exercise it in a pre-intentional mode, beneath any intentionality of a project or an object, as a free modality in a space that *transposes* the space of our public transport. This blank page before me, open and unsurveyed, of whose *incipit* I am yet ignorant and on which I cast my dice, breaks the environment that encircles us and in which, too often, we must content ourselves with the *stimulus-response* schema. In this microcosm entrusted to its keeping, each of us replays for himself the birth of the world. Indeed, writing is in league, like the world, with being qua being. It breaks with the necessities, which are imprescriptible besides, of "being-for-me." And if it must serve, which I have no need to contest, it is under the sole imperative—this one is absolute—of having-to-say the being of what is. This

necessity that coincides with its freedom tolerates no prescription that would bend it to the right or to the left. Though I be a member of a Church or of a party, writing subjects me to the ethic of probity alone. The blank page [*page blanche*] is in no way, certainly, the "subsisting whiteness [*blancheur subsistante*]" of old. It has no need to compete with the Immaculate Conception. But beneath these claims that could be ridiculous, we must repeat that it is metaphor. It is the right and power to displace oneself, to disrupt limits or frontiers that would enslave us again to the destiny of the environment.

When I refer to being qua being and to the world, I mean nothing other than this ineluctable autonomy.

4. Coming back to the verb *to write*, I discover in it multiple dimensions. In its intransitive form, it has something in common with the verbs of displacement: to go, to come [*venir*], to occur [*advenir*], to befall [*survenir*]. It implies a free becoming in a milieu that I have imprudently baptized "scriptural space" to highlight the expansion that we associate with writing. The ancients, as we know, likened the intellective soul to a *grammeteion* or writing-tablet on which, nothing having yet been written, everything was to be written. And because the *soul* is in no way [*n'a rien de*] "a determinate nature, because it is not a simple being among beings," it is "capable of becoming everything" by virtue of knowing. The conjunction of this nothing [*rien*] and this potential everything defines, by a consubstantial metaphor, one of the particularities of human being. It expresses just as well the condition of the scribe who surely also has his individual or social limits but who, within these avowed limits, enjoys an expanding space whose frontiers he pushes back indefinitely. What enchants us in the poet, less bound in this regard than the prose writer of science, is precisely this capacity of always-renewed peripateticism that he makes us share. In this sense, we recognize in him a metaphoral power.

Deepening the ancient metaphor that led us into temptation, we reach a second dimension. Before tracing lines in the blank space that he imparts to himself, the scribe experiences, if I may say so, a moment of relative void. There are perhaps fortunate writers who already possess in their inner word, in the form of a predetermination that by its weight pushes forth its own exteriorization, the virtual plenitude of that which they have to write. Fortunate, I say, supposing they exist. For they accomplish in their own way and unbeknownst to themselves that passage from essence to existence that was reserved for the onto-theological argument. Such is not the case for the majority of mortals, among whom I stand. Before inscribing on the writing-tablet, like the laborer in his intractable field, the furrow of ink that sets down a decision, the hand hesitates among several directions. Even if an East point in the distance signals to us, more than one road leads to paradise. One can take this or that detour, shorter or longer. And there is no absolutely sufficient reason that cuts through the uncertainty. What we call the sense of a phrase sometimes amounts to the modesty of a remark [*propos*] that forms a proposition [*proposition*]. Signification is born, in its final determination, a bit like the dove from the ark that seeks to land, at the point of convergence of an audacity that affirms itself and a lassitude that accepts itself. Certainly if there is, in the present case, something rather than nothing, that is because, in the end, a wanting-to-say intervened that indeed says something. Automatic writing is but the supreme ruse of a reason that claims to be [*se veut*] an absence of wanting [*vouloir*]. But though intentionality could not, whatever one says, be erased, we must recognize that it appears at the end of oscillations where the *being-toward* that roams the blank page stretches out in multiple diversions. None of these routes is strictly equivalent. It is banal to restate, after so many others, the illusion of synonymy. And the logician has some supplementary motive for calling it into question. For the gaze that sees from afar, differences are abolished in a complicit fog. The writer who ended up choosing is not a victim of his choice. He knows that he limits himself and that by limiting himself he forgets something else, that other displacement that he will abandon to the field of possibles. But what did not take place wanders in the interstices to remind him that he inhabits a space of transport that, before any precise use of metaphor, imposes on writing a *metaphoral* condition.

A third dimension of the verb *to write* is perhaps the most novel and the least acceptable. In the style of a logician, I will say that it implies a reflexive relation: *x writes x*. An old master, taking up again the image of the *grammateion*, corrects its apparent passivity and, with an audacity that heralds future times, gravely pronounces, "The soul is indeed a writing-tablet (*grammateion*), but a writing-tablet that writes itself."[2] For all that one may want to lose oneself in the play of writing or to erase from it what, recently still, was called the "author," when one has discerned the role of social conditioning and of influences, it will indeed be necessary to admit that "all this did not make itself on its own." The product (and I insist on this word) betrays, despite the refusals, a "producing itself" that is entirely other than impersonal. Consequently, the scriptural space and the world that comes to light there, as well as the set of preliminaries that accompany or precede the inscription, cannot not testify, by a certain aspect and a certain style, to a more or less visible authority. This, even if it is illegible or unnamable, places [*pose*] and affixes [*appose*] its signature, the signature of a singular. It remains, however, that this singular, which it is impossible to avoid, is not the absolute master of its writing. Its writing can lead it where it does not want to go. For one never knows how far such and such a line that we have traced, without measuring its consequences, will lead us. The one who forms is therefore formed in his turn by that to which he gives form. This reciprocity, which without being reducible to it makes one think of the "action-reaction" pair, brings about new displacements that modify the scribe and that, on his presumed identity, or on a familiar face, draw unforeseen "turns." I will speak, in this sense, and concerning the activity of inscription, of a metaphoral existence.

Public transport has introduced us to displacements in a space of writing. An analogy, perhaps more suggestive than convincing, has allowed us to draw out, in a first approach, the most salient aspects of a freedom of transit. The verb *to write*, at the end of a superficial analysis, lost its apparent simplicity. We have become aware of a generic metaphoral that reveals the multiple dimensions of its *power*, its *condition*, its *constraint*, its *mode of existence*. In a new digression, we will have to pursue our fumbling research.

Digression on a Particle

In the *metaphor* of transport, the prefix *meta*, when we isolate it from the compound that supports it, invites us on a voyage. Freed from its substrate, become, as the saying goes, *syncategorematic*, it does not signify anything in particular, but it mobilizes the heavy substantives that always risk immobilizing movement. There is no question of taking inventory, by means of a dictionary, of the adverbial or prepositional applications that influence its use in the language of origin. Greek plays *meta* in innumerable forms. On the words that it makes iridescent and that it traverses like a lightning-flash, this electric particle seems to deposit an uncertainty principle, a slight quake and something like an evening breeze, the one the prophet Elijah felt at the end of his ascension. Could it be the sign par excellence of that *being-toward*, immanent to the poetic and to poetry?

1. Nonetheless, I cannot forget the grave suspicion that weighs on its history. The singular fortune that incorporated it forever into the term *meta-physics* also explains its disgraces. The Latin transcription that commands our lexicon of *transcendence* and the *transcendent* further compromised its destiny. The image of a *beyond* and the complementary one of a *below* indeed hardened, by an irremediable cut, the fluidity suggested by etymology. Considered as the "shepherd of being" by a prestigious philosophy,[3] man could no longer gather his sheep in a single territory. The schizophrenia that was feared had repercussions

on the unity of being and of the world. Thereafter the shadow of an afterworld systematically mortified our terrestrial *joie de vivre*. Christianity, Platonism for the *vulgum pecus*[4] as the saying went, could but consolidate these mortal dualisms. It is understandable that, faced with such dramatic threats, the so-called "modern" consciousness rebelled. In the same thrust that is maintained intact in our critical dogma, one was obliged to condemn, in the name of a more radical thought, in the name of poetry, and, for some, even by virtue of their faith dissociated from religion, an ensemble of images and concepts. This ensemble allowed one to define the essence of Western metaphysics ("Western" being, moreover, only a redundant addendum) by an onto-theology that is forgetful of what alone is necessary. If I recall these details of a commonplace exegesis, it is precisely in order to make evident, without accepting its legitimacy, the massive repoussoir[5] that, by a shock phenomenon, sends us back to less rudimentary interpretations.

2. From the particle *meta*, entrusting myself to the very movement that it spontaneously induces, I will retain above all, without concerning myself too much with a rigorous justification, the dynamic factors that it seems to me to imply. First of all, what surfaces from its major indicator is the idea of instability or the idea of an impatience that shakes up the establishment's solidities, be they from nature or culture. A sort of "ether wind" penetrates all that is and makes it tremble on its stem. If I did not fear the theological bias that underlies my work, I would gladly say that the prefix *meta* is, in language, the shadow of the Holy Spirit. This Spirit, of whom the Gospel tells us that we know not "where he comes from or where he goes"[6] and who is represented as a breath, is less the spirit who creates (*creator spiritus*) than the subtle irony who *uncreates* or who undoes. In the history of the Church, those who assigned him to the "third age" of the economy of salvation entrusted to him a delicate mission that defined him, in the least worst manner possible, as the authority who disturbs and who opens other ways. Without opposing him to the Word, the place of ideas and the principle of order, and still less to the paternal principle that produces this Word, they considered him as a principle, unnamed and unnamable, who calls into question the too-well-established order, the "tranquil kingdom of laws,"[7] fixed names, and acquisitions for all time. I am not surprised that he hovered over the prophets and—why not?—the poets. He has the gift, so precious for our intelligence, of the question mark that on the one hand worries our dogmatism and that on the other hand hints, beyond or below our permanencies and our conservation axioms, at an abiding that is less visible than our abodes and more fundamental than our foundations. A spirit of poverty, he is more fond of the

minus sign than of the *plus* sign, as if subtraction, contrary to our common estimations that are so favorable to riches of whatever order, were the most originary of our operations. It is this whole semantic set that I read implicitly in the delicacy of *meta*. The Greek noun *Metastasis* that we have turned into the term *Metastasis*, frightening ourselves with it at times, secures, in the constancy of an appellation, the *being-toward* of an uncertainty that is not yet a movement.

3. In a second meaning, on which I have had occasion to comment, the adverb *meta* makes explicit a movement that fulfills the prior Metastasis. *Metaphora* is generally translated as *transport*. And it is known that this latter word conjoins the extremes of a banal displacement and the shudders of ecstasy. At the neutral point, where we must situate ourselves, the *translocation* that it designates includes all the possibilities of *Metaphor*. Thereby it signifies, as I have said, that elementary freedom of whose degrees a simple nomenclature takes inventory. *Being-toward* is indeed multiform. Like the Heraclitean fire, it contains various tropes and tropisms. The directions and orientations that it evokes demarcate a play space whose top and bottom, right and left, front and back I love to name. It would be much too restrictive to limit its expansion to what is called, in opposition to the figurative, the literal sense. Why should this so-called figurative be second or secondary? The *infra* and the *supra* are of a piece, despite the special allocations that, in the complexity of a structure, distribute over several levels the rights of precedence and the position of the consecutive. It is better, in the present case, to refuse a dualism for which we reproach the metaphysics of the ancients—those poor ancients, one moment viewed with suspicion for having divided too much, and the next moment dismissed as prelogistically archaic for having conflated too much. We will therefore leave the *meta* of *Metaphora* to the happiness of polytropism.

4. A final term, the third in our group, announces its color under the same adverbial regime. Almost a literal calque of its Greek antecedent, the French equivalent, perhaps the most expected, joins to the first two the idea of *metamorphosis*. *Metamorphosis*, because of what the ancient poets made of it, seems closer to a mythological context. The word *transformation*, by virtue of its connections to transformism,[8] is more appropriate for scientific use. And if we speak of the metamorphoses of *libido* or desire, rather than of their transformations, it is perhaps because these Proteusus of our modern world, more mysterious than the ancient *appetite*, are crowned with an unreality that is rather near to the fantasies of myth, even though the knowledge that tracks them does not exclude them from its power.

Whatever the case may be with these nuances that it was useful to indicate, the *meta* of *metamorphosis* appears, at first sight, more bound in the thickness of the real than the superficial metaphors of displacement. It has its center of gravity in that other Proteus who, in Greek, bears the name of *Morphé*. *Morphé*, form, often confused with the figure that supposedly is, according to the well-known images, its expression or exteriorization, is part of the essence whose principal, Apollonian element it represents. I do not have to retrace the transformations [*avatars*] that form has known in the history of Western philosophy, which would already suffice to testify to its power of metamorphosis. The problems related to form and essence, however important they may be, will be left in the background. I have no need to discourse on the dichotomy of interior and exterior, which recently exercised the critics' sagacity. I highlight two features that are closely related to the idea of metamorphosis. First of all, because form, by its potential universality (already identifiable at the semantic level of the predicate), transgresses the individuals that singularize it, it presents itself in a multiplicity of faces, or let us rather say figures. But more profoundly, and in spite of the principle of identity, one would say that it is troubled by itself. Not only for the young poet is "the same" also "the other." This power of alterity and alteration is of itself unlimited. Like the intellective soul of the ancients in the order of knowing, form can become anything in the order of the real. Impatient with its limitation, it tends to exceed the wise contours that its ontological position assigns it. Everything happens as if, to respond to the metastasis that undermines it from the inside, it had to traverse a milieu of variation that forbids it no possibility. There is nothing, in these archaic dreams, that foreshadows the idea of evolution. But that humanity dreamed the universe before knowing it—this merits a moment of reflection. If one accepts what I have said about the emergence of a world that breaks with the environment, and if one also grants that what is in the world [*au monde*] is bound, as a "total part," to the cosmic context that envelops it, then one will not be surprised that even a rudimentary thought can interpret this universal connection as the necessity that each determination refer to the very thing it excludes or even that it transgress itself to *transit toward* its other and become what it is not. Metamorphosis is the wondrous dream that makes the most, unto the frontiers of the unbelievable, of the *being-toward* that inhabits, as a carrier wave, every "being coming into this world." This dream does not arise only from the poor in spirit. One finds it in the philosophies that thought the *whole* as a type of sympathy or resonance, as well as in the first attempts at cosmogenesis that were a prelude to more scholarly descriptions. This imaginary perhaps constitutes what has always been understood as the complement of form: I mean matter, the substrate that rebels against the concept, which is in no way what is but which introduces into all bodies, simple or complex, an indefinite power of substantial mutation. And this introduces my second remark. Every form emerges against a background of matter, meaning that it is fully brought into relief only by relying on a basic indeterminacy that supports it and that it cannot saturate. I will not linger on the various modern transpositions of this shadowy element. We must, however, note in passing the affinities, often highlighted, between matter and *nothing*. The idea of nothingness, which fascinates and repels, absurd for some, divine for others, hesitates between a "nothingness of excess," with a mystical inflection, and a "nothingness of defect" that rejoins matter. The creation *ex nihilo* of which theologians speak is situated between these two extremes, which lend themselves better to the ruses of metamorphosis. The apparition of the negative in this third dimension of *meta* is in no way bizarre. We will see later that the poetic is not foreign to it.

Meta-stasis, meta-phor, meta-morphosis: the rudimentary semantics that I have risked spells out the various powers of *meta*. It permits no deduction of one or another of these elements from any one of them. One will nonetheless observe that meta-stasis plays the role of a base or a preliminary condition. The ordered set of these powers constitutes what I call the *Meta* function.

The *Meta* Function

The term "function," in the context in which I take it up, could surprise. Is it not indeed reserved for the language of the logician and the biologist? And yet poetics and poetry belong to an entirely different genre. Could this unwarranted crossing [*passage*] be a sophism? But is not the poet that audacious one who fears no coming together? A brief crossing into another region, without abolishing differences, will help us deal with them in more depth.

1. The propositional function, to begin with what is most abstract, is not a proposition. It becomes one when the variables are replaced with the appropriate values. In this sense, it is a matrix of propositions, a *propositionifical* schema, as would have been said in the time of Rabelais. "$f(x)$", for example, states nothing, strictly speaking; it "proposes" the law of structuration for an infinity of propositions constructed on this model.

The biological or physiological function, which is more concrete than the preceding one, concerns an organism's mode of acting. This acting can be understood either as consecutive to a previously formed being [*être*] or, more radically, as the movement that forms the organism itself. I do not separate the two meanings, even as I privilege the second.

These two functions, so disparate at first sight, seem, however, to be related. They have in common that they are not saturated by any one of their concretizations. They transcend, in this sense, the contents that fill them. Respiration can be ensured by various organs (lungs, bronchi, skin pores). And let us say nothing of a logical function that indeed opens an infinity of substitutions. The gap between the two functions is marked by a feature that is not a mere detail: the former accentuates a law of structuration, or at the very least it is *this* above all that the logician insists on highlighting, doubtless because acting, by its resonances of an operating subject or of psychologism, seems to offend the purity of logic; the latter, in contrast, seems to imply, in addition but essentially, a structuring energy, a dynamism of construction and actualization. To tell the truth, these two aspects do not appear to be dissociable: an acting without a law would be condemned to anything whatsoever; a law that did not contain its power of realization would be immobilized in an abstraction or in a pseudo-Platonic subsisting idea. The play of dominant chords, if it is justified, tolerates no separation, as works of generative grammar have recently reminded us.

2. The *Meta* function, which I connect with the poetic and with poetry, in accordance with the full extension that I confer on them, indissolubly unites energy and law of structure. Each "poet" has his own unmistakable manner of practicing the *Meta* function. But in its unrepeatable singularity, which does not enclose it in an iron corset, this practice carries out a function that traverses him more than he masters it. The hypothesis that has guided us consists of transferring to the *Meta* function the various components with which the semantic analysis—a very biased one, let us admit—of a particle of major interest has supplied us. The generic *metaphoral* that served us as a point of departure thus attains a relative precision that cannot rival the rigor of a body of knowledge.

The *Meta* function first of all integrates the factor of Metastasis. In a work of poetry, be it literature or graphic art, what most strikes us, to the degree that it speaks to us, is precisely the instability that mobilizes all its elements. Each of them, as it were, is waiting for what it *will be*, impatient with its temporary limit, in a situation of liturgical Advent where that which must come is announced. It is not only a matter of passing from the everyday use of words to their poetic transfiguration. In the very interior of a poem, whatever it may be, they seem to tremble on their semantic stalk to transit toward an unforeseeable elsewhere.

It is true to say of them, when they are truly in situation and when they belong to the movement that carries them away, that they verify the definition of relation: "They consist only in their passing." And it is here, when one gives back to inspiration the breath [*souffle*] it loses when it is no longer anything but an impulse from the theater prompter [*souffleur*] hidden in the wings, that inspiration is not a vain word. Nothing better illustrates this pneumatic condition of terms than Van Gogh's famous quasi-Pentecostal painting in which the wheat bends its colors and its stems beneath the wind that bears its vegetal immobility away toward an unknown and cordial elsewhere. River of fire, undulation of waves, immense smile of an ecstatic nature, freed, in a Bacchic delirium, from the constraints of a wanting-to-say that submits them to an economy of necessity. The reader who enters into the dance participates in his turn in a single shuddering, in which the sons of the word become brothers of the free spirit.

3. Thus launched, by the very leap of vertigo, on the path of their becoming, all these elements set off toward the universe where they have their place without ever being frozen there in an essence. Too often, traditional semantics imposed on them a sort of choice between the rigidity of the univocal and the disgrace of equivocity. It forgot, under the constraints of a binary logic, that they have to traverse a "universe interval." It is in this traversal that they say fully that which they have to say. Or if they lose their sense, it is not to go mad in some wretched asylum or to be extinguished in the "anything whatsoever." *The metaphoral law* that governs them is not external to them, as if the poet's arbitrariness alone decided, by its violence, on a distortion that would simply be endured. In reality things are less simple; they are so far from being simple that one struggles to take up, without adding anything, the language of heteronomy. But to grasp their complexity, we must return to a fact of extreme banality and great import.

It is a fact that words, and not only words, are subject to multiple uses. Our dictionaries uncompromisingly record the non-coherent pluralism of their significations. The backward theoretician would attempt to discover, beneath their semantic multiplicity, a principle of unity or a root that would justify this dispersion. To him, one most often objects that usage is the sovereign ruler and that it would be ridiculous to introduce a principle of reason that would be liable to bind this rhapsody of contingencies into a strictly and totally ordered set. I duly note this sage positivism. Nonetheless, without entering into the debate that opposes the zealots of the empirical to the fanatics of the rational, we must recognize, as we have so often been reminded, that a language is also "the proposition of a world." And yet, if one grants that this is so, why would it be unreasonable to also accept its consequences? Below any determinism, and whatever the importance of chance may be, a world is not and cannot be the pure procession of what happens. Be they as distinct and separate as the conjunction *and* at times suggests to us, the coordination that unites things and events in a single world betrays, by the very weakness of its connections, the impossibility of absolutely isolating a single one of its elements. Let us go farther. And supposing that each element is made the unique member of a world, that unique singular that is called singleton would itself be intelligible only by the *other*, that is, the infinity of other worlds that by contrast make it unique. Whatever one does, the self-sufficiency of which one dreams founders on the shore where one hears the indistinct murmur of what is excluded. Likewise, each semantic element of a language resounds with what it is not, as if the whisper of its wings and the impatience of its having-the-power-to-say needed the breadth of the earth. That which I have pompously named the metaphoral law signifies nothing more but nothing less. In its advanced formula, I will express it in the following manner:

a) every element of a language is metaphoral because it refers, by the very lightness of its insufficiency, to the universe by which it is influenced in order to be fully significant;

b) to be realized, this open possibility calls for its transit by a universe interval. Concretely, and whatever may be true of the accidents of history, it is not an accident that the "dog-animal," to take up an established example, became the "dog-constellation." Certainly, a well-distributed common sense will always be surprised, be it a matter of realities or of words, that the familiar doggy can bark among the stars. The poet is less subjugated by the prudence of our dictionaries that content themselves with an average frequency in the semantic variations of a single substantive. He senses by instinct that free association, where everything that must surprise us can happen, is something wholly other than the weekend pastime of crosswords. And even though he does not use the language of the "total part," his sensibility renders him connatural with the "paradoxical implications" that, on another plane, the logician, sometimes to his surprise, recognizes in his turn. One can therefore propose a third version of the metaphoral law;

c) the sense of a word paradoxically implies an unlimited sequence of senses. Yet the poet himself, however attentive he may be to the plasticity of the "word," fulfills its expansive power only partially. This is only a *de facto* limit that in no way cuts into the *de jure* possibility. This finitude awakens, what is more, in the theologian who sometimes dozes within the poet, the dream of a *Logos*, of a universal link, of a word that would exhaust in its unique said not only the universe but the very power of saying it. I do not care to make his human analog the competitor of the god or one who is nostalgic for an impossible necessity. This theological precedent invites us to better understand, by this passage to the absolute, a practice whose import would escape without this horizon of the unreal. The poet will never say in a single word everything that word would want to say [*voudrait dire*].[9] He says it. He says it partially in a succession that remedies, after a fashion, his infirmity. I will therefore complete the explication of the metaphoral law in one last turn;

d) the semantic power of a word affirms its inductive universality only by the mediation of the verbal universe of which it is a part.

This semantic lability of words, which the metaphoral law codifies, implies, contrary to what one could fear, neither a tautology of strict equivalence, nor the indifference of the anything whatsoever, nor the erasure of values of signification in an indeterminacy where everything would mix together in an inextricable confusion. Though poetry obeys other rules than logic or science, it has not for all that taken a vow to re-establish chaos and plunge the unidiversity of the world into chaos again. The diverse remains diverse. Each word has its weight of sense. In the image of the total part, it reflects the whole only within its relative singularity. It is thereby that it is capable, exceeding its temporary frontiers, of sheltering in the hollow of its future the successive figures of its becoming.

4. The third dimension of the *Meta* function adds to the preceding one a determination that is just as much its restriction. In the particular meaning that I have reserved for it, *metamorphosis* follows a precise line of evolution. *Metaphor* causes the passing from one order to another order, for example, from mineral to vegetable and from vegetable to superior stages in a hierarchical series that, moreover, varies with cultures. In contrast, *meta-morphosis* imposes, on the semantic transit, the law of the same genus. Though it is true that the poet is not subject to the rigidity of our frameworks, it remains that he is not foreign to a certain regulation that we observe, without too much artifice, in certain works. When the inductive word relies on an animal or vegetable determination, it is not rare for induction to open a homogeneous series, however limited it may be, that specifically lists those who belong to these respective worlds. Metamorphosis moves in a certain milieu. It leans on the vertical line of ascension where the

transpositions of meta-phor are brought about; but it retains, in each case, only the anchor point where the transversal lines of expansion, at the different levels, originate. It should also be added that the poet never makes use of the totality that he theoretically has at his disposal. More or less pressing reasons have limited the *et cetera* that the initial term called for to a few representative specimens. The evocation of the gazelle by the wife's name does not ordinarily require the rich profusion of Noah's ark. And this suggests to me a last, more general remark. Whether it be a matter of meta-stasis, meta-phor, or meta-morphosis, the space that the multiple components of the *Meta* function generously offer to the scribe remains subordinate to the choice, to the selective elaboration of an agent that we must indeed call by his name, that honorable name of *author* that has seemed, since several years ago, to have fallen into disuse and disgrace. What I have said of the scriptural space, far from proscribing it, demands this authority. For it is what it is only by the work that makes it a world, a single world, yet beneath an ever-new sky.

The Song of Songs

I have chosen the Song of Songs to render sensible this *Meta* function, of which it seems to me to be an exemplary fulfillment.

1. Abandoning problems of traditional or non-traditional interpretation to the specialist, I will consider only the naked text, such as it offers itself to the candid reader. The first impression, for a cursory reading, places us from the outset within the poem's movement. One is ceaselessly drawn away from one form to another, and the genius of metaphor adds to metamorphosis the unforeseenness of its transpositions. It is this that the nonbeliever himself notices, who one moment follows a rather linear track and the next moment follows a sort of ascensional force that makes him traverse a universe. This universe plays out on the body, the body of the wife, the body of the husband, which thus becomes a microcosm and atlas in which are marked out, by a play of correspondences, the riches of a nature that is helpful and obedient to the suitor's call. From the animal world that would seem, at first sight, to be most adapted to the free mobility of a mad love, the writer has retained the gazelle and the "young fawn," who are soon relieved by the dove and the turtledove. It is as if the earth, however light it may be for the supports that it lets bounce back in a burst of momentum, aspired to erase itself in the immateriality of an aerial space. When, changing register, the springtime vegetation of Palestine offers the variety of its essences, these forms

themselves attenuate the precision of their contours to be exhaled in fragrant essences, the last effort of a "spiration" that restores to the quasi-nothingness of a breath the fixity of their designations. This is only one example among others of these metamorphoses that take the most unforeseen paths. Mountains and hills, stars and sun, all this mute world, infant[10] from birth, receives from the lover the gift of the word and of communication. One would say that nature entire aspires to resolve itself into a universal north wind: "Arise, O north wind, and come, wind of the south! Blow on my garden, let its spices be wafted abroad. May my beloved come into his garden and taste its delicious fruits" (Song of Songs 4:16).[11]

I have sometimes meditated on that "living flame of love" in the rose windows of Notre-Dame that distribute the enchantment of their colors over several concentric circles. The Song of Songs is not submitted to a geometric structure. It invites the major apparitions of a cosmic feast to the dance. The round of the seasons, the conspiracy[12] that from one extreme to the other joins the elements and the parts of a universe, verifies an autarchy of the world that adequately responds to the autarchy of a subsistent love in its perpetual becoming. One passes from one circle to another, from the earth to the sky, from the inanimate to the vegetal, from the flowers of the day to those of the night, from the lightest animality to its volatile dream, but the metaphoral transition, however abrupt it may be, never negates continuity. Each of the circular lines that carve out a region and that constitute the quasi-latitudes of the poem is subsumed under the meridians that recall, over and over, the unity of everything. Metamorphosis and metaphor, under the impatience of metastasis, define the fervor of a footrace, wandering and competing in its fraternal dispersion. A haughty regard, much taken with positivity, would doubtless pose, concerning this admirable delirium, the impertinent question of a sage positivism. It would perhaps reproach the pair of lovers for the naïve anthropomorphism that makes "everything" revolve around their august navel. From there to invoking, as a decisive argument, the "Copernican revolution" there is but a step. Too heavy a memory is, I admit, scarcely favorable to the heart's ecstasies. And the charges of egocentrism would add to the first charges the critical supplement that attributes the exuberances of an inspired youth to the infantile representation of the world. One cannot but be disarmed before the severity of such a gaze. Perhaps, and this would be the poem's meta-critical lesson, this lucidity that mistrusts too beautiful a light makes but a single error: taking itself so seriously that one adheres in one's turn to one's own representation. It could be that the poet is the child who in order to say himself needs to cause beasts and precious stones, "myrrh and aloes, with all the finest spices,"[13] to speak. Does he thus spread through fragrances the archaism of a henceforth abolished rhinencephalon?[14] Each one is free to thus interrogate the "children of paradise." But the adult who today takes up the paths of the Song in his own manner would be more than skeptical of the awakened man's assurances. For the love that thus spreads out, from orbit to orbit, over the elements of a universe, is a transpersonal force of which the frail beloved is but the passageway. What she feels in herself, in a fundamental sensibility that accords with the being of the world, is precisely the power of this transit that makes everything that is "consist" in a reciprocal reference. And it is thereby that the Song exercises, in a major key, this *Meta* function that sums up, in the inevitable abstraction of a formula, the different powers of *being-toward*, which I have temporarily isolated from *being-in*.

2. Meta-stasis, meta-phor, meta-morphosis: this operative trinity is not limited, let us repeat, only to the domain of writing, still less of a literary writing. It should be, at certain moments of happy plenitude, the Song of each one of us. The necessities of life have converted existence into the impossibility of existing. The Song of the Sun that, in Francis of Assisi, connaturalized the soul with the fraternity of the *cosmos* is now only the exception that confirms the rule. This is why a sorrow, whose cause is not perceived, seems to traverse every poem, as if it had to be pardoned for the beatitude that bears it and that it diffuses. The presence of the chorus in Greek tragedy, but also in our Song, lets us guess this sorrow. As different as it is in the two cases, its role is irreplaceable. It reminds us of a simple and imprescriptible demand: for the poetry of the world to be felt by each one of us, we need the complicity of all gazes upon the light and shadow of things, common participation in the joy and woe that they spread, the conspiracy of all spirits in a single body of benediction or of pity. On this condition alone would the poem be completed.

In this way, one better understands what the spectacle signifies, so frequently identified as an accidental pastime, a simple appendix that would be added from outside the work.

Yet neither reading nor spectacle are, strictly speaking, additives. The poem, be it made of stone, of sounds, of colors, or of words, is truly constituted and attains the "stature of its perfect age" only by that excess of overabundance that makes it exist in us and by us. It matters little whether the author did or did not foresee the posthumous history of his work; it matters little even whether he accepted or wanted the destiny of solitude. The gift that he gives to us is not truly received unless the receiver adds to it, by his welcome, the glory of its future. In this sense, everything that is durably inscribed on our earth awaits the "revelation of the sons of God"—I mean that noble appearing that has nothing in common with the illusions of appearance. The sorrow that I invoke and that, in the peace of the seventh day, envelops the rested expanse of completed work measures the distance between what should be and what is, measures the gap between the poet's universe and the universality to which, by a necessity of essence, he can aspire without being able to renounce it. Unlike the God of Genesis who, at the end of his creation, "saw that it was good,"[15] the poet does not have at his disposal the supreme assurance that would affix to his world the definitive *Amen* of the concert of spirits. He can but share the bitter beatitude of those who already know that they will not be consoled.

3. This opening of the poem on its improbable future obliges me to complete what I was saying about the *Meta* function. We must consider it no longer only within the internal economy of a work but also within the totality of relations that refer it to its possible recipients, which amounts to enlarging considerably the field of its different factors. Meta-stasis afflicts, henceforth, the later becoming of the poem with a ring of uncertainty that will never be totally dissipated. The subsequent interpretations project onto the thing, written or inscribed, a supplementary mobility that at times renders the original version unrecognizable. None could be surprised by this save those—and they are yet numerous—for whom "sense" has the fixity of an antique essence, immutable beneath accidents. Yet "accidents" are so little foreign to substance that substance, at the limit, seems to be reabsorbed into the non-ordered set of all that happens to it or that can happen to it. Without sharing this radicalism, for the written thing has also its weight of day and of night, one cannot disqualify this ring of the unknown that makes it the point of intersection of itineraries that are as varied as they are improbable. Who would have foreseen what the books of the Old Testament would become? They have been translated and indefinitely commented on. These transformations [*avatars*] are so many paths that no providence could have anticipated. The lines of possibility could well, retrospectively, be drawn on the background of the past. They say in the past tense only the present whose contingent future they will have been. If we take the case of simple translation, we are not unaware that this passage to another genre is something wholly other than an equivalence. The supposed correspondence between the two linguistic sets betrays, beneath a postulate of synonymy, the metaphorical power that displaces a text toward an unsuspected elsewhere. This more or less abrupt leap from one universe to another is repeated along each of the transversals that develop this or that type of metamorphosis. The spiritual exegeses of the Song have permitted

us to dream in turn of the precious stones that it makes gleam, of the scale of fragrances with which it enchants the atmosphere, of the zoological and vegetal series that punctuate, with their successive emergences, the beloved's footsteps, etc. One can freely choose other examples. Whatever the styles of the adopted variations may be, one finds again in them the constants that, clumsily, I have conceptualized under the name of the *Meta* function.

4. The poem, in the diversity of its genres and modes of expressions, remains for us the uncontested paradigm of *being-toward*, which therefore indissolubly unites meta-stasis, meta-phor, meta-morphosis. We will have no need to contest this connection. Nevertheless, nothing prevents giving one or another of these components an elevation that, without isolating it in a chimerical in-itself, indicates its importance and originality. The problem that from then on solicits our attention would be stated in the following manner: are there not quasi-symbols that exemplify, in a striking manner, each of the factors of which the *Meta* function is a living unity? The question is perhaps not as strange or wild as its abrupt formulation could incline us to believe. It remains to find the *respondents* that could, possibly, assume this symbolic value. I do not pretend in this search to get hold, as the saying goes, of universal invariants. More modestly, I have retained three elements that seem to me, rightly or wrongly, to illustrate, by their recurrence in our cultural milieu, the different powers of the *Meta* function. Their names are not mysterious. The *mask* schematizes meta-stasis; the *angel's wing* frees the movement of meta-phor; *fire*, more familiar, evokes, in my immemorial memory, the lability of meta-morphoses. The analysis that I will devote to them will complete my study of *being-toward* in the poetics of the sensible.

3

Mask and Metastasis

The mask, which comes to us from the four corners of the world, as if their enigmatic identities were hiding under this mysterious double, demands, to be understood, a first reflection on the face. What is striking in a face is the extreme mobility that does not permit us to liken it to the simple repetition of a figure traced once and for all. This mobility is inscribed within the interval delimited by the point of origin and the final point, birth and death. The dead person's face was perhaps the first sketch of the mask. In what sense is it still a conclusion, a proposition, a last *prosopon*?[1]

The Face of Death

1. What unites the first walk-on apparition that comes into the world to the disappearance that leaves it, after being released from it, is that both have closed eyes. But whereas the closing promises to the beginning an indefinite future, it signifies to us at the end the necessary impossibility of opening ourselves to it. Metastasis is the interim of variation that unites that *incipit* and that *exit*. I do not forget, however, that this restriction of the form to the face brings about a real reduction. By what right does one sum up the human, in his psycho-somatic density, in a facial undulation, and this undulation itself in an ocular point that fades away in its turn in the imponderability of a gaze? Could the gaze be what lifts up the weight of things and of the body in a movement of immaterialism? Could the sin of idealism have been, for all time, embedded in optical privilege; could it be this acropolis that fixes the reflection of the immortals to the summit of the hill and to the vertical axis that joins the earth to the sky?

The meta-stasis that pushes upward the terrestrial heaviness of the body and the world is indeed prolonged, indefinitely, in the face. Whether it wrinkles with waves provoked by the slightest shock; whether it hardens in decision; whether it affects the mimics of the actor; or whether it relaxes in a child's sleep, which remains for me one of the most admirable spectacles, the face is in a continual transit, as if it also had to become all things to be what it is. Great art was often tempted to surprise it. And Cézanne himself, when he painted the Sainte-Victoire mountain at various hours of the day, kept an eye on that denuded mass, watching for the restlessness of a living thing, the uncertainty of lines that trembled in the wait for a visitation, in order to insinuate in *Physis* itself the consciousness of an invisible passage inviting it to rise ever higher. And yet this face is extinguished in death. Fires extinguished, the deceased is promised to the ashes. But before being dispersed in them, he seems to brace himself against himself, in a last jolt, in order to persevere in his being, in the form of a solid with a suspended sentence. I do not weary of contemplating this fixity without return that signs with an *Amen* the definitive *adieu*, this writing with bumps and hollows that points to an ultimate elevation on the flat horizon of a finite world. It is a sculpted writing that disdains the details of existence in order to gather up, on this block of yellow marble with purplish veins, the essence of an existent, an essence that no longer has to become, that no longer invites to that "exit" that the verb *ex-ister* signifies.

2. The face of the last hour implies something else, however. It speaks of a repose whose *Requiem*, Gregorian or Faurian, will be the Word of liturgy or of austere splendor. This repose of the face in the eyes that are closed forever is perhaps less the absence of the gaze than its last unfolding (unless it is the first), a new trope that turns it toward the interior, toward an East that one cannot anchor because one lives from it too intensely to spread it out in the space of an object. This gaze that gazes at nothing but that an invisible light obliquely illuminates, this absent gaze where the figure of the world gathers itself, whose radiant point and fragile lightning-flash it once was, indicates, beneath the agitation [*agitation*] where our acting [*agir*] is divided, this indefinite place of a fundamental *abiding* of which death, in the most ancient dreams of our old humanity, remains the most singular manifestation. The end of a man, of a face, of a gaze, is ambiguous like the "end" itself that, in our tongues, says pure and simple cessation just as much as fulfillment. The famous Hegelian *Aufhebung* perhaps draws its force and its prestige from this prestigious equivocity that the preface of the dead sang in the Roman mass. The *Requiem* of death does not, indeed, impose any positive faith. It holds us on the brink of an indecision that refuses the dogmatism of the *yes* and the cutting blade of the *no*. And it is doubtless in certain overwhelming images that Zen Buddhism offers us in its monasteries in Kyoto that I most felt the grandeur of this indecision that marks, below any ground, a certain depth of being, of living, and of thinking.

The Face of the Child

At the other extreme point of the bow that meta-stasis draws, there is that ball of fire, tempered by its enclosure, that we call "baby" by a redoubling analogous to that which gave its name to the surprising theater usherette that the old man himself still calls "mama." The child's closed eyes shelter the growth of a nature that makes grains burst to give to them also this quasi-gaze on the world that evokes, in complicity, that other gaze, thrown from above, that we confide to the stars. It is, moreover, only by convention that we determine a life's beginning. To tell the truth, the child-infant is at the zero point only by the absence of word and vision. But from all time he was on the way, also a pilgrim of the same becoming, on a route like no other. Metastasis is thus articulated, virtual and unlimited, over this initial void where the first tremblings of the fledging who tests his wings in the premonition of the first flight are risked.

The motivating incoordination waits for the signs of the commandment and the constraints of order. But already about this rigor to come the plasticity of the origin poses the question: what will this child be, and what will he make of what is and of what is imposed? The question mark half-opens the royal door of existence. Beyond empty indetermination, beneath the firm features that limit possibles, it casts toward the future the indistinct lines of a hope. It is thus that metastasis lets dream, on a child's face, a poetry in act that hesitates over its writing. What has been called *essence* is already there as "what is to be," in this flesh shaken by a Brownian motion. This quivering of a breeze over the sleeping waters of closed eyes awakens the festive memory of Fra Angelico's Annunciations and the impending lightning-flash of primroses in the mild warmth of spring.

The germinal metastasis is also heavy with multiple metaphors. The vegetal extends the shadow of its muteness over the *infant's*[2] silent growth. But the beautiful animal becomes agitated without delay, as if to refute the immobility of the beginning. He drags himself around, rolls about, and rolls himself into a ball, for he must crawl before rising up in a defiance that lifts the head and before taking leave of a too-long sleep. He gropes by trial and error in the course of his metamorphoses. But when his eyes are fully open in a last *adieu* to a life's dawn, the tacit decision that verticalizes existing will sign, with an irreversible writing, the end of innocence and the exile from paradise. And the adult's gaze will fix, on this new avatar of interminable metastasis, the melancholic and categorical imperative: Pass, you too, and die.

The Face and the Mask

Between death, which erases meta-stasis, and birth, which inaugurates it, I situate, after a fashion, that surprising artifice of which Africa and Asia deliver to us the strangest specimens. Our poor carnivals reverberate, with a dying echo, their immemorial fascination. What does the mask say to us?

1. I read on the mask the fixity of the cadaver, a dead face that has even lost those extinguished eyes that nature grants, for a time, to those who have left forever. I read there also, as on the child's closed eyes, the infinity of an inaugural metastasis. In this coincidence of opposites lies the mask's heart, its secret, and its challenge.

2. I am using a very equivocal, and too scholarly, expression: "coincidence of opposites." It is an abstraction that the naïve understanding [*entendement*] interprets as a synthesis in which the respective and contrasting qualities of its elements would be canceled in an eminence. More subtly, we should grasp what the supposed reconciliation of opposites lets us hear [*entendre*]. Simply put, in this paradoxical conjunction that we translate by the particle *and* the irony of the mask murmurs to the sensitive [*sensible*] ear: *neither this nor that*. The mask is in no way what we, by a poverty of intelligence and of imagination, make it say by lowering its enigma to the level of what we have already seen and of what we know. The mask invites us to a surpassing of the familiar landscapes that surround, between two extremes, the eloquent and visual mobility of a gaze fixed on a face.

In place of the eyes, there *is nothing* but the void of their possible place. These holes of shadow seduce and make tremble. The mask's immobility disqualifies movement only to shelter all its surprises, without containing them. Say, if you like, "immobile movement." But on one condition that I specify at once: in this mysterious immobility the unpredictable future of a world, of a history, and of a character takes root. Nothing and everything. *Todo y Nada*. The *nothing* of withdrawal and silence, like the mathematician's indifferent or neutral element, accompanies everything that will come to pass. From this black cavern, and from this open and snickering mouth, there emerges only the impossibility of stopping and of settling somewhere. The fear and the fascination that they unleash arise from this nothing, from this *ex nihilo* from which every creation proceeds and this spectacle that a divine comedy will make the theater of marionettes and illusions, the game of chance and calculation, the vital space of the ridiculous and of tragedy. After which, if you have looked well upon this mask at the midnight hour, reread the finale of Plato's *Parmenides* that served as an exergue and a motif for this work: "'As it seems, whether one is or is not, it and the others both are *all* and are *nothing*, and both appear and do not appear all things in all ways, both in relation to themselves and in relation to each other.'"[3] I emphasize *everything* and *nothing*, and I return to the mask, which the philosopher had perhaps found again when he wrote these exultant or despairing lines.

3. The mask worries because it is in man the inhuman place of all metastases—or, if one prefers, metastasis itself. This masked man is, like Odysseus, the man "of a thousand devices [*tours*]," the *polotrupos aner* who was perhaps in Hellas the true ancestor of the pagan and Christian *Logos*. This is why, if one asked this masked man who without moving twists and turns his terrible fixity in every direction, "Tell me, what is your name?" he would doubtless answer, if he could answer: *I am called* Personne.[4] *Personne:* the same word, among us, that signifies *none, no*, that cancels every person [*personne*] and that at the same time reestablishes him in his signified. Curious destiny of a word that should tempt, for a philosophy of the mask, the defenders of the person [*personne*] and the partisans determined to surpass him. This forbidden pentagram that says the gathered-up violence of a bloody freedom in the form of its negation in a degenerate matter is a word as decisive as Cambronne's,[5] a destinal word that says at the same time the nothing and the everything of the person [*personne*]. It is to be meditated on indefinitely, just like being qua being, also an expression "of a thousand twists [*tours*]." "Tell me, what is your name?" "I am who I am." A Biblical word that it would doubtless be sacrilegious to liken to the Odyssean answer. God and being and the person [*personne*] (the nondescript person [*personne*] that I am, like the *uomo qualunque* of the Italians of 1950, like the *Niemand* or the *Nobody* of the fifteenth century or the strange captain *Nemo*)—it is the same mask that from its "mouth of shadow,"[6] if it could close it, would say to us again, "I am called *personne*" or nothing; "I am who I am." Being and mask, God and mask, the person [*la personne*] and his mask. *Of* and *by* this immobile fixity there are only walk-ons, schematizations, metastases. And on all these voids of an originary *No* theater unfolds the macabre or joyous feast of our processions. I am surprised that a young philosophy, really young, has not yet undertaken a serious reflection on all these quasi-*nothings* of language, these indefinites, as they are called, or these poor decadent remains (*one, some, none*), these holes of shadow where names are lost and which open the space of a post-philosophy, the post-philosophy of the "syncategorematics," these abandoned ones of our common dereliction that have not yet found their *metaphysician*. After substantives (where the old substance nested); after verbs

that said the glory of action *in the beginning*; after prepositions and adverbs that said relation and transit, the quasi-nothing of passage, we must, "going ever farther" toward our evanescence, make a decisive place for all these, language's little ones, that we should finally have come to us. I well know that the logician is not a stranger to them when he speaks of quantifiers. But *quantification*, as the word indicates, remains within the molar domain of quantity. And the particles of nullity such as *no, none, nobody* [*personne*] look just like a piece of refuse that indicates less the possibility of a source than the extreme point of our vanishing. For affirmation, so it is believed, is first, like addition. It is all this that would invite us to reexamine the meditation on these particles of extreme poverty that are in language the equivalent of the mask—I mean these linguistic voids in which arise, in the dailiness of our words, that which puts them at a distance and calls them into question. They are, in daily bread, the yeast that makes its substance rise (it is in this sense that they are supersubstantial) and refers it to that void that cloaks and shades our various plenitudes.

4. If I am proposing a round trip between the mask and the syncategorematic, with an eye to illuminating the one by the other, it is precisely because the mask has no sense or content by itself. It makes every sense and every content tremble. It is the meta-static possibility of a theater of characters. By linking, through the mediation of characters, the meontology of the indefinite pronoun "nobody" [*personne*] to the ontology of the *person* [*personne*] that it covers with its shadow, it suggests a mysterious power of all becoming. Over the singular that bears a name and at which one points in a demonstrative, it lets the indecision of the "unnamable" and of the "omninamable" hover. More exactly, the nothingness of the mask *roots* the being of the *person* [*personne*] and obliges it to proliferate in the multitude of figurations in which is affirmed, without being exhausted there, an ever further that will never be completed in a *nec plus ultra*.[7] The meta-stasis that the mask thus makes imperative for all temporary stases of figuration signifies two things to us: the impossibility of fixing once and for all in a role or function the being of this singular whose face the mask infinitizes, and the necessity that pushes it to *proceed* indefinitely, to go from figure to figure and from shadow to shadow in order to equal the world-universe that it must *face up to*.

But in its most enigmatic aspect, the mask reminds us that being *inhabits a place* outside of all ontology, a utopic place that disqualifies all circumscription of essence or form. And this non-localizable place of the mask is less a protection than an unsurveilled freedom that judges, without appeal, the lability of our metamorphoses and that refuses to take seriously whatever is imposed on us by the principle of an importance. It is thereby, by that fringe of non-being, that the mask evokes the divine.

5. The relation between the mask and divinity is in no way artificial. We know, indeed, that the god reveals himself only by concealing himself. The *deus absconditus* of Judeo-Christian theology is a power of distance and judgment. He frees a "cloud of unknowing"[8] that defies any will to representation and manipulation. One can henceforth wonder—but I advance this hypothesis timidly—if the mask might not be the secret and poetic matrix of all negative theologies.

Perhaps it is necessary to go further. Ancient theater, more than ours, used the mask. And comedy still more than tragedy. It has also been possible to say that comedy was the death of the gods. Death in and by derision. This is a rather well-founded opinion, but one that it is important to understand well. The ridiculousness of the gods, at a certain critical moment of cultural evolution, consists in their too-great likeness to the human world of their creatures. They imitate too well those who ought to have been like them—so much and so well that they look thereafter like the hypertrophy of an existence that tragedy still maintained in its loftiness. Comedy had the great merit of highlighting the impossibility of dissociating supposedly positive qualities from their necessarily defective modes. It shows with a sure but unconscious logic that the anthropomorphic postulate will not tolerate any decisive division.

The principle of redoubling having once been posed, it is necessary to grant to the immortals, so that they can descend unto us, all the flaws that their essence refuses but without which they could not exist. Just as they surpassed us in virtue, they must inversely transcend us by the excessiveness of their flaws. The mask, in its turn, takes on another form. Derision indeed demands the enlargement of traits and the reversal of transcendence in the swelling of the negative. Comedy thus plays its cathartic role. It invites us to eliminate the gods whom our laughter sanctions and, for an analogous reason, those who make us tremble, to the degree that they are only the exaggeration of our power or our violence. But, ridiculous or tragic, they remain, under the masks in which theater decks them out, the contraries of a single genre. And such is, it seems to me, the ultimate lesson of comedy: leaving the *genre* that brings them together into a single community of human finitude. The two masks with which comedy and tragedy dress them by turns are but the sides of a single *breadth* [*travers*] that we are shown at work so that we might have the courage to *traverse* [*traverser*] them. Beyond these antithetical figurations, comedy suggests to us the derision of powers and the necessity of re-ascending, in order to not be victims of them, to the pure and immobile mask that, in its immobility of the last judgment, holds them at a distance and denounces their vanity. It pronounces the death of the gods only to elevate us to that sublime and neutral point that gives rise to their frolics, but without conceding to them the right to the absolute.

Pure and faceless mask, mask of tragedy, mask of comedy. If, renouncing facile representations, we wanted to think them at the level of their functions that are in solidarity, we could explicate the sense of their reciprocity in a quasi-group of operations. The pure mask that dominates, to give rise to them, the figurations that it makes possible indicates, beyond beings and being itself, the unfigured abode, the space of serenity and height where the spirit rests. The mask of tragedy sums up the world of characters and functions in their more or less solid determinations and their possible evolutions: it renders sensible the indefinite procession of figures. The mask of comedy unties [*délie*], in a judgment that brings them back to their origin, that is, to the pure mask, the solidities of the establishment that confirm the characters' seriousness. It symbolizes irony, the astuteness [*délié*] of a spirit that does not let itself be fooled or taken in by anything at all. These three masks are, I repeat, the symbols of the fundamental operations that articulate the movement of a free being [*être*]. If we designate them by letters with indices M1 M2 M3, it is easy to note that M3 is possible only by M2 and M1; analogous connections would be valid for the other terms. This amounts to saying: if we had no place where our hearts abided, we could do nothing, we could judge nothing. Freedom, supposing we retain this oft-debased word, is the Trinitarian unity of these fundamental movements, relations, and operations to which I assign approximate verbs: abiding-inhabiting, transiting-producing, putting at a distance-judging. A pure abiding would be death; a pure doing would be dispersion; a pure judgment would be a non-judgment. One will excuse me from schematizing the various combinatory possibilities. For the masks thus understood I know not if there is or can be a dance, bergamask or not. But I would not be at all surprised if some audacious one is caught up one day by their incantation in order to render sensible, in music and movement, the originality of their fundamental acting.

6. In Christianity, would it be rash to see in the mad [*fou*] and infirm God of the *theologia crucis* a mask of divine comedy? Is the judgment on the world and its attractions not, as Saint Paul implied, a derision? The highest gods, who are identified with Wisdom or with Power, the most spiritual ones if you will, are there designated as the supreme authorities by which it is no longer possible to be taken in. They too have been nailed to the Cross. The new god takes shelter under this sign-mask; he takes leave of the former figures. And his death symbol, so badly understood in spite of all that has been said and repeated

in these past decades, is, truth be told, the mortification of all that is and all that was. By making, in turns, folly appear as wisdom and wisdom as folly, or infirmity as power and power as infirmity, he delivers us from our positions as from our negations. Beyond, indefinitely beyond, without our ever being able to stop, somewhere, the movement of withdrawal, the astuteness of a freedom for which the bird-catcher with his nets will never be deft enough. The fools [*fous*] for Christ understood this well. They knew that the Cross is the feast of a worthy folly. But if they understood it thus, it is doubtless because the mask of divine comedy, derision of our pretentions and swellings, brought them back to the pure mask, to that eminence, or to that hollow of the Calvary-rock, to that void that one inhabits, not to loaf there or to there take delight in a bleak identity, but in order that everything begin there and that nothing be completed without making a return to it.

4

The Angel's Wing: The Feast of the Ascension and of Metaphor

I will speak of the angel because *that* has for a very long time been forbidden to us. It is not a current consideration, and theologians themselves seem no longer to have the courage to revive it. But at the moment of explaining myself, I experience more than ever the fear of being naïve, as if I were constrained, faced with the free spirits who walk without crutches, to hide beneath my coat the wing that bears me. And yet the angel has the means to charm. He has charmed this or that poet who has generously opened to him the threshold of his abode. Without entering into the details of a debatable angelology, we should remember that these spirits who do not strike,[1] who glide in the murmur of the lightest breeze, are part of the poetics of the sensible. Without them, something heavy would envelop the world and prevent it from rising or taking off. Even if prudence forbids us from believing in separate substances, each one of which, so it was said long ago, exhausts its species, this strange condition that the logician, with his customary precision, would raise to the abstract dignity of "singleton" could induce more than one dream. The painter who in his piety questions light has the cordial certainty of an instant that will not return, of an "angelic salutation" that also saturates the set to which it belongs according to the language of extension. And if criticism hesitates, before this new winged tribe, to grant it the right to and the grace of existence, at the very least it has a duty to suspect that on earth as in heaven there is *perhaps* something else. *Perhaps*, this adverbial particle, as tenuous as a breath, passes over our heavy affirmations to awaken them to a more courageous mobility. The tongue of angels perhaps contains only this little word, which they have let fall within the interstices of our most decided words. And this means also that we must not too quickly enclose ourselves within the *diktat* of our impossibilities. *Impossible*, so it was said, is not French. It could indeed be an axiom of laziness, a lack of imagination. At the very least, before pronouncing it we should weigh our words and specify their context. Many things have appeared impossible that later on were less absurd than had been believed. But if the angel suggests to me the modesty of the *perhaps*, it is not to plunge me straightaway into a dogmatics of his existence, as if, to avoid the outrageous excess of the negative, I needed the energy of so presumptuous an affirmation: "there are angels." The angel is subtler. He is less *what there is* than that which allows me to think the "there is" in a multiplicity of registers that do not exhaust our nomenclatures of the real. This is why, thinking of the weight of matter that we feel passing over our shoulders, this weight of ourselves that we bear in all our walks and gaits [*marches et démarches*], I make the angel the wing that bears this heavy matter, the poetic turn of phrase of this weighty sensible that is our sensing body. To be brief, I would be tempted to say: the angel is the immaterialization function of this matter that I experience as the body of the world and as my body.

The Body and Metaphor

Fundamental sensibility, of which it was a question at the beginning of these investigations, concerned the world above all. We must return to it with an eye to more in-depth study.

1. The "sensory" body, divided according to the diversity of these powers, themselves distributed among the correlative organs that scholarly or spontaneous languages assign to it, is not what is essential to that which is aimed at here, even though it remains [*demeure*] its light side in the interplays of perceptive intentionality. I leave to the side, however interesting it may be, the ancient doctrine of *common sense* as the power of connection or synthesis of the multiplicity of sensibles along one "identity pole," designated by the name of "thing" or "object." I am speaking of the body, but of the body gathered onto that neutral or null point on the basis of which there will be distances and objects. This sensing globality, beneath the commonplace dichotomies body-object, body-subject, I express anew by the intransitive *to sense oneself*.[2] As I hinted above, beneath the modalities that specify the verb by the adverbs of modality *good* or *evil*, *sensing oneself* is the null operation, the neutral element, in which the activities of inside and outside devolve, an intransitive operation where they collect themselves, as the far-Eastern exercises show us that gather the body in a position of rest, thus converting it into that immobile movement where its functions draw their energy. It is an operation that *lets be*, in a fundamental serenity, the being qua being of the sensing body. The verb *to sense*

oneself, in the middle voice, indeed does not imply any reflection. Reflection points to the subjective pole of a route that follows in the opposite direction, the path from Thebes to Athens. It does not make us change frameworks. And yet that is what is essential. It is a matter of a rapidity of the body that experiences, in its crossings to different levels, the power of its own metaphor. The poetics of the body, abstracted from what literature tells us of it, and rejoining what the old East suggests to us, consists above all in this free mobility that has become more and more difficult for us because of our fixation on the world of our quotidian representation and our common worry. Every allusion to the condition of the resurrected bodies, whose subtlety and glorious transparence a religious tradition exalted, seems to us as chimerical, and for the same reasons, as the angel's wing in mythologies or the rapture of flight in the fantasies of a waking dream. I do not wonder about the possible verification of this quietism of the body in the diverse cultural contexts that have attempted to practice it. What would such a verification signify, besides, since by definition it must hold itself within a framework of the object and of objectivity that disqualifies in advance any other possibility? This rigidity, which claims to be without appeal [*appel*], calls for [*appelle*] no other sanction than its own limit and the impossibility of guaranteeing, by virtue of its own criterion, the absolute on which it prides itself.

2. However chimerical it may be, the way that the voices of the West or of the East trace for us, in their invitation to the impossible, at the very least has the advantage of suggesting to us the vision of another abode. The utopia that lightens the body by freeing it from its familiar places, at the extreme edge of a simplifying analysis, does not, however, presuppose the exploits of an asceticism of torsion or contortion. An exasperated will would never have obtained that marvelous silence and that grace that one admires in certain statuettes of Buddhist art that, for lack of anything better, I baptized long ago with the equivocal name of "thinking Buddha." When one contemplates them, one believes one knows that no scholarly decomposition into elements would have obtained that serenity "beyond all sentiment" that foils our ruses of reason. To experience the impact of this re-linquishment and this unbinding, one can, by contrast, refer to the famous thinker that Rodin fixed on his pedestal of marble in a tension where all the available energies swell the flexions of a musculature ready to bound onto the forces of the world to make them the docile and strong support of a statue of freedom. The two bodies, the one Western, the other Eastern, are equally at rest. But in the former the rest is but the virtuality of an act or of a drawn bow, an effort that gathers its powers. In the latter, power itself is put at a distance and is as though ignored by that sovereign peace that exceeds it too much to

grant it the frontal situation of an object of judgment. However infirm our words may be, I can well speak in this case of a transcendental body, so relieved of all heaviness that it blends with the meontological depth of a beyond of the will. If one sought, for these complementary experiences, which distinguish so cleanly the possible turns of our poor flesh, a terminology more adapted to the global situation, it would be necessary to speak of levels of corporeality, arranged from the most epidermic to the most radical (or "pneumatic"), passing by the cosmic, or "cosmopoietic," median that Rodin's sculpture schematizes. The somatic empirical realm is the most familiar to us. Against the world's horizon it cuts out the contours of a figure, indissolubly organism and *psyche*, with its passions, its projects and its objects, its sufferings unto death, the works of its days, and the shadows of a destiny, itself inserted into a universe and a history that overflow it on all sides. This margin of *et cetera* that pushes it beyond itself, toward the infinity that precedes it and that will follow it, expands its borders to the ends of the earth. The cosmic undulation of *soma* has two aspects. One can, indeed, accentuate the set of forces whose necessity it suffers. Conversely, as one sees in the surge that the sculptor surprises in its will to conquest, one can read on its lines the energy that transforms into accomplices the servitudes that it must endure. Would it then be in the world without being entirely of the world? This is a question that is always to be posed, though never resolved, except by faith in a power that defies without ceasing the resistances that it opposes. But beneath this empirical realm of simple evidence and of that creative freedom that gives itself the world as the means of its power, the far-Eastern calm plunges the body into an ultimate instance, where its apparent disappearance is equivalent to the East of its origin. In this movement without end that descends and reascends its course, we admire the metaphoral, evolving mobility of its more or less slow degradation. Would not the secret of great art be precisely that it lets us suspect, in the lineaments of a morphology or the backwash of an existence, the force that makes an indomitable will stand up straight over the world and, more radically yet, the great calm in which, in a null and substantial acting, the figure of the "son of man" is revitalized and brought to peace? I would not want, indeed, by a bureaucratic mania for classification or tidying, to abandon this poor body, in advance broken up into three stories, to the various specialties that make it their elected domain. I do not see why painting should limit itself either to drawing the geometry of an organism or to describing the vicissitudes of a life. I have no reason to grant to sculpture the revelation of essence. And the privilege of the Christian icon does not make it the only witness to a beyond of existence and even essence. Simply, by referring to the models that inspire me, I try to translate what each of them, in this or that mode of manifestation, makes us guess about what it does not say in order to permit us to hear it. What is essential is to restore, in the apparent stasis where one or another of these images seems to linger, the restlessness that mobilizes it and that induces, in the spectator himself, the metaphoral power by which he is inhabited. The immobile movement of the Eastern icon is not to be refuted since it founds the heroic virtuality that throws itself into an attack on the world. The pictural form that takes pleasure in the charm of the flesh or in the most significant details of a story has taken no vow of empiricism or positivism. It contains a sufficient opening to not mortify in the body the free mobility that traverses the body. If we could, by the effect of a simple juxtaposition, journey through these different levels in a lightning-flash gaze, the simultaneity that gathers them would then reproduce the logic of a poetry that makes all three of them stand within a single dynamic circulation. The angel's wing does not only watch over Jacob's ladder. It animates, in the corporeal microcosm, the divine instability that makes it a living metaphor.

Matter and the Immaterial

From the body to matter the crossing [*passage*] was, from all time, too easy to not leave us indifferent to their possible relation. When one thinks of everything that was said of it over the course of a long history where science and philosophy mix and divide their waters, one cannot prevent oneself from seeing there a striking illustration of the *Meta* function.

1. I will not seek beneath these variations the invariant of content that, from far or near, inspires, from time immemorial, the multiple principles of permanence or conservation. It is doubtless better to retain from *matter* another type of invariant that makes it a matrix of movements. The most tenacious opposition is doubtless the one that tears it asunder into two contrary vections: heavy matter, light matter, according to whether it is terrestrial or celestial, sensible or intelligible. From these dualities, we have too quickly inferred the separation of two worlds, the latter being, as we know, the domain par excellence of the religious or metaphysical soul's waking dreams.

We can neglect the critique to the greater advantage of the dream it condemns. Yet this dream, as old as humanity, ever since man, strengthened in his vertical station, stood [*se tient*]³ on his ground to gaze upon the stars, has traced for all time the vertical axis that joins the earth to the sky, mortals to the light of the divine. We have spoken, in this regard, and by a sure estimation of the values bound in language itself, of "gravity and grace." The play of contrast marks very well the essential correlation that unites the low and the high, and the reversal that ensures the crossing from one extreme to the other. Matter, in the most unsophisticated imagination, is therefore less that enormous thing, obscure and ready-made, than a sense of movement in an oriented space. Below any semantics, and in order that there be a semantics, these signifying lines that orient us, starting from an East point, are first necessary. By raising itself from the earth *toward* the sky, heavy matter tends *toward* its own immaterialization. Inversely, in its descent *toward* the earth, the immaterial *tends* toward its own materialization, as if the destiny of light *were* to make itself flesh in a depth of night.

2. Truth be told, the inversion of the movements is more and better than a simple and prosaic round trip. The interval that separates the contraries is also the milieu that makes room for their reciprocal transformation. It is therefore necessary to glimpse, underneath the duality that established them long ago in separate substances, the constant circulation that suggested to the poets the ring of gold where the nuptials of the two matters are ratified. Nothing is easier, in these conditions, than the imagination of an eternally turning movement that a subtler mathematics will later convert into a rotation group. On this imaginary wheel, and starting from a neutral position of rest at zero height, free for each one to follow and gradate as he pleases, above and below the reference line, are the variations of the ascent and the descent. Materialization and immaterialization thus define the becoming of an energy of which the variable intensities trace, on an ontological ladder, the degrees of perfection that situate each being [*être*] at the level of its essence in a universe interval. Could what we call *being* be only the solidification, temporarily stable, of a forgotten movement?

3. To this high matter and low matter, two rather different functions have long ago been made to correspond, in a certain intuition that does not lack profundity, in order to justify an irreducible opposition. The first, more linked to light, is a space of transparency where, in the broad daylight of the sky, those redoubtable and loved East points where men read their destiny play. The second, which we associate with the weight of the real, is the material of which one makes vessels, instruments, machines. It is addressed above all to the hand, and no longer to the eye. It obliges us to come closer to things, to touch them in order to pass again over their contours and verify their solidity. The hand and the eye are not separated for all that. One can, it is true, make their difficult conjunction the sign of a break between two classes or of a division between spiritual work and material work. This partial analysis is far from being without foundation.

Intellectuals—too often, alas!—for lack of familiarity with that of which they speak, see things from far away, through what was and is said of them. And this is why knowledge [*savoir*], though it originates in a seeing [*voir*] according to etymology, has had to join forces, as it became more demanding, with ever more precise manipulations. But this said, and we should not forget it, it would be as ridiculous to do without the eye as to cut off one's hands. Without a distancing, that which celestial matter imposes on us, we would never have known the critical spirit that we can no longer dissociate from the very essence of our freedom. Without the work that puts one's hand to the plow, we would not have known the intoxication of our conquests. We must at the same time be able to both involve ourselves in things and distance ourselves from them. We need the matter-space where we breathe and the matter-material that gets our hands dirty. If the junction of the two matters must be an ideal for the very functioning of our body, it is possible to perceive a foretaste of it in those alabaster amphorae that one admires in the museum of Athens. Amphorae, so well named since they evoke the two arms that surround and embrace. Amphorae of benediction that reconcile the gaze and the hand. By their transparency, they free the celestial space where they wave to the stars. By their heaviness that softens light into luminescence, they tell, through the energy they commemorate, of the initial heaviness they have vanquished. Heavy and light, shadowy in the brilliance they filter, they announce, in a mute sign, the hope of a world where the two matters would henceforth be only, as they have always signified besides, the top and underside of a single movement.

The Angel of Metaphor

It is in connection to matter and the body that tradition has thought the angel. He is at once *immaterial* and *incorporeal*.

The two negations that prefix our adjectives and that say, in simultaneity, *neither* this *nor* that define an original type of mediation opposed to the current conception, called integrative, which arranges the respectively assumed natures in the unity of a subject in which they coincide. The angel carries out the mediation without being a mediator properly so called. He makes no synthesis. But he makes communicate. In this sense his nature is essentially rapid. And this is why the well-known image of "Jacob's ladder" that the angelic cohorts ascend and descend maintains its decisive signification.

1. Jacob's ladder refers us back, from the familiar image, to the philosophical representation that itself takes up a very widespread hierarchical thought. Doubtless transcribed from the social order where it ravages in the manner that is known, hierarchy makes us forget its origins, of which it preserves what is essential. Whoever says hierarchy indeed evokes a scalar arrangement where differences must be simultaneously thought as brusque qualitative distances (apparently without intermediary) and as a sequence that invincibly marks the indispensable continuity. The static relations that one can deduce from it refer to a strict order that tolerates nothing but the property of transitivity alone. They are translated in the double mode of the comparative (x larger than y, in a definite order of perfection) and in the superlative, both absolute (very large) and relative (the largest or, inversely, the smallest).

2. Hierarchy therefore presupposes a plurality of elements ordered according to a strict order, a principle of order and of excellence or perfection, capable of indefinite gradation, the degrees of which define a series where none of the terms can be *ex aequo* or interchangeable. Mathematically, one can see in it a realization of Zermelo's axiom.

The difficulties that one can oppose to this vision of the world, be it a matter of the *cosmos* or of society, are authorized by two diametrically opposite considerations. In the name of a certain egalitarianism that attenuates differences to the point of denying them one can, indeed, disqualify all subordination, which seems essential to hierarchy. This position appears tenable only with difficulty: how to deny *differences*, what does *equality* signify? For, even in the simplest identity proposition, $x=x$, one can wonder by what right we posit two x's if the first is not distinguished from the second. And how would they be distinguished if they did not have a minimum of difference, of differential determination, present in one and absent from the other? To say *other* is, inevitably, to call into question an equality that, pushed to the limit, would have to rejoin indifferentiation. Indifferentiation again puts us in mind of that initial formless state that cosmogenies posited at the origin of the world and that our principles of degradation glimpse as an end of death at the extreme point of an evolutionary process. When there is no longer any level, nothing can happen, exchanges cease, all plurality is abolished in the silence of non-being.

The tacit postulate that underlies this position would be expressed in the following manner: *differences necessarily imply subordination* or, inversely, superiority. And yet these relations of superior-inferior are intolerable. Therefore difference itself could not be tolerated.

3. The second thesis-antithesis refuses the preceding postulate to also infer the refusal of all hierarchy. But this generic characteristic does not prevent a variety of motivations.

Some emphasize the *subjective* character of the options that command the hierarchy. More and less would be linked to *comparisons* of a preferential character, the arbitrariness of which thwarts any objective criterion. In this it is like *taste. Non est disputandum*. Each one has his manner of tasting, of choosing his elect and his supreme one. The hierarchical order therefore obeys no necessity. It betrays the contingency of our education, of our cultural milieu, in a definite space and time.

If one confines oneself to the perception of *difference* as such, one notices that it tolerates no subordination by gradation. Here it is necessary to evoke the entire problem formerly known by the designation "quantification of qualities." I will suppose that the objections and replies are known in order to confine myself to what here appears essential to me. A difference is based on quality. And yet quality, so it is said, disqualifies any concept. One senses it in its irreducible originality, and the artist experiences it with a singular emotion. The Sainte-Victoire mountain, at various hours of the day, will never have the same color. Each qualitative instant is a *Hapax*.[4] It will not return; one will never see it twice. In sum, a critique of the scientific spirit in its measurement procedures is thus signified to us in the background of this verdict. Science measures effects of work, consequences, or exteriorizations. It could not measure anything qualitative, not because this would be difficult or impossible, or even because it would be contradictory, but more profoundly because it would not make any sense. A measurable quality is a nonsensical expression, of the same order as a "very green number." Moreover, these critical limits that science must accept to remain within its proper field do not prescribe any limit to scientific work. It is simply a matter of not going to the wrong address. The quantitative of the qualitative remains perfectly measurable, and there is no question of doubting this. It remains to know exactly what one is measuring. And it matters to the scholar, in a self-limitation carried out by knowledge itself, that he be exactly familiar with what he is doing. The intensity of qualities then becomes either a manner of speaking corporeally of that which is not a body, as Pascal and Spinoza complained, or an approximate manner of saying difference in a register that is not its own but that, being more familiar to us, remains the only one accessible to us, at the risk of creating a sort of transcendental illusion to be perpetually corrected. Qualitative differences are not aligned on a scale of intensity. They could not be subordinated to each other in a strict order that would make obviously manifest the reign of quantification according to more and less. The social origin of these conceptions is, moreover, patent. Society doubtless needs inferiors and superiors. This is why egalitarianism is socially impossible. But in the true order of things, this manner of conceiving can appear only as a concession to our weakness or as an anthropomorphic transposition.

4. These theses and antitheses are not reconcilable. I will therefore propose neither a synthesis nor a compromise. On the contrary, I judge it necessary to push the analysis farther. If we see through to the end each of the hypotheses envisaged, it will be necessary to say alternatively: one thinks only in and by the equal or the same, all difference is reducible to the one, difference is only an appearance to be dissipated. Truth be told, in the terms of the Platonic *Parmenides*, we would then have *the very impossibility of the other*. Inversely, the thought of differences ends in the pure dispersal of incomparables, without any possible relation, for any relation-rapprochement risks contaminating the exception of the unique and its property. It is therefore necessary, not to resign ourselves, but much rather to rejoice unto elation over this pure, unorderable, and non-relational multiplicity, for in the end every relation supposes a comparison, comparison a certain similarity, every similarity an assimilation, every assimilation a march toward death by in-difference.

This is why all these conceptions of metaphysics are conceptions of death (and it is not by chance that they are born of anguish). Should one speak of being or of the one, should one oppose as much as one likes henology and ontology, one subjugates oneself, whether one wants to or not, to the reign of the one. Plotinus is right: being is the trace of the one. One could not better state the attraction of in-differentiation and this will to death that would, in philosophy, be our deepest instinct, and the instinct that, moreover, condemns us to paradise: since it is blessed indifference, it definitively absorbs us into he who is all in all [*tout en tous*].

Thus I find again the ending of Plato's *Parmenides*: "'As it seems, whether one is or is not, it and the others both are all and are nothing, and both appear and do not appear all things in all ways, both in relation to themselves and in relation to each other.'—'Very true.'"[5] Between the *one-one* and the *to alla* or pure power of dispersal, of which the Jewish *diaspora* would here be the most moving symbol, the dialectical spirit sways without hope for a solution. But, truth be told, must we accept this double paroxysm of the pure one and the pure plural?

5. I fear that we have hypostatized functions even more than hypotheses. The impossible of the one and the impossible of others, frozen into absolutes, are indeed separate substances. And there is no longer any question of reconciling

them. But why, first of all, should we want to reconcile? If one thinks the *one* and the *to alla* of others as vections, they escape false substantialism and become principles of thought. If one reifies them, they become, for an imaginary, the two poles of impossibility between which the Odyssean *polutropos aner* must navigate. Perhaps, and it is in this sense that I will restore to the imaginary its dignity, it is indeed necessary to harden functions into absolutes or quasi-substances to better mark by an artifice that *on the basis of which* the work of thought actually works. But if I willingly accept this sculptural figuration, or this dramatization, I cannot but disqualify the mythology of primal antagonistic forces that, whether one wants it or not, either by excess of the *one* or by excess of the *other*, *both* end in the same phraseless death. I prefer, then, to find again, with my familiar angels, Jacob's ladder, a rapid and indicator [*cursif et curseur*] world whose rapidity and metaphoral power our discourses have too much forgotten.

6. I will posit, without justifying them, the following requisites:

— whatever one may say, we have left, for a world that is for us the world, the regional diversity of environments;
— in this world that is our world, every being, whatever it may be, is indissociable from the world in which it is;
— in consequence, by virtue of this world in which it is, it is and is thinkable only in and by the cosmic reference that envelopes its singularity;
— in this sense, and by virtue of this fundamental relation, it is necessarily encompassed in a whole (for the whole is inevitable) that is not reducible (is it necessary to repeat this truism indefinitely?) to a sum or to the juxtaposition of arithmetical unities in addition;
— by virtue of this re-ference to the whole, each of the singularities that inhabits this world is drawn (as the German verb *be-ziehen* says eloquently) toward precisely that which it is not. If one will permit me this logico-mathematical transcription, it has for a complement the set of precisely that which it excludes qua this or that determination;
— such that the world is not added to it but *remains* [*demeure*] the *neutral* that necessarily bears it without altering it. I will say, therefore, substituting for the world the symbol E, indicative of the neutral, and making A the symbol of the "singular element" (that we could conceive as a singleton): $A \cup E = A$. The world is not added to the singular, any more than being [*être*] is to the being [*étant*]: Being [*être*] plus being [*étant*] = being [*étant*]. The world being in *no* [*rien*] way a being, this nothing [*rien*] does not modify, by the addition of a determinant, what it *bears in itself*: simply

"it makes it be" or it "gives it to be." Inversely, if I think the world as the "whole," I will find again the theorem A ∩ I = A: I being the symbol of the "whole," I will therefore write: the intersection of the whole and of the singular restores the singular to its singularity. *Todo y Nada*. Finally, to transcribe complementarity I will permit myself the theorem A ∪ Ā = I;

— if I avoid the formula A ∩ Ā, it is to do justice to difference: a rose is not an elephant. Which, I hope, the most critical spirits will concede to me, in their moment of lucidity;

— although, in another sense, I can say: every being necessarily implies in its advanced formula precisely that which it excludes by virtue of its difference. In this sense, the attraction (*be-ziehen*) of each being to each being, of each being to *every other being*, is verified;

— the relation-transport, thus posited, therefore does not annul differences. It necessarily presupposes them. Relation is therefore not primordially a relation of likeness. Contrary to what the proverb says, it is not obvious that birds of a feather flock together. They can "flock together" without being "of a feather." I will even add: the more distant beings [*êtres*] are, the more they attract each other by virtue of their difference;

— attraction, in a poet's optics, is inversely correlated with similitude. The more different things differ, the more they belong to each other, the more they get along [*s'entendent*] for a poetic understanding [*entendement*],[6] listening for the voices of the world;

— but difference always marks a *distance*. A distance is *that which is to be traversed*. And yet an interval to be crossed must join that which is nearest to that which is farthest. Everything thus lives [*habite*] farthest from itself;

— there are, therefore, and there must be, relations among those that are near each other [*de proche en proche*], and these relations punctuate the interval to be crossed. By right, I postulate that every being, to go to the ends of itself, must thus traverse a "universe interval," to the degree that it belongs to a world that is its world;

— a universe interval is therefore a milieu of differences. A milieu of differences that come one after the other, little by little [*de proche en proche*] constitutes what I call an order, an ordering. I cannot avoid the verb *to order*. And yet, whatever may be true of the etymology, which is the least of my worries, one can *order* [*or-donner*] only beings [*êtres*] that are capable of *giving* [*donner*]. They can give only to the degree that the recipient is not on the same level as the giver. Every being [*être*] thus has to give what it is to the other that it is not. Insofar as it has to give to that which does not have, a shift is brought about that *sub-or-dinates* [*sub-or-donne*] to the one who gives [*donne*] the being *to whom it is given*. This image of giving or gratifying sub-ordination is not juridical obedience. According to the Latin word *obaudire*, obeying is setting oneself to listen attentively, disposing oneself to welcome that which, in one manner or another, we have to receive. Every being [*être*], in the space where the gifts of an overabundance are ordered, thus creates the un-leveling of a subordination. It is thus that we must understand hierarchy;

— unless one posits a sectarianism of greed as an axiom, nothing forbids, *a priori*, conceiving of beings [*êtres*] that are more apt than others to give. It is not wealth that is damned but its divorce from the gift. Positing as a postulate that the more a being [*être*] is apt to give, the more degrees of freedom of movement it has at its disposal, I refuse the divorce established by some between quantity and quality: if we do not measure the intensity of a quality when we quantify its effects, the fact remains that the latter could not be foreign to the former. I will say in this sense that it is better to give than to receive. And as it can give only as a function of what it is, I affirm greater-well-being [*mieux-être*] as the ground of a more extensive having-the-power-to-give;

— the profound idea that animates an entire tradition, symbolized by light's radiance, is that being is indissociable from a giving act. It is perhaps this that, in the obscurity of semantic progressions, would explain the German *es gibt*, whose importance in a certain literature is known;

— what complicates things here and makes us suspicious with regard to an ideology of generosity is the spectacle of a human history in which hierarchy, like class divisions, has too often masked, in the form of superiority, an egoism of exploitation. This bad memory that is at the origin of a legitimate resentment has subsequently cast a maleficent shadow on hierarchy taken in its generality. One has come to be suspicious of the very ideas of excellence and of a perfection "that it would be better to have than not to have," which is an idea or postulate that underlies certain forms of the ontological argument. Furthermore, and following the same line of thought, the position of a *maximum* at the summit of the hierarchical interval (more and less, so it was said, can neither be said nor exist save in reference to a *maximum*) awakened the specter of a "supreme being" that devoured with his eminence all that, proceeding from him, existed only in him and by him. God thereby became the hypostasis of a superlative of language that, politically and theologically, could not be innocent. The theological dimension, by overdetermining the ontological dimension of the problem, whipped the debate into a frenzy. Tacitly accepting the logical connection between the affirmation "of more and of less" and the affirmation of a supreme being, the calling into question of the consequent necessarily brought about the calling into question of the antecedent;

— this reversal, which does not bring us out from the same regime of thought, would suggest, by contrast, the possibility of another way. The merit of neo-Platonism is to have understood that the position of an order does not necessarily imply the transposition of excellence in the *Arché* of the origin. It glimpses in a lightning-flash that this by which there is something—that is, a world in the dripping cascade of its ontological levels—was in no [*rien*] way what it made possible. Whence the paradoxical expressions that, in the Middle Ages and for want of anything better, designated by the term "nothingness" what was formerly called the supreme. The addition to this *Nothing* [*Rien*] of a corrective such as "*nothingness par excellence*," *uncreated nothingness*, risked, however, diminishing over time a severity that drove understanding to despair. Without any wavering in the fundamental thought, the necessity of speaking could have left the impression that the excellence of the supreme flowered again in the very austerity of the desert, whereas the original aim attempted to exceed as much the negative as the positive of ordinary languages. The most delicate problem is that of the link to be established between the Nothing, or the "beyond being and nothing," and the giving authority for which people praise it;

— for its part, Christianity, with its mad [*fou*] and infirm God, beyond wisdom and power, linked the folly [*folie*] of the Cross to the radiance of grace and of *Agapé*. The halo with which it enveloped that which does not exist and which must nonetheless confound "what is" did not call into question a chain of beings [*êtres*]. The Christian egalitarianism that today is spoken of as the supplier of supposedly aberrant doctrines had no need to deny differences. It simply signified that one cannot treat as mere means those for whom Jesus Christ died, without distinction of condition, sex, or power.

7. There remains, one will say, the enigma of a giving that gives nothing because the giving authority is nothing and has nothing, of a giving that, in consequence, consists in making be what one is not, what is not the origin, the greater glory

of that original authority being henceforth to allow to be, in the upsurging of a *hapax* that no pre-existence deflowers, the being of what is. Consequently, in hierarchy, whose different degrees are giving authorities, in what will the gift consist? In making be in their turn beings [*êtres*] that are not their giving authorities. Let us take banal examples. It is commonly said, and not only by the good people of the schools, that the inorganic is the basis of the organic, that the vegetal organic is the basis of the animal kingdom, and the animal kingdom the basis on which the human world emerges. And yet it is clear that the basis does not pre-contain what emerges from it; it makes be what it is not. Inversely, in a descending perspective, what is called the superior does not have to contain, as was formerly believed when it was said that the inferior is contained in the superior, that which proceeds from it, as if from the one to the other the development went from the implicit to the explicit, from the folded umbrella to the unfolded umbrella. Every gift is, in this sense, the effacing of givenness before the emergence of a *novum* that it does not hold under the influence of something contained. The kenosis of the gift is precisely to render possible below itself the improbable star that will be the Biblical marvel of the "here we are": being-there, at a sort of call from whence emerges the East that glorifies it with an unhoped-for overabundance. Being-there in a "there is" that alights there. All this doubtless obliges us to correct what is said to us of the image in the Christian tradition. The image does not reproduce a pre-formed antecedent. It is a novation that excludes all pre-existence, however subtle its conception may be. The image is produced in the likeness of God who produces himself in his manifestation. But this supposes, at all levels of creation, an original dynamism, as foreign to an identifying assimilation as to a causality of simple conditioning. The enigma of the causal link, which has tormented more than one thinker, thus refers us back, by the newness that it contains, to a giving authority that makes be, in the manifestation of a *quasi-I am!* and in the trembling joy of a primrose, something that is not the principle.

Beings [*êtres*] are completed to the degree that they call, in the exclusion that grounds their distinction, precisely to that which they exclude. It is therefore in its dimension of non-being that the same awakens the other, as if, in order to blossom open to itself, it needed what it is not and what it invokes in a sort of creative and optative sigh. In a still more precise manner, I will say that non-being hollows out in things that margin where precisely that which they cannot contain and that bears them away beyond themselves emerges.

8. Thus understood according to the discontinuities it requires, as according to the vertical axis where its emergences are inscribed, hierarchy can no longer

be that bogey of militarization that has been and that remains the object of a just resentment. For all beings [*êtres*], whatever level they belong to, necessarily remain [*se tiennent*] amongst themselves. In this sense, they are completed on the scale of the power of alterity that extends them beyond themselves. Each one of them is as indispensible to all as all are to each one. This is why each one of them is just as much a giving authority. Qua giving authority, it marks a gap or a difference of level, a gap that is more or less great according to the distance that situates and that draws away. The more and less of which the ancients spoke thus chant an interval of alterity that has a double meaning. Overabundance and poverty, it causes to arise in the void of the "less" a "more" that would be its recompense. It seems to me that it is in this register that the ancient idea of *glory*, as well as the infirm terminology that speaks of inferiors and superiors, is fully brought into relief. Jealousy is henceforth unthinkable in a world that is as giving as it is given [*donné*] and ordered [*ordonné*]. The mathematical conception that permits us to think this hierarchy according to the relations of order and strict order cannot, obviously, express this universal diffusion of generosity. It would be just as ridiculous to banish it as to content ourselves with it.

What I have said up till now prepares the way for the entry of the angelic metaphor.

9. What bothers us in the idea and the practice of hierarchy is the image of a fixed order, of a bureaucratic tiering of levels in a panorama, a sort of *Panopticon* that unrolls the universe according to the necessity of its self-sufficiency. One thus supposes a universal *pax romana* that harmonizes beings [*êtres*] following a pre-established arrangement. Such a clichéd image can only, so it is believed, lull to sleep or justify the *status quo* of the present. There would be a double error there. On the one hand, that order takes into account only the static relations of inferior to superior, or inversely. On the other hand, even if one dynamizes the levels, the genesis that one attempts to re-establish most often disregards the dimension of forces in conflict. It is necessary to think the universe, so we are told, as a system of forces in continual antagonism. It is this agonistic version that people have wanted, in various contexts, to bring to the forefront. Such an exegesis smells of gunpowder. What could the angels possibly be doing there who, by definition, have nothing in common with a perturbing element? Would they be condemned, at the summit of the world, to beatifically proclaim peace for men of good will, objects of divine benevolence?

10. If, despite everything, I obey the permanent charm of the angel, it is because, contrary to the received traditions, he is no well-behaved child sitting

tranquilly on the architecture of the world. I prefer, for my part, less reassuring images. I will rapidly evoke, as an introduction to metaphor, angelic "metastasis."

What is striking, indeed, in the angel's status is that he is less a being [*être*] than a breath; less an immovable position in the hierarchy of nine classic choirs than the interior pressure of a passage, of a perpetual transit. This relational being illustrates well the definition that enchanted me long ago: "relation consists in a certain passing." Because he is, essentially, a passing, the angel is essentially "metaphorical."

The metaphoral of transport introduces in every position an impatience for transposition. What, indeed, does the metaphoral signify? Beyond the semantic order, which the disciplines of the sign deal with, it indicates, in each thing, its power of passing. Transit and metabasis, the angel bears what is away toward its elsewhere and its beyond. The metaphoral, from this perspective, exceeds the linguistic condition of metaphor. The metaphoral, which I distinguish from metaphor, as the "floral" is distinguished from the flower, is also ontological; one should rather say "ontogenic," to the degree that it affects the very genesis of the being [*être*] that emerges from its hold. I say its "hold," for the metaphoral is precisely that which opens the being [*être*], in its density of being [*être*], to the immensity of what it is not. We should therefore add a new specification to the preceding remarks: if the beings [*êtres*] that are ordered in a hierarchy pride themselves on a giving authority, the authority in question is not an accidental excess; it is integrated into their own genesis. Without this power of transport that is the metaphoral, they would wither, as is said of a plant that withers when it lacks the pure air, that which is unsurveilled in earth or sky, where it abides and which it must inhabit in order not to die. Of being, which the metaphoral imbibes, one could affirm, as of relation, that it "consists in a certain passing."

11. A "certain passing," for the being of what is does not pass in just any way. To the thesis here developed, one could object, not without some reason, that it delivers us over to the arbitrariness of anything whatsoever. Paraphrasing, in a sense that is foreign to it, the famous proposition, "The world is everything that happens,"[7] it would be all very well for the objector to conclude: the metaphoral is the world itself, that is, everything that can happen to whatever being [*être*]. And if the angel is identified with the metaphoral, how could we not add: the angel is conflated with the everything of anything whatsoever by an indifference that resembles, to the point of being easily mistaken for it, the isothermy of death. The angelic floral that we were promised rejoins the original fog from which, by an insurrectional gesture, the figures of difference had freed themselves.

To avoid such a catastrophe, it is important to recall a simple principle: difference stands out in its fullest relief when one faces up to the set of what it is not. Far from conflating everything, the metaphoral therefore cannot but ensure for it the full measure of its originality. Moreover, between everything and nothing, the interval conserves a rich array of proximities and distances. The poet is not ignorant of this. I come back to the Song of Songs that has served me as a frame of reference. In the fraternal course that, along the footsteps of the wife and husband, carries off flowers and stars, precious stones and the leaps of the gazelle, the bond of "everything to everything" does not signify the blend of chaos. Without saying so, the scribe practices an axiom of choice. This precious stone is, by its color, closer than that other one to narcissus or to saffron's fragrance, closer to this animal than to that other one, closer to the apple tree in flower than to Jonah's castor-oil plant. In the space of the metaphoral, there are therefore several abodes or, if one prefers, series that are more probable than others. The poet is the one who knows how to discern, in the "power of all becoming," the veins that are best suited to the efficacy of transit. It is not necessary, for all that, to respect a normal gradation—that, for example, which goes from the simplest to the most complex. It is possible that the link must skip the intermediaries that good sense would think obligatory. The miracle arises when the metaphoral brings about the most improbable bond, the one that makes the extreme of the remote coincide with the closest intimacy. The logic that unites these diverse things is not that of the logician. It arises from a flair that is not satisfied in the least with marriages of reason. By this exceptional stroke, the metaphoral draws closer to the angelic condition. The angel, indeed, is not only the *metaxu* that travels Jacob's ladder from top to bottom and from bottom to top in order to affirm, with its protective wing, the fraternal diversity of the qualitative orders. It is also the non-subsistent lightning-flash that throws common sense off balance, the suddenness that blazes at the horizon in an annunciatory light. But this irruption has nothing in common with a juxtaposition of incompatibles, be they contradictory or contrary, as if the "poetic" art could affirm its excellence only by delighting in square circles or in a teratological exercise. The "coincidence of opposites" with which religious literature abounds is something else entirely than an ostension of monsters or of shameful concepts. In its manner, which is not that of the poet, it says and practices the stellar friendship of the closest and the farthest.

12. At the risk of being overly meticulous, I therefore suggest the distinction between the metaphoral and the metaphor. The metaphor is nothing other than the metaphoral power's passage to the act. More exactly, before bearing on an expression that would be elevated to another semantic power, the metaphor has an ontological sense that invests things and, later on, language. It marks out the metaphoral interval that separates a being [*être*] or a term from its extreme possibilities. One would willingly make it the pontifical gesture that casts a bridge, the arch of a bridge, for a new covenant, from one bank to the other, be it a matter of the elements of the universe or of semantic elements. The support, the thrust, the falling back, and the inverse movement: such would be, in a round trip, the dynamism of metaphor, its efficacy of transport. But that said, nothing forbids taking a less long course—the poet does not always live at the extremes. If one postulates the universal bond, by virtue of a complementarity as much of wealth as of poverty, of each element to the immensity of its excluded middle, we would have to add: the universe is the set of the lines of metaphor that traverse it in every direction.

In these conditions, one will ask, what difference separates the metaphoral and the metaphor from the great Platonic genuses: being, the same, the other, movement, rest? I would be tempted to reply: the philosopher tries to fix in concepts an experience that each one has the right to practice on his own scale, an experience more capricious than the *Odyssey* and that, even as it there takes on a new sense, exceeds the human order. For things and beings [*êtres*] also have their experience of travel; it is their manner of "gazing at each other," in a *respect* that the old Latin *respectus* (translated by gaze, respect, and relation) said so well in order to highlight the regards that, in a single golden chain, refer all the parts of the universe to each other. On each one of them, one would say, trembles a flower of angelica that throws them beyond their identity.

If I had to transpose the Platonic terminology into the metaphoral and metaphor, I would suggest the following translation [*version*]: every being [*étant*], in its being of being [*être d'étant*] and in the repose of its difference, is the support of a perpetual soaring that opens the same to the destiny of the other by a movement in which, under the arch of a bridge, the world lines that traverse it are allied.

13. It is not too hard, henceforth, to relate to the present reflections what was said earlier about matter and the immaterial, about the body and its multiple levels.

Each thing has its weight of matter, its gravity: a cat is a cat; no artifice can make it not be one. It is this weight of being that makes it abide in itself. A word is a word: "rock" is "rock," and it is necessary to build on this "rock" the arch that one will cause to emerge from it. But if the one and the other were only what they are, if they were isolated in their identity, they could no longer differ; they would die of their indifference. To exist, they need the exodic thrust, the angel's wing, that raises them above their heaviness, toward a light that bears them toward their elsewhere and that exposes them to all translations [*versions*]. Every being [*être*] in the universe, every semantic element in the language, is this bird (or this angel) with folded wings that hides in its immobility the worry of a free becoming and that confers on its relative fixity its weight in gold and stars. One has the right to speak in favor of the corpuscle's precision. One could not refuse it the associated wave that throws it to the remoteness of the constellations.

In other words, closer to an old memory and to mythology, terrestrial matter invokes the *fiat lux* of a celestial matter that falls back on it in a rain of stars and gazes.

14. As for the body, whose human dough the flexibility in the dancer's gestures lifts up, it follows in its turn the same metaphoral movement. The path that leads it, by the mediation of the *cosmos*, from its empirical realm to pneumatic subtlety is, in its way, a "song of ascents." Ash Wednesday, which casts the body back to the dust of its origin, does not only say what it was made of. It says above all that the body is a member of a vaster body. By breaking its limits, death restores it to the peaceful universality of the universe. This is why, when we read on a tomb the poor name that our regrets contest, for a time, against the voracity of wild grass, we wish the departed one rest. The *adieu* cuts the moorings and confides the ship to the swell that takes it again on the last day. But if we believe with difficulty that everything is finished, this is because, somewhere, an East point signals to us, like the angel on Christ's tomb, to assure us that "he is no longer here"[8] and that the world would no longer be if a single one of its elements had definitively deserted it. The spiritual body, metaphor and metaphoral of such a frail creature, gives us a new idea of what faith calls "resurrection." "He is not here." Of every being [*être*] and of every word, we will say, "It is not here," in the limits in which we had enclosed it. It is elsewhere, always elsewhere, always "being-toward" without our knowing what we must understand by finitude. I will end by believing that finitude is only a truism, as debatable as the others, a lack of breath and of imagination.

Metaphor is the spiritual body. Like "celestial matter" in "terrestrial matter," it is, in an empirical realm, born away toward a body of the world, the seed of all transpositions.

15. "Do not be surprised that I say to you, 'We must be born from above'; the spirit (or the wind) blows where it will, and you hear its voice but do not know where it comes from nor where it goes. So it is with all that is born of the spirit (or of breath)" (John 3:7-8). Over all that is "you will see heaven opened and the angels of God ascending and descending on the Son of Man" (John 1:51).[9]

> Jacob came by chance to a certain place, and he spent the night there, for the sun had set. He took one of the stones of the place, put it under his head, and slept in that place. He had a dream, and behold, a ladder was placed on the earth, and its top reached heaven, and angels were ascending and descending on it. (Genesis 28:11-12)

The figure of the angel that has inspired me all through these pages takes shape and is completed in these Biblical *passages* that bear their name so well, for they have the wondrous power of making us pass. They tell of this "flower of angelica" of which I dreamed in metaphor and that I in my turn confide, for a new adventure, to those who will have accompanied me on the same path.

5

The Metamorphoses of Fire

Everything has been said about fire and reveries by the fireside. Waking dreams, sexual symbolism, hushed talks that waver between good-natured confidences and the political ruse of persuasion, intimacy of the hearth that lets another song of the world be heard in the distance on earth and sea. Fire reassures. It is surrounded by a protective wall. Domestic fire, bound to our cares, to our timidities, to our fear of living. It is a force that the demiurge bends to his designs in the arts that rob the volcano of his flame of thunder. I will not venture to perform the exploits of a psychoanalysis, too much the slave of our fashions, too attentive to the reader's wink. I will take fire in the savage state, when it frees, at the whim of its flashes, the flux of its metamorphoses.

The arbitrariness that determines the presentation cannot be avoided. Along each of the lines where I will be led, I will endeavor to maintain the unity of direction. Fire has the instability of metastasis. It lends itself to the games of vertical metaphor. The angel sometimes arms himself with a sword of fire. But he does not enter the furnace. I will consider above all a power of transformation. In the nomenclature that distinguishes, among rocks, the three groups, igneous, sedimentary, and metamorphic, it is the first and last that furnish, so it seems, the most precious directions. They suggest a first orientation.

Eruption and Irruption

The myth of "living fire" has from all time nourished the imagination. It involves, even today, an art of the sensible. It establishes a modality of "being-toward." This *being-toward*, in the present case, remains subject to a double register. Depending on the initial choice, one will be attached either to a native force or to the evolution of forms. I will follow each of these ways, one after the other.

1. The Heraclitean expression "fire that causes to live" (or "that gives life") is based on an immemorial experience. Cold stops all circulation. It makes an

organism that is sensitive to the cold and that struggles to survive curl up on its reserves. Cold spares only a reprieve; it delays the inevitable that announces itself in the trembling of contingency. It is not in vain that one speaks of the chill of death and of cadaveric rigidity, of dry ice [*neige carbonique*].[1] Absolute zero is the image the physicist gives us of the impossible. The lightest gas does not resist this temperature; its volume disappears. A gas chamber of this sort would be the antichamber of the null set.

This minus sign says a great deal. The degrees of heat would thus be a rather beautiful illustration of a degressive hierarchy. One would then imagine two fundamental unfoldings of *being-toward*. One is enchanted by its ascents, by its burning-bush sparks. The other goes away toward the definitive "no-place." It answers in its fashion the question: why is there something rather than nothing? When the poet situates himself, by refinement, beyond being and non-being, beyond joy and sorrow, he savors a strange power. We would be wrong to neglect it. We must always have at the horizon of thought this extremism on which the ending of Plato's *Parmenides* comments in its way. Not, certainly, to better savor the happiness of living or the grace of being-gift, but to understand at what point a certain excess through defect is congenital to our human condition. Too easily, we have rid ourselves of so-called negative ideas. Nothingness, without being declared taboo, remained the outcast that it was necessary to not name. Unnamable, it named that ultimate from which one does not come back because one cannot come to it. Nevertheless, these damned doors of a new hell have been crossed. It is necessary to tarry there an instant if we want to seize this will of the fire that traverses all our enterprises, of whatever order they may be.

2. What interests me in this meditation on nothing as an introduction to the living fire is not exactly the reference to death of which one immediately thinks. Death is itself thinkable, and terrible, only to the degree that all is finished and nothing remains. We should, therefore, reverse the habitual perspective and make a return to the negative par excellence. I will draw no cross of non-being on the diverse philosophies, or religious spiritualities, of East and West. I ask myself only two questions: What function does nothing assume in a regime of thought? What would be its schema in our language of today?

One can see in it, I admit, the simple sentiment of the void, often observed in some clients of psychoanalysis. And this would suffice for some who would willingly add: the cause is understood. Or else, by way of negation and denial and their origin in a psychic conflict, one tries to follow its genesis again. These explanations have their worth, and I will refrain from maligning them. But I still fear that these learned analyses, for lack of a reducing agent, would take themselves for the absolute. To avoid naivety, which would compromise the critical spirit and thereby knowledge, we should accompany them with an ironic "I think" that spares them from the disgraces of dogmatism: "There is this, but it is not everything." This "yes but" that, beyond all determination, intimates something else spares, by right, no explanation. Every explanation must foresee its beyond. Should one imagine, in a unified science, the perfect elucidation finally realized, I would think the totality that is thus offered me only by exiling myself straightaway to take cognizance of it. Is it not strange that, to think the whole, of which we would be, so it appears, only a link, we had indeed to secede, take our distance, and wonder about the value of that which is thus presented to us? All knowledge is born of a recoil that could not come to terms with precisely that from which one moves away in order to judge it. Perfect knowledge would thus coincide with an infinite power of withdrawal. And yet, what I find in these aberrant thoughts, which conform so little to our affirmative spontaneity, is the impossibility of fooling ourselves into believing them, the impossibility of a saturation that would bog us down in its exhaustiveness. The interrogation that springs up from anything that encompasses prevents us from sinking into it. And these thoughts of evening and of despair that energetically disqualify all naivety, even scientific naivety, comment, in their manner, on precisely this impossibility. The nothing of their apparent disenchantment is, in a work of literature, only the expression of a power. The orchestration they give of it is doubtless unilateral. Some liken it to a morbid negativism, to the perturbation of the "function of the real," or to the rhetorical pose of a disinterested spectator who sees, passing beneath his window, the innumerable crowd of those who have believed or who yet believe, however different their faith may appear. These are grave and facile accusations that in their turn betray an impatience that it would be useful to survey. It would be improper to see in this one or another of the multiple forms of skepticism such as, ordinarily, the stereotypes of textbooks present them to us. To tell the truth, it is not at all a matter of skepticism but of a more radical attitude, beyond the nomenclature of affirmative, negative, or doubtful stances. It is a matter of an attitude that is summed up, once again, in the impossibility of adhering to anything at all. Nor is this "nothing," as an aberrant power, conflated either with the "nothingness" of the mystics or with the engimatic *nirvana* of Indian traditions. I would see its distant analog in those formulae of the logician that identify all judgments of existence with the following statement: a certain set of x is distinct from the null set. In order to think any supposedly real thing, a reference to zero, to nothing, would thus be ineluctable. It is this ineluctable that our intrepid ones claim to follow, but while adding to these bloodless formulae the fervor of a *step back* that is the movement of a lucidity without pity. The despair that is displayed in the foreground is but the deceptive other side of a freedom that does not say its name because it is not in the service of any cause. One cannot deny that this refusal to serve can be associated with the acrid joy of a free mobility that is due to "nothing." One does not produce a work in the lukewarmness of the "anything whatsoever." I will therefore read, on these disenchanted landscapes, the anonymous burn that retained from the living fire only its power of incineration.

3. Without being named, it is this last image that seems to me to best schematize what is said obliquely in the meanderings of a certain discourse. The acid smoke of the feast of ashes remains, however, in the cloud that is exhaled from it, beyond the more or less learned designations that denounce sadism and its contrary for complicity, the festive testimony of a paradoxical poetics. The power of undoing is no less intoxicating than that of creating. Binding and loosing [*lier et délier*] cannot be disjoined, as a Gospel saying that associates them on earth as in heaven reminds us. The inverse movements betray the double understanding that unites them in a single destiny. Ascension and descent, anabasis and catabasis, the living fire is, in a single burst, that which determines life and death. Before the falling back that deposits them on the continuousness of a calm dust, the grains of ash could, for an instant, in the flame that rises, shine with a spark's lightning-flash. It is thus that the burning bush (*buisson ardent*), without being consumed, regenerates without end the dancing atoms that it delivers over to its ardor (*ardeur*). This incandescent monad that "reflects onto itself," without being consumed, its "own fervor" needs this "cinder mountain"[2] in order to there sacrifice itself and rejuvenate itself. But for that which is going to die, the ultimate light that crowns the fall of ephemera with a setting sun is necessary.

4. By thus restoring its Eastern side to the night in which a certain West takes pleasure, I do not claim to balance, in a happy medium, the lively forces of the original fire. The old fable cares little about reconciliation. On the slope of one of our most antique reveries, the same path leads from Athens to Thebes and from Thebes to Athens. Flux and reflux are the two faces of the god. Turned in opposite directions, they preserve, without being able to anchor it, the enigma of their metamorphosis. Their gaze seems, though, to extend beyond the mystery that ignites them. We will not ask them the question: Why is there something rather than nothing? They would not answer. The "flowers of fire" of which the "Chaldean Oracles" speak also flower without the permission of a reason, simply "in order to flower." Whence do they come? To sustain their

youth, they need only this nothing that theologies have made the equivalent of a quasi-matter. If there were not, in the distance, this void against which their arabasques are outlined, nothing would happen. Curiously, and like the logician who invokes the null set to secure an existential proposition, fire burns against the background of night or of nothing. But fire has from all time found this nothing that we seek to enclose, since fire bears this nothing within itself as its own power. Everything and nothing [*rien*]. It is thus that the soul of old, in order to be all things, demanded its dauntless vacuity. Had fire therefore foreseen the soul; or else was the soul already the soul of fire?

But if, in order to be everything that it becomes, fire is in no way [*n'est rien de*] that to which it gives birth, it is in order to be reborn without ceasing from the nothingness of ash in which it appears to fade away. Would ash be the mobile earth that fire needs in order to be elevated anew in a rhythm of *arsis* and *thesis*, of position and elevation? One would then find again, from myth to myth, this bond between the heavy and the lightweight, between weight and the imponderable, and, to be honest, between matter and light, of which physics itself, unto these recent times, gravely testified in the commonplace titles of certain celebrated works. But here, and thanks to a singular coincidence, one can no longer isolate the support in a prior exteriority. Matter and form, efficiency and finality, include each other reciprocally in a circle of asiety. The mysterious *causa sui* that haunts philosophies translated, in a difficult concept, this paradoxical immanence. Fire is by itself its own father and mother both. It sufficed unto itself. Would it thus awaken in an unsophisticated consciousness the originary "fantasm" of a pure birth, delivered by the radicalness of its genesis from any reference to everyday generations? This is a dream of the absolute that certain sick people, so it appears, betray in their symptoms. From there, it is but a step to identifying the delirium of a disheveled imagination, of a wandering planet abandoned to the drives of desire, with a profound perturbation of the real. Philosophy and religions are thereby, finally, in the same boat. They too, however different they may be, obey a single nostalgia that the poets of myth narrate and transmit, for an illusory domestication, to the work of metaphysics and of faith. Fire, be it dreamed in the proximity of a hearth or in the distance of a doctrinal statement, would assemble under the same sign of unreality the idle dreams of the origin, which find themselves at the same sensible point, at the same libidinal epicenter whose authentic nature sex, in its transcendental energy, would establish. This time the serpent has a name even if he dissimulates, beneath the undulations of his ruse, a power that is unnamable and capable of all names. Fire has no other magic than that which gathers, in the clarity of a body of knowledge, the new

Prometheuses who drove it to this ultimate avowal. We would be ungracious to turn away with a disdainful gesture those who, supposedly, have forever put an end to the dance and music of fire. Everything that, in one manner or another, calls our poetic naivety into question has the right to our gratitude. Explanations will always be welcome when they open a new space to the course of a *being-toward* that disqualifies only a single verdict: that of a final authority that would take itself in its turn for the definitive absolute. But if the elucidation that one lavishes on us adds to fervor the grace of a lucidity in which its light would be finished, it would be audacious and senseless to there abolish all interrogation. If the energy of which one speaks is capable of such feats, would this not be because its most distant results reflect, as it were, onto their principle and confer on it, retroactively, a "capacity for all becoming" that belies too easy a univocity? By enlarging to infinity the circle of its metamorphoses, the original center is detached in its turn from the overly precise definitions that would rivet it to one zone or one function. It becomes the Proteus that relieves the ancient indetermination of the soul capable of all transformations. The animal, so it seems, is ignorant of such an attractive ray of dreams. Would this not be because, from the outset, the "desire" or the *x* whose appellation one tries to control reveals human workmanship and shakes up, *a priori* so to speak, the narrow environment that one would prescribe to its magnitude? Its extension covers the breadth of the human only by virtue of an understanding that exceeds the confines of a strict meaning. In audacious terms, which reiterate the conclusions of my first investigations, I risk the following hypothesis: the imagination springs from desire only because desire, already, was pregnant with an imaginary, such that it is engendered in its turn by precisely that which it should engender. I do not claim, with these simple remarks, to resolve the question. Timidly, I open it to a horizon that forbids us from too quickly confining to house arrest an energy whose conquering dynamism equals, by right, the unlimitedness of the universe.

5. The circle of fire that the imaginary traces therefore has, at the extremities of its axis, the two poles of impossibility that I clumsily signified with the terms eruption and irruption. These are two manners of saying that fire, despite the material practices that seem to feed it, surges forth only from itself, by a suddenness that allies it to thunder, and that it irrupts in a play space conflated with its own movement.

The metamorphosis of the first degree, the most profound one since it concerns fire considered in itself, consists in this single gush that makes it at once come out of itself and abide in itself. The eruptive force indeed is a thrust of exodus only to the degree that it retains fire within the domain that maps out for it its power, as if the space promised to its essence were conflated with the very sense of its movement. The originality of this condition, as much dreamed as thought—but we are in a register where our customary distinctions are erased before a more radical foundation—would be rather well marked out by prepositional phrases, with which French, less supple than Greek, is more miserly than prodigious. To express this exceptional condition that philosophy and poetry conjoined have attempted to circumscribe, it would be necessary to unite a double modality of specification with the *being-toward* that indicates overtaking and transit. On the one hand, at the point of origin, the indication *by virtue of itself*[5] would highlight the fervor of a fulfillment that disqualifies any condition other than its own boiling. Meister Eckhart, with expressions that are inexact but rather faithful to the course of the imaginary, speaks of an "internal bullition" that is extraposed as *e-bullition*. The "I am who I am" of Exodus would thus in the "burning bush" have its cosmic context of radiance. On the other hand, at the opposite extreme, which specifies less a reticence than the internal condition of an irradiation, the formula "in itself" accentuates, in the exodic pressure, the characteristic of immanence, which the terminology of "introversion" would translate badly. The semantic ternary "stasis," "extasis," "enstasis" has the advantage of a correct formation and an imperative brevity. Its pretentiously technical nature discourages its use. Consequently, it is better, in order to signify the essential without masking it with useless jargon, to modalize *being-toward* by the two polarities that overdetermine it at the limit points of a vertical axis. The configuration thus specified by the propositions "from," "toward," "in" suggests what was intimated by the ancient paradox of an "immobile movement," which the neo-Platonic definition of spiritual being—"that which, abiding in itself, proceeds from itself and returns to itself"—explicated. This philosophical abstractness betrays what I would dare to call, apologizing for an unusual conjunction, "the igneous induction of thought." If what was inadvertently named "metaphysics of the Exodus" was born on the edges of the burning bush, we should add at once that the common translation, "I am who am" (whatever the always-enigmatic content of the original may be), justified the static ontology of "subsistent Being" in advance, by a first forgetting of its fiery context. Restored to its environment, as Eckhart wanted, the "generating monad" finds again the youth of its first fervor. The classical triad, "being, life, thought," which displayed its advanced formula, gathers the breath of a Trinitarian dynamic that invites us to think not states but movements, relations, and operations.

6. Being, whose loss we exhaust ourselves salvaging in the cordial memory of a forgotten difference, is inflected in an intransitive and substantial acting,

in a "being-in" that in no way alters the "being-toward" that it sustains and to which it seems to add itself. To tell the truth, the sequence is as irreducible to a succession as it is to an additive juxtaposition. The logician would doubtless propose a recourse to reciprocal implications. These are precious but insufficient auxiliaries, whose merit is to remedy the heavinesses of language. For a disheveled life whose being, thus understood, would no longer be the point of anchor would exhaust itself in the chaotic multiplicity of the "anything whatsoever." "Thought" has precisely for its function to reflect the wandering flame onto the source from which it draws. The mobile unity that places together what is distinct awakens, in proximity to the fire that is not consumed, a circulation without end that freezes the inert image of the circle into a closed line. The first metamorphosis, such as it is profiled against the horizon of our efforts and our failures, draws a destiny of the real and of thought. One can certainly escape it by freeing one or another of the factors to fix it in its sufficiency. But one day or another the fire "that causes to live" denounces our partialities. Being risks shriveling up into a principle of conservation. The dispersal of life no longer has anything but the appearance of wealth. Thought itself is isolated in the void of the nondescript object. There remains for the poet-savior, faithful to the play of metamorphosis, the irreplaceable grace of the "burning bush."

"The Flowers of Fire"

The expression "flowers of fire," borrowed from the Chaldean Oracles, has known a certain fortune in the course of the centuries. I take it up first for its beauty and above all because it revives this meditation on fire by opening for us the other royal door of its metamorphoses.

1. "Flowers of fire," but also, to take up again a metaphysical-spiritual phrase, this "flower of the soul," of which the mystical Middle Ages made a spark. The burning bush cannot but burst into a procession that indefinitely goes through bushy terrain.[4] The "flowers of fire" indeed inaugurate another course of things that indissolubly mixes man and the *cosmos*. At first sight, one could not submit them to a precise regulation. It is not difficult, however, to discern a certain order in this multiplying madness. Overabundance, certainly, proliferates solely for the joy of proliferating. But this furor of giving traces, on the interval that it imparts to itself, certain directions that order the flux. Without imposing on it an "absolute structure," one can determine some axes capable of guiding reflection.

2. To say this profusion, whose grace is hidden from itself, popular language offers us a first indication when, in a certain context, it declares, "It goes off in all directions." The "it" is eloquent, first of all by the very neuter of an unnamed authority, as if any personal pronoun would restrict by its limits the pressure of generosity that traverses it and that traces, with all its eddies, the contours of a singularity. The power of this impersonal, like the sun of the Gospel that shines on the just and on the unjust, has for measure [*mesure*] only its own immoderation [*démesure*]. That is why this power goes off in all directions [*sens*]. Beneath its semantic meaning, sense [*sens*], in such a universe, precedes any word. Or, supposing that we grant sense a word, it would be in order to open it on the path of light that infallibly inscribes in an existence the imperative *fiat* of its own possibility. The space that it illuminates indeed is in no way an inert container that its objects would fill from the outside. It can await only precisely that which it gives itself. And the first givenness consists exactly in these lines of expansion that distribute its riches. Flowers, if they are born without reason and like unto no other, shine in their differences only by a succession that situates them at their level and in their place. Their distinction would be effaced if each of these sparks did not add to a common origin the gap of a precession or a consequence. The unique itself requires, for its own splendor, the minimal opposition that refers it to its other and that completes it in its beauty. The stars, from all time, emerge in constellations.

3. The burning bush disregards, however, the apparent fixity of our stars, which appear to fade away when we see them from bottom to top, in a wide-open gaze like that of certain icons. Immobile on its vertical axis, with incandescent branches, the burning bush throws before and behind itself, to the right as to the left, upwards and downwards, the profusion of a permanent benediction. These "Easts" that cross at the same center and that flee it as they return to it can then shelter all the birds of the earth and the sky. Imagination would exhaust itself following this *diaspora* that a second thought arranges in a more or less learned hierarchy. But the detail matters less than the dream of love that leads the dance of its metamorphoses. Each of the "extensions" that inaugurate the movement promises to the improbable figures a sequel without end. In the succession that pushes one toward another, the flowers of fire distribute an energy that "does not tire of providing."[5] The philosopher has sometimes hesitated between the *same* and the *other*, between the fascination of dead identity and the discontinuity of a plurality unbound from the constraints of the one. Fire brings us back to that state of indivision where the plural and the singular are not yet two distinct genuses and where we have no need to choose

between the absolute of the unique and the indefinite dyad of a dispersal without measure. And this is, in the final analysis, the sense of metamorphosis.

4. Whether we follow it in the internal evolution of its fundamental operations abstractly defined by the ternary being-life-thought, or whether we are in sympathy with its leap in the procession of its lightning-flashes, in these two modes that the gaze distinguishes solely for the convenience of discourse, fire leads us where our prudence would not want to go. I understand that Van Gogh did not dissociate the ardeurs of summer from the breath that put the wheat to bed in the morning of a cosmic Pentecost. The tongues of fire of which our Scriptures speak burn in the being of things as in the voice that announces the beatitudes of a new world. And the fall that ashes proclaim does not refute the ascent that lifts up their falling back. One would understand nothing of the resurrection myths if one did not discern, beneath their variations and precisely by virtue of their diversity, that irresistible thrust that substitutes, for the states we oppose, the fluidity of forms and the active genius of their metamorphoses. The distinctions that administrative necessities multiply matter little here. Poet or theologian, philosopher or artist, craftsman of language or demiurge of colors and sounds, all those who take on the responsibility for a world always to come have been, one morning or evening, traversed by that flame whose heralds and servants they are in their manner. And each of them, in his native language, hears, for better or for worse, the old prophet's word: "Son of man, do you believe these bones can live again?"[6]

Do the powers of being-toward, at the different levels of the *Meta* function, let be foreseen, for *being-in*, a lookup table that would offer us its inverse? We rightly fear the artifice of parallelisms or of false windows. Instead of subjugating them to the contraries of a single supreme genus, I will therefore leave the two sides of the poetic to their diversion. Each of them has the grace of its state. If they must play alternately or in synergy, it would be an excess of happiness that I have no need to rush.

The figures of *being-in* that I propose are not deduced from any *a priori*. They emerge from an experience from which nobody is excluded. But if I ask nobody for permission to give rise to them, I recognize that there are many abodes in the "Father's house." Diversity is too beautiful to confine it to our partialities.

If an order takes shape in these analyses that is not one of simple succession, nothing prevents us from breaking it and preferring to it an independence that tolerates ill any subordination. What I bind can always be loosed. The essential is to not be a slave and to grant oneself enough space to rid oneself [*se défaire*] precisely of that which one does [*fait*]. With these reserves that are not mere politeness, and without delivering myself over to a dialectical exercise, I will follow, in the course of the induction, the path that led me from flavors, fragrances, and colors, by the intermediary of the abode, to the icon of the face.

6

Flavors, Fragrances, Colors

If I associate these three terms, in a single aim of *being-in*, it is because the first two have as much right as the last to the high esteem that has hitherto been refused them. In contrast to the East, which has succeeded so well at taking advantage of their differences, in the West the primacy of the optical tradition, united to the tradition of hearing (emphasized more particularly, in the Christian world, by the demands of the Reformation), has confined flavors' supposed coarseness to the background. If fragrances have been better treated, they doubtless owe this to a certain subtlety that offended a misplaced delicacy less. And if one wonders why such a persistent, unfavorable prejudice has been strengthened, the most obvious explanation, which from Greece through the Middle Ages has made its way to our era, detects in sight's immateriality the reason for its supremacy. When the *Critique* treats of sensibility in a so-called transcendental aesthetics, it sums up sensibility's definitive traits in *a priori* intuitions. And as intuition is linked to space, time itself, by necessity, had to conform to spatiality's demands. One conceives of space only through the eye's surveillance. Such a limitation indicates an aristocracy that savors in the gaze the domination of a distance taken. Indeed, however useful it may be for the necessities of life, sight has for an imperative the *noli me tangere* that even today the balsam names,[1] that sensitive plant whose fruits burst and fling out their seeds as soon as one touches them. What is more, and by a thought-provoking interference, this power of distance that the Latin expression, adopted by the dictionary, signifies to us refers us back to the Gospel scene in which Jesus, resurrected, refuses the Magdalene the sensible consolation of a contact that would inaugurate, in the softness of a caress, the cool of the new world on its first morning. Confirmed in the excellence of its immateriality by the pneumatic condition of *resurrection bodies*, accessible only to sight, the eye is not, however, unconditionally beatified. The faith of those who have not seen, but who have believed without seeing, can dispense just as much with the verifications by touch that, to appease his doubts, the hesitant if not unbelieving apostle required. The new heaven and the new earth that Revelation envisages remain nonetheless the crystal spectacle promised to the sight of the blessed. By way of philosophical or religious habits, the purity of the optical is assured, like an elixir for long life, in the beatitude of the pure in heart, the only ones who *will see God* without dying.

Against the current of these historical necessities, forgetful of their contingency, I would wish for a promotion of the humble ones that have the right to more and better than a backup diaconate, which one hastens to relegate to the obscure corners where *eating* is kept.

Flavors and the Gods

1. One thinks at once, to introduce this redemption of the poor in spirit and of the captives, of the famous saying, the Heraclitean *logion*, that places "the gods in the kitchen." The Christian, familiar with the Eucharist and the real presence, "in the species of the host," is not so far from this archaic thought. Archaic, not in the sense of an archeology, but of an *Arché* that has nothing to do with the meditation of bone or stone, for what is said here joins with that which the terms *commencement, principle* designate after a fashion. By these two ways, whose convergence was not foreseen, a profound thought is affirmed of our being-in-god and of god-in-us. *Being-in* is therefore signified to us by the modesty of bread and of the place where bread is cooked beneath ashes. But bread is really what it is only by disappearing in the flavor that allows us to taste it. One can explain without difficulty the listeners' hesitation before the Gospel discourse on the *bread of life*. Whereas sight does not dissolve, or seems to not dissolve, for it leaves that which it sees to its transcendence, one who eats consumes and uses up [*consomme et consume*] the god whose infinite distance forever separates him from this quotidian destruction. The very coarseness of the interpretation should turn a normal sensibility away from any sapid approach to the Absolute. What is strange is that theology itself seems to have oscillated between the flavor of wisdom and the optical requests that, however refined they may be, still come to light in the language of the *invisible*. Contraries being in the same genus, it is not overly surprising that they finally opted for a hidden presence, shielded from the gaze but thereby offered to a faith destined to vision. The negative locutions have, over the course of centuries, been the decisive sign of a timidity in or an incompetence at thinking otherwise than in terms of vision.

2. This impotence has become the well-distributed common sense of philosophers and artists or poets who have also retained only the cultural

dignity of the two higher senses. This bizarre insensibility does not seem to have been called into question. Abstracting from any theological reference, it is easy to note that the manner in which the thought of being and of the world is today renewed tolerates only the unshaken prestige of light and the voice, of sight and hearing. Consequently it matters little whether one overturns representation, in favor of a before whose forgetting representation would perpetuate, if the context is maintained that renders what one refuses and what one wishes to promote equally legitimate. Why and by virtue of what could there not be a flavor of being and of the world? This would today be one of the major questions that the thinker's reflection truly has to weigh [*peser*] and to think [*penser*]. Every way out that would dissipate the apparent strangeness of the questioning with disdain or a shrug of the shoulders would be too obvious. Arguing from the coarseness of taste or flavors would be but a poor recourse; one would unconsciously re-establish a dual condition of sensibility that, by its noonday division between the blessed and the damned, would confirm a break between the higher and the lower, the illusion of which has been denounced so many times. Once again, why this choice that is also forgotten?

3. I am willing to admit that the taste of the world or of being, this flavor that refers to no food and no soil, seems very abstract. But are we any better off when light or the voice is invoked to make us sense, beneath any concept, the thing, supposedly essential, of thought? Whatever may be the discourse in which we engage, we are in the same boat. Thus persists, without being stated, the tacit presupposition that exalts a traditional and omnipotent clarity in light and in the voice. And yet nothing we call human (as I recalled in my earlier pages), whether of the body or the spirit, is exiled from the human condition. For the flesh is spirit, even, contrary to what was sung, in countries that lack wine. Consequently, we have no need, in the present case, to call for a vivisection that I deem schizophrenic. One will perhaps wonder to what specific factors a flavor of the world would be tied. The error would be precisely in positing a privileged experience whose exultant character, by lifting our empirical realm above itself, would *ipso facto* confer on it the perception of the essential. Here there is no quasi-miracle that, breaking with continuity, would for an instant make us leave our limits. The ecstasy that is called for is closer to quotidian calm than to a stammering drunkenness. When one has for years suffered hunger and thirst and finds again, after such an extended fast, these poor foods that in our home [*chez nous*] the Eucharistic prayer names in order to transform them into the body and blood of Christ, one knows with a knowing that is the very joy of life what the world in us is and what we in the world are. *Being-in* is at once refined by the reinvention of each day's bread and wine. Their flavors have the discretion

of a neuter that, far from erasing the contours of things or adding to them to alter them, exalts their form, brilliance, and depth. By passing into us, through a conversion that the theological formulas relating to "transubstantiation" recall, they designate, well and truly beyond the objects we fix in place, a manner of welcoming, a disposition that places us in accord, in *accordance* (if I may be permitted this old French),[2] with the universe of men and things. And if there is a despair with which alarming news about our distant brothers overwhelms us today, it is because, in their excessive destitution, they will have known of the world only the impossibility of inhabiting it and of life only the jolt of a last breath for greeting with a *viva la muerte* a last end without finality.

4. I do not want thereby to reduce the flavor of the world, that sweet fervor that makes us inhabit it, to the bare minimum of the indispensable. As far as I can know them, the multiple cuisines that have not taken leave of the gods know how to diversify pleasure. One finds in them, without artifice, an accompanying quasi-indeterminate, a sort of permanent "I am tasting" that gives thanks to their varieties. Rice is not bread; millet is not rice. It matters little; the function remains that anchors the palate in a sort of relatively immobile base where the omnipresence of being and of the world is schematized. The art of flavors consists, consequently, in marrying the "base" to the changing forms that fulfill our hope. I will not be so ridiculous as to recall in this regard the difference between being and beings. But there are forgettings that are no less mortal. By a sure instinct, absent in our philosophers, the ludic activity to which these culinary inventions testify is exercised in the obscure regions of the hearth where "thought" rarely descends. As it has been pointed out, serving tables, as an art of cuisine, was abandoned to women, who gave their names (their first names, rather) to marvelous dishes that were later taken up, under the trademark of their advertisements, by great chefs, concerned above all with substituting their brand for those names.[3] Books on art and the history of art still disregard this kind of creation that baffles their nomenclature. I do not have to be scandalized by this. One tastes a novel or a poem. But to taste a Bourgogne or a Bordeaux, it does not suffice to read the label or to consult the menu, even in an armchair. And yet, whatever may be the distance between such remote kinds, how can we not recognize that a certain taste of the world is affirmed, there also, in the genius who composes their bouquets? The thanksgiving of our Eucharists celebrates a little-known grace that gathers in the host and the chalice the slow germination of the universe. The gods have not disdained this gesture of offering and libation that raises above the ground, but so near to the earth, a fleeting abode where their passage is announced in the delicacy of a flavor.

Floral Essences

1. From flavors to fragrances the distance is so slight that the East has crossed it from time immemorial. But if the distinction is attenuated by the nearness, the differences are reinforced by their evident proximity. Whereas flavor deepens our being in the world in the mode of an incorporation, fragrances create around us an ethereal milieu that seems to thwart the multiple weights of which we are more or less the unconscious or complicit victims. If I risk in this regard the expression "floral essences," it is partially to correct what the vocabulary of "essence" ordinarily implies in a certain tradition. Essence defines a being [*être*] by a set of indications or properties that, from the most epidermic to the most fundamental, constitute its ontological record or number. Even though, in the course of the centuries, the function that has fallen to it has varied in its contents, the passage from substance to relation, and from relation to a system of relations, or even what has been called the mathematization of quality have hardly affected its initial composition. It is and remains a principle of limiting determination. Yet in the common vocabulary another sense comes to light that is more consonant with our subject. When one speaks of essence of lavender, of violet, of lemon, etc., one evokes something light, like a spirit of things that is not unreminiscent of the quintessence of old. It seems that every being [*être*], to accomplish its destiny, must be dissipated in a breath. A floral grace, which would be the glory of the evening, thus immaterializes in a sigh the indispensable grounded socket. The ancients discoursed on "the flower" or the "summit of the soul." The East universalizes, by extending it to the most opaque realities, what the West reserved for human nobility.

2. That is, however, only a first approximation. At the limit, the world itself is transformed into a floral essence. Without being doubled by an afterworld, it is metamorphosed into a subtle or pneumatic body that is not so far removed as one thinks from the more familiar themes that our terminology of resurrection shelters. This spiritualization, far from diminishing it, refines it in its power. When the art of fragrances, responding as it were to its call, marries together its attractions, it will fulfill what it is and what it should be: the space of freedom in which we are and live. For this "poetics of the sensible," which cannot be invalidated by attaching it retrospectively to a supposedly outmoded stage of our evolution, indeed tends toward such an excess. We must not malign "rhinencephaly." The hunting animal's sense of smell follows the track of the coveted prey betrayed by its odor. We are not at that point, although it is doubtless necessary to attenuate with a *perhaps* this too-confident assurance. But if it is so, that is because, from the environment to the world, the qualitative

rupture providentially condemned us to a necessary transfiguration. The artist who, by "making them give up their spirit," gathers those wandering atoms that flowers give off prolongs the play of the world with itself. The sphere that we inhabit is thus enveloped with an atmosphere. And if it is true that fire itself is, according to an old master's saying, only a "burning smoke,"[4] we should add that this smoke must also dissipate and, even if it is white, lose its color in an aromatic transparency that makes itself be forgotten.

3. Odors and fragrances bestow around us the imponderableness of an unsurveilled air. Strictly speaking, they propose nothing to us. Beyond essence and form, they let hover a *je-ne-sais-quoi* that refuses any circumscription. In their way, and by their very discretion, they oppose to the eye's representations a refusal that calls the extent of their empire into question. By their presence alone, and without even a murmur or a wanting-to-say,[5] they say a depth of things that could not be the horizon of a gaze. The sensibility that they caress rather than agitating is there freed from any object. It seeks there less a refuge than this unhoped-for [*cet inespéré*] that escapes our hold. And that is why certain philosophies, and not the least of them, have not disdained these almost-nothings, which in their delicacy are more in accord with a "nothingness par excellence" that pushed their language to its breaking point. The spiritual in their turn has taken the same path. The god they invoke inhabits neither the sumptuous colors nor the harmonies of the earth or the sky, and incense would be too much if it were insistently affirmed and spread. To the abrupt questioning that would worry about their abode, they would have no other answer than a certain inflection of body and spirit where the beatitude of "being there" and not elsewhere is discovered. The untranslatable term *Gelassenheit*,[6] which still very recently has known a certain revival, sums up this experience of the ungraspable. It is not a matter either of a simple relaxation or of a prolonged ease that rewards labor, and still less of a negligent "anything goes [*laisser-aller*]." Contemplation [*recueillement*], when it concludes an effort, would risk troubling its quiet. For lack of anything better, one will speak of "letting be [*laisser être*]," in order to abide in it, a generous insistence that gives not its name and that flees every face.

4. Is not, however, the raising of fragrances to this mystical sublimity an artifice far removed from the ordinary, but just as removed from that very East that has succeeded at taking advantage of their charm and their equivocity? Analysis must accede to a less inhuman condition, without for all that diminishing their necessity. To the degree that they create a milieu of respiration, beneath any word, they are in league with the everyday verb "to find oneself, to be located [*se trouver*]."[7] "Finding oneself, being located" is not synonymous with "being-in."

In the middle voice, beneath the passive and the active, it indicates a state that is in no way static or inert. It signifies, in brief, the reverberation or the resonance in us of abiding. This is the reason why I do not dissociate it from the positive and negative valences that it connotes in its common usage. Finding oneself is always finding oneself well or finding oneself ill.[8] The axiological turn of phrase defines the fundamental manners of *finding oneself* and the polarities of *being-in*. In this regard, the nuances of vocabulary are not to be neglected. In a sectarian work that had great success in the last century, a Catholic writer,[9] by a deliberate contrast, opposed *Les Odeurs de Paris [The Odors of Paris]* to *Le Parfum de Rome [The Fragrance of Rome]*. Let us leave to the side the easy jokes and mockeries that would amuse today's readers. The two titles define fairly well the anonymity of an ambiance that, depending on the case, leads us to say "that smells good" or "that smells bad." The poetics of the sensible can, at each person's discretion, be fastened to one or the other of these sides. More refined people would doubtless add a precision: odors rise, fragrances descend. We will not destine to the eccentric's disgraces the one who prefers rising to descent. Without excessive partiality, it seems to me that descent better corresponds to the indefinite grace that envelops, that gratifies, and that makes flourish. But if we opt for the positive, an image arises at once that binds fragrances to woman's charm. This association is not without danger. The danger, nevertheless, is not the danger at which one guesses and which transfers the serpent's ruses to a body's troubling volubility. Masculine prejudice always risks—but it is a wholly other risk—dissipating the feminine, when he deigns to think it, either into the ancillarity of an indispensable service or into the apparent gratuity of a supplementary luxury. In any case, one way or the other the conclusion remains the same: "woman does not exist." This is an assertion with a double meaning, like the nothingness of the medievals that slides from nothingness "by defect" to nothingness "by excess." Non-existence can indeed oscillate between the effacing of the "lord's little handmaiden" and the quasi-nothing of a presence that is annulled in precisely that which it causes to exist. Could the feminine, conflated with fragrances, therefore be condemned to the same evanescence? This disobliging suspicion cannot but draw the famous and sharp retort, "I am not an atmosphere!"[10]

5. The feminine condition, reduced to a sort of kenosis for the use of right-minded people, serves too well, I admit, the dominator's ideology. A poetics of the sensible cannot, therefore, be content or satisfied to repair the sin of omission with a Platonic "inspiration" that would whisper to the demiurge the invitation to speech or to writing. Writing and speech remain macroscopic places, favorable to clichés. The muse has too often figured as the adventitious

one that the seriousness of creative work neglected at once. It does not malign woman to wish for her another mode of existence. It is more difficult to situate her in her true place. The Christian faith spares her a place between the angel's wing and the shadow of the Most High. This double patronage is not innocent. Perhaps it masks, in this vocation for the sublime, the uncomfortable position of a submission without appeal. If, in contrast, we decline the woman's personal index that individualizes her in favor of a "feminine" neutral that seems to exalt her, then diligence in the kitchen, with children, or in the Church immediately recalls the prose of days and of night. By sparing her, in the heights as it were, this place that none can wrest from her, will we then liken her to the excess of happiness that delivers us from boredom by the distraction of sabbatical hours? These extra coins would aggravate the scorn. The gesture of offering retains the odor of sacrifice. And if there remained only this incense to justify the burnt offering, the rest of the seventh day would join Ash Wednesday in dominical calm. Without falling into feminism, the hoped-for promotion should fulfill another level of aspiration.

6. The East that we mistrust, so much does the nagging image of veiled faces upset us, has perhaps better understood what we seek but are unable to grasp. If I also make a return to floral essences, it is not to fall again into the discourse of banality or the artificial ease of salons. Rather, it is to recall that a poetics of the sensible must, like the East, *meet* woman to the exact degree that it must think, by reflection on these neglected sensibles that are flavors, fragrances (and, as I will soon add, a certain mode of existence of colors), the feminine essence of the world. This feminine essence of the world is what makes us experience it (*experience* and *find ourselves in it* [*éprouver et s'y trouver*]) as the fundamental *there* in which we are, like the *precondition*, apparently immobile, whence proceed all the movements that will convert it into a space of conquest and work. The East had the intuition of this fundamental rest, thus reversing the familiar optics that places the Sabbath at the end and not at the beginning. The feminine is therefore that which makes *abiding* possible, which grounds us *in* and *on* a habitable universe. This is the *second birth* that makes us be-in-the-world (*être-au-monde*), and the woman is for us responsible for this birth. The feminine is this envelope of transparency that remains inaccessible to those who are born solely "of flesh and blood." Feminine essence certainly has not deserted woman, and I do not claim, absolutizing the neuter, to justify a divorce between the essence and its rightful subject. But if, at the risk of forcing the abstraction, we claim this neuter that transcends the individuality of its individual bearers while not disregarding it and even while leaving it its inalienable function of

schematization, it is because its forgetting would be for us the irreparable loss of a human quality of the world, without which it would become unbreathable. This relaxation that would seem, to the busy ones that we all are, a slow death in the void, is therefore not a supererogatory luxury. The gratuity of this grace is the most necessary of necessities. One will perhaps object that the earth was given to us to dominate and not for a half-sleep of idleness. Certainly, it would be ridiculous to dismiss this unalienable component. But would not the most beautiful freedom be that of judging power itself and, in the highest consciousness of the mastery that it grants us, of putting it at a distance and as if beneath our feet? In this volatile ether where fragrances dance, the dreaded image of a maternal authority that devours its children to deprive them of all force of understanding and of lucidity is also erased. Between Martha the strong woman and Mary who does nothing, should we choose? If I refuse the choice, it is not to be deaf to the ancient word: Mary has chosen the better part. A poetics, sensitive [*sensible*] to what is beyond forms and powers, cannot disregard this part, best in the division of the world. And if there yet remains a hope, it is that this part will not be taken from her.

Of Tastes and Colors

Are colors a last-minute addition only for the pleasure of composing a new trinity on earth? If I add them, it is because flavors and fragrances need, in order to spread, a milieu that tempers light's brilliance with its heat. I include here, for the same reasons, both the sonorous background, so avidly sought today, and the diversions of a touch that is sometimes too eager to not trouble the serenity of the envelopment. But why colors and not, as one would expect here, that festive "whiteness" of whose pure subsistence our fathers dreamed long ago?

1. It would indeed be erroneous to believe that, however tempered it may be, white light, as it is restored by complementary colors, could be the neuter that in no way alters what it surrounds. If the medievals were able to believe it was, that is because in their scholarly naivety they considered the luminous to be the immaterial that, far from transmuting beings [*êtres*] or things, makes them appear in the originality of their elevation and their contours. Yet when it is a matter of *being-in* and of *abiding*, the very lightness and the discretion of its emergence ill tolerate a clarity that is hardly conducive to penumbra and that, however attenuated it may be, would free a percussion effect. In contrast, I attribute to certain colors, when they cause themselves to be sensed without

being conflated, a power of radiance that, on flavors and fragrances, places the light touch of a climate.

2. In order to attain this degree of silent omnipresence, they also require a prior purification. They must be detached from their substrata and must thus acquire, by being simplified, the status of an abstract that is in no way conceptual. It is red or blue or green as such that are invited to the rendezvous. Freed from their objects, they find again that immateriality that harmonizes so well with the anonymous givenness of a world, just as irreducible to the limits of a thing as to the presumed infinity of a sum of objects.

To complete these remarks, I cannot but return once again, and indefatigably, to those rose windows of Notre-Dame that, at the hour when the sun declines, invite you to the dance of the last rays. The violet and the green, the red and the blue of the Biblical scenes seem to wait for this hour for the intimate feast of the mirror. At the point where their face to face in the transept gives way to the happy medium of their encounter, the colors have lost the memory of the figures who were attired with their attractions. They are now nothing but the essence of the decanted color of a first existence that bound them to the vicissitudes of history. The evening light then gathers them for a second birth at the very center where the edifice joins the arms of its cross. An attentive gaze still discerns the chromatic differences in these divine frolics. But none jealously demands the right to its private property. They seem to die of not being able to die. No synthesis imposes on their interferences the law of their necessary unity. The exultation of being themselves in the impossibility of being alone is sufficient for them. If there is a case where being recovers the gift [*don*], it is indeed in this marvelous instant when each one of them breathes its other in a spiration in which they give up [*rendent*] their spirit. It would be ridiculous to add to their sigh a hypothetical resultant of their forces. Without calculation, midway along the distance that separates, in the heights, their circle of irradiation, they find themselves there, and their softness descends that our joy might remain. Perhaps *being-in* needed this ultimate power of reciprocal transparency so that fragrances and flavors, by raising themselves above things, might make of the world a feast of the transfiguration. Nothing would be more foreign to their tenacious and impalpable presence than their insertion into a hierarchy where they would occupy, respectively, the base, the middle, and the summit. It is better to leave them to their quality of elements, in the broadest sense that designates less a "component" than a milieu in which "we live and move and have our being." For it is a matter of just that. And that for us is sufficient.

7

The Abode

Flavors, fragrances, and colors free an ambiance that, closest to *abiding*, defines its power of radiance. But if they tell us the conditions of *inhabiting*, they leave full latitude to the diverse ways in which abiding gives itself, in the midst of men, the consistency of an abode. The passage from the verb to the substantive does not signify the forgetting of the substantial acting, and neither does it signify the degradation of function into substance.

The body's beauty does not scorn the finery that, far from effacing it, enhances its brilliance to highlight its attractions. The home, in its broadest meaning, also extends, by lending it a place, man's body into its world-body. Too often, it is true, the circumscription that the home evokes suggests the walls of a prison or, at best, the imperative of a preservation or conservation principle. The image of stability and tradition confers on it, in addition, a sort of femininity, even though care for classification and tidying, operations of the understanding, are not exclusively domestic. When, moreover, uniformity shows its severity, the heaviness of stones becomes the symbol of boredom, of this fog in which everything is gray, in which the newness of the morning fades in the repetition of gestures and phrases that do not speak, of movements that cross paths without meeting, this fog in which fidelity is exhausted in the return of an everyday that begins again only to never have begun. This summary analysis, which seems to give the lie to essence in the tepidity of existence, invites us to ascend again the slope of a degradation against which there is no absolute recourse. How can we make a poetics of the sensible that renders abiding sensible cross over [*passer*] to action?

Force and Impotence of Abiding

The varieties of the human habitat discourage by their overabundance. The history of art and of techniques describes and classifies their forms, explains their evolution, possibly seeks to understand their finality. Without being foreign to me, this preoccupation remains lateral to the reflection I am pursuing. In contrast, the pathology of *inhabiting* recently offered to us, under the name *sarcellitis* (from the famous commuter town of the Parisian *banlieue*, unworthy of the web-footed bird whose name it copies),[1] the highly instructive case of an environmental sickness, an affliction that one could call "ecological," of which we would have to take advantage. This negative exemplariness of an abode in which it is impossible to abide could be the initial shock that, by contrast, puts us on the right route. The gravity of the situation indeed exceeds the blunders of an uncertain urbanism or the treatment of one dysfunction out of so many others. It affects those depths of the human being who, in this domain, today suffers from a veritable crisis of grounds [*fondements*]. The problem is no longer solely one of architecture. It cannot be resolved by the treasures of ingenuity of which contemporary artists are no more bereft than their elders.

1. It is not a matter of foundations [*fondations*] or of the simple arrangement of territory. It is quite simply a matter of knowing *where one is*. And this *ubi*, this *there* that grounds [*fonde*] us decides what we *will ground*. If sarcellitis rages, as a sign of the times, it is to the degree that it translates, in a sort of schizophrenia, the divorce between a fundamental question—*where do you abide?*, a question whose forgetting exacerbates, in the unconscious, its irrepressible urgency—and the answers that elude it in our diversions. If I had, without trampling on the rights of a body of knowledge, to define the regulatory principle that would orient in the past the tasks of an art of building, I would risk the formula: every architecture, however rudimentary it may be, is the solution to a metaphysical problem, a problem that philosophers encounter or skirt and that concerns as much a depth of things as a ground of existing and a reason to live. Plants secrete their protective sheaths. Animals dig their refuges. Foxes have dens and birds have nests. But the Son of Man has, from the beginning, nowhere to lay his head. For it is indeed from the head and the heart that the artifice proceeds from which we have made what remains [*demeure*] today of our contingency. Necessity and freedom unite to draw on the sand, on the sea, or on the rock the home where the right to live and to die is affirmed.

2. The right to live and to die, immanent to existing itself, arises in a *sortie* that, over the shadows or over the clarity of things, raises the *I am* of an act of being whose audacity and fragility an *I think* assumes.

This fragility, at the origin, found in the rock's crevices and the hill's grottos the precarity of a shelter and the remedy for the gropings of a power. As power over things grew firmer and action verified in its successes the anticipations of an autonomous providence, man's work accentuated the distance that separates him from his environment. Be they ever so humble, these ancient abodes where the gap is affirmed still move us today by the testimony they have left us of their indecisive victory. A simple raft then secured, on the mobility of the waves, the first steps of a courage of being that heralds from afar the inaugural walk on the moon. Everything that is becomes already, at the limit, the support for a decision, while awaiting the pedestal of a conquest. Being and beings thus mark their ontological difference. The lakeside cities will subsequently reinforce an austere experience that has not known the time of discourse. In these efforts, in which the fear of the worst and the hope for the best are indissolubly mixed, a more or less submissive nature answers, by its substance, a young liberty that holds itself[2] and keeps itself [*se tient et se maintient*] at a distance from precisely that by which it sustains itself [*se soutient*]. People have discoursed much on the *substratum* and the *subject*, while too often forgetting what is in question, as if the venerable texts that nourish us would henceforth dispense prosaic and precise references that the wisdom of the scribes merrily sacrificed to the delights of leisure. Beneath the abstract categories that name the forms of judgment, there is all this movement of *being-in-itself* that is affirmed in the act of grounding and of grounding oneself, an act itself bound to the care of clothing oneself, preserving oneself, defending oneself, in short holding oneself in a place, the breadth and quality of which, in their relation to the world, constitute the more or less happy totality of a circumscription adjusted to the necessity of existing. To the question *where do you abide?* men have had to reply on the scale of their savoir-faire and of the inclinations of their love.

3. The more or less hypothetical succession of stages matters less than the originality of the modes of being and of sensing. I conceive first of all, so much does it still speak to me today, of a wandering abode that would take on a temporary consistency only at the moment of the day or night when an excess of fatigue compels the fall into the horizontality of sleep and of death. *Being-in* and *being-toward* alternate there without being able to find an equilibrium, even in the instable figure of nomadism. The Biblical Feast of Tabernacles marks, on this vanishing line, a halt that is less hurried by the departure but that still remembers the long march in the desert and the impossibility of establishing, somewhere in a stop, that musical and forever unfinished *there* [*là*][3] where our hearts rest. The booth of branches emphasizes still more a movement that is not conflated with our modern itch for change. The bird on the branch is here more than a symbol. It celebrates an impermanence that does not forbid song, that seems on the contrary to push it to its limit in the joy of a ceaseless soaring.

4. These abodes of times gone by say the being-in-itself of abiding. They say it, however, in the foreign element, scarcely transformed. They seem to obey the childish happiness of a certain insouciance. It would be ridiculous to compare them to our exploits that have at their disposal a wholly other capacity. But, however dubious the idea of progress may be when we apply it without discernment, we must at least recognize that this economy of the *minimum* lets be discerned a less rudimentary regime where the certainty of being and the security of having would be less exposed.

The home, in its most common meaning, henceforth evokes, inscribed in a solid matter, the affirmation and the ambition of a right to property. *One's own* [*sien*] makes the *self* [*soi*] manifest. By contrast, and to better realize the import of this, it suffices to look toward those shameful parts of our towns where, outside the walls and in a predestined non-place, the habitations of misery and chance are spread out, where the necessity of living rubs shoulders each day with the impossibility of existing.

The histories of art disregard this rubble because it has been agreed that art is the slave of the beautiful. And the beautiful is what is pleasing to the eye. We must not offend the "calm of the gods."[4] The painter who passes by that way, pushed by his evil demon, in order to anchor his phantoms under a rainy sky, sometimes discovers there children's laughter in a furtive ray. This grain of happiness wrested from despair by a miracle of grace irresistibly recalls the thrust of life that, at the extreme limit of the possible, and to the explorer's surprise, would arouse the germinal elation of an unforeseen microorganism. There is nothing so wretched that it does not hide an atom of radiance. But this certainty that honors cannot console us from unhappiness, nor justify, by the joy of escaping from it, the necessity of wretchedness.

5. I have known, near New York, a garden of paradise that held, right in the middle of its delights, a simple villa in discreet colors, well made for sheltering the religious silence of a fervor of study and prayer. Contemplating it from afar, I could not silence a melancholy. From the vision of a splendid nature, cloistered by the unrefusable respect of mine and thine, there lacked the complicity of innumerable gazes in which the beauty of this little world would be completed but which, alas! would never see it. I would not want to mix with this sadness I know not what base resentment that blasphemes to the point of wanting to destroy that of which we have been deprived. Wishing, for the home I love, an extension of love that no longer reserves it for fortunate loners is not, however, acting as a facile demagogue or threatening the glory of difference with the possible degradations of equality. The analogy of knowledge could be illuminating;

its propositions are truly valid only if they are valid for everyone, and strictly speaking they are valid for everyone only if each one, *de jure*, is able to prove it by recognizing its truth in an actual verification. This is a chimerical ideal, certainly, and quasi-paradisiacal, but it is one that appears indissociable from scientific work. Likewise, a work of art and this humble home that, at the cross of our paths of sand, makes the sign of its shadow to the morning's passerby need, in order to be affirmed in the possession of the world, a gesture of benediction, an amen in which the innumerable gazes of those who have eyes to see meet, in which every vision resounds with what is absent from its beatitude. I will say later on what would be, or what was, the universal home that schematizes the world-abode or the abode-world. I must come back to the singular abode. How does it merit the honors of a poetics of the sensible?

6. Every designation (which would class it, according to our canons, in the category of the fine arts) having been abstracted, and within the very limits of its singularity, it stands out against the anonymity of the nondescript earth and of that "nondescript object" where being and nothingness exchange their idioms. Its first merit is precisely to exist, that is, to renew, by its manner of holding itself over and against a horizon, that first insurrection that made the human, facing the forces of nature, a being [*être*] that stands upright in the defiance of its verticality. It seems to say, *I abide* and *I will maintain* [*maintiendrai*], as if the *now* [*maintenant*] whose instants it tells[5] and holds together already had the validity of a universal. We no longer see anything there but the banal hearth, hunched over a narrow and too-often vacillating flame. But if the jaded eye remembers, by interiorizing it, this becoming that the abode immobilizes in a gesture, the splendor of *abiding* and of *holding oneself* [*se tenir*] speaks a forgotten language anew. *Holding oneself*, holding oneself in oneself: this poor tired verb, worn out by too long a lexical stanza, had regained a new vigor in the sorrowings of the *Stabat Mater*, of the "Mother upright at the foot of the cross." Holding oneself is something wholly other than doing nothing or not walking. Against a fall that always threatens and that is, as the saying goes, "caught," it is assembling the diversity of our limbs and dispersed forces in a stability [*tenue*] and a continuity [*teneur*] where, from the base to the summit and the summit to the base, the serenity of a substantial acting that is exempt from all action, but in order to become its ground and its depth, passes and passes again. The home, it is true, has its juridical status. It is the sign of a right. It is the *at-home* [*chez soi*] claimed by a *self* [*soi*] that calls itself "I" and whose name is inscribed on the registers or Tablets of the Law. It is perhaps by this legal mediation that a "consciousness of the subject" appeared in the West for the first time. And law [*droit*] arouses

suspicion because it seems to be exhausted in the canonization of the private, that is, in property by right [*de droit*]. Yet there is nothing less poetic than this inflexible rigor that reiterates, without finding again its floral freshness, the balsam's *noli me tangere* and that seems to have retained nothing of the flower but its irritability. But once again, though we should not be duped, it would be dreadful to sacrifice the originality of that which was in its way an origin to the indubitable contingencies of a local and dated history. By paying tribute to the home-abode, I would like, one last time, to there hear the confession of this human footstep that made of these stones, erected and intertwined together, the recollection of a passage or of a rupture, the exodic passage that makes us leave the den or the nest. If the *abode* is *there*, and with such insistent gravity, it is to commemorate a being [*être*] that alighted there, and not for five minutes only. The substance of the substratum exalts the condition of an "I am who I am" that sums itself up there by resting on itself. There lacks only, I acknowledge, the terrifying proximity of the "burning bush." If the home were possible, would it not in the end be in order to avoid the burning of this flame that tolerates only either the distance of a march in exodus or the heroism that flings itself into it with furor?

The Temple and the Cathedral

Beyond the singular home, the familial hearth, I will pay a word of tribute to the more ample, aristocratic, or familiar home that today, under the name of "culture" and "admiration," gathers a less homogeneous population in which the multiple faces and trades of the city are reflected. This home of the people is only moderately popular. Though it elevates the singular beyond its singularity by acceding to the language of right or the language of the spirit, it has no way to retain the singular. People cross paths there, multiplying one by another their essential indifference. They read, listen, see the procession of a kaleidoscopic present or of a past whose memory one vaguely establishes without truly interiorizing it in an authentic ontogenesis. The optimism that made us believe for a moment in the recapitulation of the species in the history of each individual ended in the disenchantment that the famous phrase "Nothing is deeper in man than his skin"[6] expressed rather well. The epidermic rejoins the superficiality of the outer membrane. The town hall, which the village's prose has made into the mayor's office, emphasizes the official with empty solemnities only to sign the marriage or death certificate with this same objective and disinterested air that presides over births and funerals. It is a funereal echo of the "sunken cathedral."[7]

1. I will unite the temple and the cathedral, the Greek genius and the Christian Church, the Buddhist marvels of India or Nepal, and the mosques of the Near East in the city of the roses that Isfahan names for the tourist.[8] In these blessed places, with such varied ambiances and styles, it seems that a single founding power pushed man to lay the ground of a home, open to all, and welcoming "to the four corners of the earth." Spirit blows where it will. And if it privileges some abode, as though it were unique, it is always by reminding us that unicity, to not be suspect, is but a manner among others of rendering homage, in the originality of the exception, to the liberality of the Universal.

I am not tempted, for all that, by relativism or indifference. But if I know where I inhabit, unable to contest the Eternal's ubiquity or the infinity of his love, the determination of my difference does not prevent me from seeing, above the home, the palm leaf that flutters and that makes a sign of friendship and respect to that irreducible other the possibility of whose name I think without being able to name it. The fraternity of the calls, inversely, forbids neither the distinction of sonorities nor the necessity of the narrow gate that, beneath the archway of Notre-Dame, leads into the great nave. These banalities, for which I do not have to apologize, so difficult are they to comprehend, must, however, to dissipate any misunderstanding, be accompanied by a corrective.

In the aristocratic enumeration that sums up several itineraries, have I not forgotten, obsessed with the historical supremacy of certain models, these "homes of the Most High" that, in the forests of Africa and of other worlds, also render homage, without the pretention of a canonical architecture, by the simple praying junction of stray branches and dispersed leaves? Why abandon, to the profit only of the rich, these humble abodes in which a gathered people, breathed in by the invisible, meet together? I have not lost myself in these immensities. But though I cannot speak with full knowledge of the facts, and though I am not keen to redeem my ignorance with a hasty appendix in which authoritative references are juxtaposed, I admit to feeling [*me sentir*] close to these unknown ones who also have elevated above things, and above their sleep, the vigilance of a lookout who awakens in every man an immemorial power of waking. What, therefore, are we dealing with here?

2. In the universal home, I discern in the first place the quasi-vegetative pole that roots it in our earth. A plant or flower, which it would be wrong to liken to the artificial expressions that display eternal regrets on tombs, it sinks

into the night. It needs the rock or stone that permits it to hold itself. It must be solid to better fill its function of solidarity. But the foundations on which it rests are but the sensible signs of a movement that goes well beyond. In reality, the founding act that it incorporates traverses all the elements that it submits to its attraction. It must thus descend, in a regressive march that confers on it an indefinite space of recoil, the successive layers that compose the universe. Nothing should escape its hold. In this sense, the universal home is the world itself as restored to its first destiny that made it the abode of mortals. But this restoration, beneath the hand that digs the earth, does not claim to pierce the earth to compile, in a new Noah's ark, the stratified exemplars of each species. In its ideal vection, the foundation sends back to the ground the universal function of the substratum that the singular home, within its limits, already exercised. The temple assumes it anew while giving to it, on its scale, the extension owed to it. One can say of it that it is the earth insofar as the earth has become, by the work that humanizes it, the microcosm in which it is reflected in a sensible thought that makes it be born to self-consciousness. For the temple is just as much the call addressed to nature as it is the answer that raises nature up in a *here I am* in which it holds itself in the stability of its waking.

3. Whose abode? one would have the right to ask. Of the dead or of the living? Is the tomb not the home of the dead, and are not tombstones the first temples? Must we oppose the law of the night to the law of the day, the clarity of masculine understanding to feminine night? These dualities are in large part artificial. The body of the world, in the architecture that completes in speech the obscure order of a cosmic interdependence, is made of what is past, of what passes, of what will pass. The temple, in the synchrony of its space, tells in simultaneity of the dispersion of the time that it redeems and that, in a certain manner, it abolishes. This is why the god it celebrates is the god of the dead and of the living. For all, it remains the place where one rests and abides, the *there* where the border between life and death is but an outer membrane that only an illusion makes into the wall of separation between the here below and the beyond. The difference would be radical only if work as the genius of transformation were man's last word. Yet it is precisely this that the temple calls into question by converting us to the serenity of an acting that does nothing but that does not for all that amount to the banality of inertia. "Doing nothing" simply marks the impossibility of reducing being to so-called *transitive* action, that which associates demiurgic ambition with agitation. This is why, in the architectural intention of our fathers, the deceased who carried out his task has a right to this rest that was at the beginning when the world, at the zero time of

its origin, was in God and was with God. And those who come after him in the sequence of becoming also have a right to this first idle "acting" that was the first moment of existence, as if before being and in order to be *oneself* it were in a sense necessary to pre-exist oneself in an original distance from oneself. The temple gathers all that is in the sublime imperfect of the verb *to be*—It was[9]—in this immobile movement, whose recollection the Christian Word reveals in the initial verse of Saint John's prologue. The foundations [*fondations*] unite in a "self-grounding" [*se fonder*] that is at once the depth of things and the ether in which they breathe their natal air. It therefore does not suffice, for *abiding*, to seat our contingency on a carpet of soil or to guarantee oneself an *at-home* [*chez soi*] that inscribes the will to be oneself [*soi*] in a conquering appropriation.

The heroic inscription that subsumes the defiance of a puny creature in the assumption of a human word is more and better than a delirium of imagination whose conceptual translation [*version*] as "*causa sui*" would join with the phantasm of a birth with no parental cause. But if this paradoxical causality has been too much maligned, it is not at all sure that its paroxystic willing is the alpha and the omega of human discourse and human being. The beauty of our temples, Christian and non-Christian, that join together in the ecumenism of their silence consists precisely in the indissoluble unity of an affirmation, creative of oneself and of one's *at-home*, and of a sovereign distance that measures their limits. If, as it has been said, every power must be vanquished, this victory is given a first testimony in the monuments to such a decisive pride that tell at the same time of the glory of power and of the impossibility of holding oneself there in order to rest there.

4. With the vegetative pole that roots the abode in the depths of the universe, I associate, in consequence, the vertical that, at the other extreme, translates, in an upward thrust of reason and faith, the wild joy of being more than oneself. Such would be the ultimate signification of the abode and of abiding. The styles, once again, are most diverse. They join together in the gaze they inspire, which traverses space to blossom in an aerial liberty that is dominant over its own conquests. In the reciprocity of the movement that descends and the movement that rises, the temple buries itself to support itself and rises to resurge. Immersion and emergence, baptism of the world that in a single complicity, and at the median point where their relations are calmed, crosses paths with the diversities that its wealth troubles. Just as mute nature speaks in the stone that represents it in order to offer it, so too does dispersed humanity draw closer in a "mystical body" that inspires matter with the anonymous breath of a universal prayer. It is there that our hearts abide.

8

Figure, Image, Icon

In this new stage that should suggest to us another power of abiding, we encounter, linked by a single semantic and stellar fraternity, the figure, the image, and the icon. The iconic has recently known, among a youth more or less enamored of the mysteries of the East, the honors of a renaissance. The enthusiasm is not necessarily feigned. It is explicable, up to a certain point, by a lassitude that does not result only from an incapacity to follow progress and to take up its conquests. It is part, so it seems to me, of a critical thought that questions the supposed apodicticity of a self-consciousness that would fulfill the contemplation of its power. The diversion to which it testifies does not respond to a need for entertainment. The leisure that is painfully won from the exhaustion of work grants a weekend of boredom or a period of idleness that actualizes, in the absence of quality, as an equivalent to the ancient Sabbath, the hard-won right to indispensable rest.

We would readily agree that this *ersatz* does not suffice. And what is proposed to us, in the name of doctrines of liberation, for elevating these moments of relaxation to human dignity is far too mediocre, in whatever sense one understands it, to call forth a consent that would not be a sigh of wretchedness. If the youths go away on the distant paths that disorient [*dépaysent*] them, it is precisely in order to find in an elsewhere that would be a true "region of unlikeness" that which they have sought in vain in the philosophical or religious ways of a West destined to the impossibility of finding one's bearings. Unlike their peers who benefit from the same age and the same intransigence, for them neither a contestation, enlarged by the body of evidence from which we have lived as from an organic substance, nor a fervor of devotion that, to remedy flagrant injustice, enlists in one or another party of the revolution suffices. What is necessary for them? Simply *to be*. But this intransitive verb is more an enigma than a solution. To wrest it from the more or less fastidious turns of phrase that have dissipated it into ontology, perhaps it would be necessary to add onto it a prepositional flexion. Which one? I have said that "being-toward" is declined according to the cases of a single *Meta* function.

It is not in this direction that a certain youth, dissenting from the other youths that I evoked, has oriented its choice. The other version that was commented on under the name of *being-in* would therefore be welcome. But is it not also captive to narrownesses that, however valuable they were, no longer satisfy a more demanding request? *Abiding* and *inhabiting* offer freedom a space that suits it. It remains to think this space. Tradition authorizes us to retain its two essential modalities: the *self* [*soi*] that the expression *in itself* [*en-soi*] secures, and the *at-home* [*chez soi*] that the abode in its major forms as temple and home [*maison*] schematizes. The "in-itself" has left bad memories. It seems to shrivel being into a slightly scrawny individuality for which the human *Ego* would be the model; and when it is enlarged in the infinity of infinite attributes, this is to absolutize, in an ocean of perfections, the hypertrophy of our preferred excellences. The *at-home* follows the same destiny. It hesitates between the patch of private land and the figure of the god in the majesty of the cathedral. In any case, the *self* and the *at-home* each fall outside the other. Yet what a certain youth pursues—if, without having the key to it, I have rightly understood the wanting-to-say of its dreams—is a beyond of these oppositions that are still too marked by the infirmity of our languages. The *in-itself* and the *at-home* verify the plenitude of *being-in* only if they perfectly overlay each other beneath, as it were, the specificities that divide them. The intrepidity of our dissidents finds the peace and joy of their abode only in an excess of transgression that defies any designation. When they take up the Buddhist word *Nothing*, it is without compromising with the analogous designations, of a Western stamp, that to them seem to mask I know not what residue of an equivocal and contested transcendence. Pure indeterminacy does not frighten them because it goes in the direction of a freedom or a *self* that adapts poorly to our distinctions and our traditional questions. But to find again this *self* that the agitation of our cares commands us to forget, they deem necessary the ascetism of a way or an itinerary. This way [*voie*] takes on the insinuating sonority of a *voice* [*voix*] and the pacifying serenity of a face that radiates, by a magisterium without mastery, that sovereign calm that the gods bestow. Could the face be this more divine abode of which the abodes of stone, of wood, or of canvas are but the distant proclamation? Perhaps it is worth it to ask ourselves this.

Figure

Concerning the face, the figure and the image fight for the right to interpret it. Rightly or wrongly, these two terms, especially the second, have aroused more than one reservation. The poetics of the sensible does not seem to express itself

Figure, Image, Icon

there in the manner most consonant with its freedom. What, exactly, is the situation?

1. When I speak of the figure, I am not aiming directly at the abstract definition that makes of it a finished grandeur, enclosed in its contours. I daydream, at the whim of my memories, of those so-diverse forms that nature lavishes on earth as in heaven. Labile forms of the clouds that pass; smoke, glowing red, from the near or far volcano; more durable forms that the regard that awaits constellations discerns; rays of honey whose hexagon the mathematician examines; nautilus shells; the magnificent remains of a life extinguished on the rock that delivers its will and testament; fruits and flowers, animal grace and force, pyramids of the Grand Canyon, or giant sequoias of Yosemite Park—such a profusion fulfills, dazzles, questions. Even before art revealed to us what we had not seen, the eye was intoxicated by a prodigality that enthralled it. Without this first complicity with the big or little games with which the wisdom of the world distracts itself, we would remain indifferent to the artist's creations that, without confining themselves to a reproduction, prolong the creating gesture of metamorphoses. A banal word, but one that it is necessary to pronounce, sums up an experience that is heavy with its globality and clumsy at furnishing its reasons. It is the word *admirable*, itself close to *miracle*. And yet the miracle, flower or fruit of the imagination, does not have good press in a context of knowledge where the miracles of science are but the worn-out formula of a surprise effect whose surprise is soon dissipated, for those who have the right to knowledge, by the clarity of explanations. The admirable supposedly coincides with ignorance of universal causality. The exception, or that which is believed to be one, is the lifeblood of superstition. Whereas the understanding seeks connections, fancy, essentially feminine, supposedly wishes for surprise or stupor, as if to be attentive to things it were necessary beforehand to exile them from the order that holds them. This reductive conception, which makes the imagination into a failed understanding, a virility mortified in the service of typically religious prejudices, has no doubt softened in these recent decades. It remains, in spite of everything, very widespread. To the degree that a poetics of the sensible could not, so it seems, economize on admiration, we cannot neglect the question that the language of the admirable poses to us regarding figures.

2. It would be easy, first of all, to oppose the artist and the scholar, intellect and fancy. We were cradled—I mean sent to sleep—by these obligatory dyads that are transmitted from generation to generation. Quality and quantity, order and inspiration, possible and impossible, even quality of life became as unendurable to us as the artificial flowers of a certain rhetoric. Unendurable precisely because

there is no longer, behind the words, that freshness of the admirable that would make them bloom anew in the morning of primroses.

Of the admirable I will maintain the connotation of the miraculous, for it is so precious. For one who knows how to look, by abiding there, at that which gives itself to be seen, each of these apparitions, which the walker tramples underfoot or which his distraction neglects, arises, like a precious pearl or a fallen star, in the exception's novelty. The identity of indiscernables, so badly named since it invites us to discernment, was the axiom of a poetics before being the statement of a logic of predicates and relations. Perception indeed blunts singularities, arranges them in a class, levels them according to a mode of use that drains away their significance. Against this flattening, justified by the everydayness of our practices, a sensibility protests that is attentive to that which will never be twice. The figure then arises in the advance of a lightning-flash that surprises us before we have domesticated it with our labels. Lightning-flash and East, the form of each being [*être*] is an island of Formosa, surrounded by water, by light, and by all that it does not say without having to keep it quiet. The Greek term *Hapax*, in the expression *Hapax legomenon*,[1] has no equivalent in French. For lack of a better one, we will leave it to its origin and its double sense, since it indicates simultaneously the originality of what is and the delicacy of a differential feeling.

3. The unicity of the unique does not, however, isolate it in the exclusivity of a private property that would render it strictly ineffable. It necessarily consists of one form, and this form, of whatever nature it may be—mineral or organic—*holds itself* within a more or less unstable border. The lightning-flash that crosses the cloud, imprecise though it be for the regard it blinds, marries the path of its blaze. One understands, consequently, that a poet's vision, by the piercing consciousness of these limits, is continually invited to transgress them. The Sainte-Victoire mountain could not be exhausted in the instant in which it is born to pictural light. It has never finished being born because the form that inhabits it endlessly overflows its individuality. All that is has a right to the infinite series of other singulars, to the unlimited series of its metamorphoses. We are here, in this sublime point where the finite and the infinite touch, at the crossing of multiple thoughts. The logician well knows that a predicate, because it is in another semantic category, always exceeds the individual variables that are liable to satisfy it. More generally, the man in the street who uses the resources of his language also practices that universality when he constructs, on the same model and with the same attribute, phrases whose similarity and diversity he recognizes. But it falls to the artist to make us feel, in all that he encounters, this mysterious contact between the closing of a form and the

permanent possibility of escaping from it. This is why, in a style which is not that of scientific objectivity, he can in total freedom believe that each thing is a home haunted or inhabited by an excess that bears it and in which it abides. That which we name *thing*, in a discredited language that only the order of poets and the order of philosophers could redeem, insofar as both are charged, by vocation, with the redemption of captives—that which we name thing, in its indeterminancy, goes farther than it seems. It signifies on the one hand that the forms, I mean the diversities that, rightly or wrongly, we connect with a certain individuality (the *this* of the ancients), are opened onto a larger front, or onto an undercurrent that bears them and in which they rest. It signifies on the other hand that this indeterminate that we no longer know how to name (thing, stuff, thingamajig) or that we name in any old way (while letting, sometimes, the god's shadow hover there) could well be the being of these beings. Being: in other words, that by which they hold together [*tiennent*] and by which they hold themselves [*se tiennent*] in the miracle of existing. If one prefers another mode of language, we could say that every figure is the point of emergence of an anonymous power of which it is the flower offered to our gazes. A mortal flower that testifies by its death to that which cannot die. Painters have so often painted "dead natures."[2] Indeed it is not difficult, in certain cases, to note, by the colors of the market stall or the kitchen, that it is indeed a matter of death, and of violent death. But in the most modern of these artists, we are no longer at the spectacle of hanged beasts and disemboweled poultry. Dead nature also means fruits, vegetables, and flowers. One sometimes adds in the dictionaries "inanimate objects," perhaps in memory of Lamartinian poetry. Have these "inanimate objects" therefore lost their souls; or is the artist there to give them their souls back, as to the dry bones in the prophet's vision? Cut off from their natal land, from their undercurrent (to do justice to the Greek term that people keep on bringing up), they need another breath in order to hold themselves. They still have great difficulty holding together. They hold together, under the spirit that vivifies them and that puts them back on the earth, that re-establishes the surreptitious umbilical cord that matter, matter and mother, ceaselessly holds out to them in the invisible part of the painting. Dead natures are not only *deceased*. In the abstraction that makes them "be for themselves," in their state of separation, they say the destiny of every being. This is why the death of dead natures is one of the strongest truths that the non-philosophy of the poets has been able to make us hear. *There is* an essential link between what is and what is mortal. It appears only in the promise of its disappearance. These cut flowers, which bleed in the water of the vase, are the force of a stronger one that they express in the immobility of their rest. I do say rest. Stretched out, rested in sleep, they signal in the distance to the unknown star that will come, to the point they have left forever in order to take their position and their face in this place that is their abode, the pre-supposition of their essence. While waiting in this void that they radiate, the pictural word resounds that echoes the Gospel imperative of the miracle of the resurrection: Little girl, get up![3] And these dead ones begin to walk once more; from dead natures they have become again natures moving toward their soil, toward that *there* of their natal home.

4. Moving. And yet they do not budge. Is not every figure necessarily at rest in order to be a figure? It must be at rest for my hand, passing over its lines, to go around it, to caress its caprices, as the animal needs to immobilize its prey before consuming it. But the artist has no need of this cruelty for the figure to be under the hand of the one who tells it what it is. He has never encountered the outdated opposition of being and movement, and with good reason. He invites us not so much to look as to sympathize, as the saying goes, with the invisible movement that animates the forms. Every form, I would say in the manner of an axiom, lets be heard under its contours the formative movement that is concluded in it. But the conclusion reverts at once into its premises. It is itself only by always exiting itself and by coming back to its departure, to its first departure into existence. This is why, and be it ever so humble, a *thing* (and how could we not find again this word with no power whose redemption is confided to us?) exists only in that dance of ladies-in-waiting that makes it turn, in a round of stars, around itself, around its pole and its axis of identity. It is then that it seems to say, I am who I am. And if we are generous enough to exit from ourselves, perhaps we in our turn will know how to dance, how to enter into that movement that cannot cease and where all things abide before they are. This is perhaps what a term of philosophers and theologians has meant, which doubtless for this very reason has lost nearly all its flavor: the word *procession*. The Parisian knows a street of the Procession, but the procession went by long ago. The procession was the Feast of Corpus Christi (since then, there has been the feast of humanity; there have been the protests [*manifestations*] that doubtless no longer say anything but the absence of manifestation [*manifestation*]). Let us risk, then, what would be, provisionally, the last word of this pale prose that tries its hand at the impossible: a figure is, at bottom, whether one knows it or not, the Feast of Corpus Christi of a real presence, where the poet abides and that remains [*demeure*], so long as he exists in poetry, the mystery of faith of which he lives and of which he dies.

Likeness

When I say *image* a swarm of pious mediocrities that in olden days awaited the devout at the Place Saint-Sulpice awakens at once. Popular piety, so it was claimed, had to nourish itself with these modest supports that did not disturb dogma and that satisfied demand. Thus a system was reproduced that required nothing of the intelligence but the aptitudes of the heart. The victim of a mediocrity without appeal, the image, in the singular this time, had to die of another death, this one more philosophical. Gravely, serious spirits hesitated, when they spoke of it, between the critique of a mimesis to which, according to them, the classical conception of art was being reduced and the vague recollection of the double that was generously being abandoned to the archaic forms of the explication.

If I come back to images, it is in the hope of getting out of cliches and out of those images of Saint-Sulpice, the most subtle of which perpetuate, by virtue of critical repetition, the sacred store. From the figure to the image, the distance can seem nonexistent. Every figure is an image; every image is a figure. If things were as simple as that, we would have only to take up, at an extra cost perhaps, what has been said. Things are not so simple.

1. The likeness is too close to the image for common language to not tend to conflate them. It was sometimes retained as the relation par excellence, identity itself being only the limit of a series of approximations. The imitation of nature, before the imitation of the ancients, was hailed as the essence of art. In the critique that was made of this theory, what determined it has perhaps been forgotten. The sought-for likeness was not the reduplication of a copy. When looked at closely, it responded to a sort of henological demand, but by a way that was not that of the mystics. It invited the artist to integrate himself in this movement or this thrust that bears nature and all things. Besides, it was not a matter of fusion, despite a terminology that speaks of "identification." Likeness is not identity. But in any case, it was indeed necessary to find, beneath the relation, the authority that grounds it. Two beings [*êtres*] are alike, but on the condition that there be an x in which they are alike. Without this additive, the relation remains indeterminate. One might as well say: the relation does not suffice. The justification of the statement of likeness risks, it is true, being enclosed in a vicious circle. Beings [*êtres*] are alike because they have the same nature; they have the same nature because they are alike.

Beneath the awkwardness of the formula, which justifies the relation by its repetition, it is easy to restore an authentic thought: that by which two beings are alike is obviously not a relation of likeness. The name of this ground matters little, provided that one recognizes it as indispensable. The beings that it joins together will, in consequence, be said to "abide in it." Be it a matter of things or of persons, the principle applies equally. Of Christians, for example, we will say, to express their fraternal bond, that they are *in christo*. This *being-in*, this "abiding in" anchors them in the soil of belief, in the midst of which they live and which bears them. And if one objects that the ground, in its turn, is thinkable only in terms of relation, we will take care to add that this relation is not a relation of likeness and that the grounding relation itself presupposes, in that which is called a ground, something other than the relation itself. I am willing for the real thing of which one speaks to be but a system of relations. The obsession with reference cannot eliminate the originality of its coordinates.

2. Likeness indeed implies a certain distance. The very fact of plurality would suffice to maintain this. If likes are several, that is because an inalienable difference makes them irreducible. Those who love measures can, in consequence, envision diverse cases in which likeness and unlikeness are by turns either prevailing or equal. The theological tradition has reserved for analogy "similarity in the greatest dissimilarity." We would therefore have two movements to clarify: the assimilation that at the limit becomes identity: $x = x$; the dis-similarity that at the limit excludes any possibility of *coming together*. Let us consider these two possibilities.

What indeed could a being be that would have nothing in common with anything at all? Strictly speaking, it would lose its validity as a being since if it kept it, it would maintain a link of similarity with the beings that it is not. It is therefore impossible to dissociate the two factors. Beings that differ do so only by an alterity that belongs to each one of them. But, inversely, what would a strict identity formula signify, since by its relational content it demands a certain diversity? Strictly, $x = x$ is unintelligible; one could even show that it is contradictory.

Consequently, and whatever the infirmities of our languages may be, we must indeed recognize the two vections that bear us, respectively, to the two extremes of Plato's *Parmenides*: the one-that-is-one on the one hand, the not-one that is not-one on the other. And we are forbidden from disregarding these two movements, which we cannot smooth into two perfectly stabilized limits that it would be lawful to posit as objects of knowledge. Even should one judge them to be contradictory, the limits toward which they push us are inherent to our thought. These are the poles of impossibility between which, as they did between the pillars of Hercules in days of old, poor humans force a passage. Yet though they are unnamable, people have tried to give a name to these two impossibles. At the limit of the henological movement, one glimpses the perfect unity that, precisely because it excludes every distinction and difference of an ontological type, will be deemed "beyond being and essence"; at the limit of the opposite movement, which I would not dare to call heterological, matter is situated in its most transcendental sense, which is "below being and essence." To tell the truth, as I was implying, these are not so much names as impossibilities of naming. When one seeks to draw them closer to our indigent mortality, we assign to them, by a logical transposition, the wretched figure of pure identity or of pure diversity. These expedients are valid only as temporary props that we will have to expel. For a proof of this I want only the strange Plotinian expression *to alla* for designating matter. Pure plurality can be said only by sticking onto it a singular that unifies it and that, in a badly formed but highly eloquent expression, sustains the necessity of thinking the impossible. Furthermore, to the first solecism *le autres*,[4] the no less strange *to hen*, which would recall the inverse necessity of thinking the one in a minimal diversity, would respond in perfect symmetry. Which signifies: we can speak of that which escapes unity by its maximal diversion only by projecting onto it the shadow of the one; reciprocally, we can speak of that which escapes diversity by its maximal unity only by pouring into it the trouble of the diverse. Could these two impossibles that the meditation on likeness suggests to us, in its two potential versions, be in the end the very image of our despair? Or else are they only the more or less rhetorical torments of aimless people devoted to the delights of the boudoir? I for my part grant them a decisive importance, and I am not sure that our time is not torn apart by these impossibles that overlay, in a perfect antithesis, the obsession with the purely diverse in the *diaspora* without a corrective and the more traditional obsession with the unitary, be it a matter of a "unified science," a unified theory, or monotheism.

From these poor reflections on likeness, I will retain a few conclusions:

— the image is not a likeness but must pass via likeness;
— the image marries the tearing apart of likeness in its double vection of assimilation and dis-similation;
— it can, consequently, either veer to the mere reproduction of a conformed copy and be abolished in the identity to which it aspires without reaching it or turn to the pure dispersal of difference, indefinitely projected and never attained;
— unlikeness and likeness, by the play of similarity, invite us to think a something, let us say x, that is neither the one nor the other but that makes use of these supports to secure, beyond our modes of normality, an unreal that is the best of our imaginary and the dream of our folly.

Along the lines that indicate these two extremes, it is possible for us to think on the one hand the image properly so called, in the most quotidian sense of our practice of images, which emphasizes likeness, and on the other hand, in the opposite sense, by an insistence on the dissimilarity that it awakens, that which we will call the *icon*, which no longer has any mission of reproduction. To tell the truth, we should say of the icon, on which we will have to comment, that, exceeding the image in a certain line of the image, it tends to abolish the dialectic that places the polemic duality of its essence in conflict.

Image

I have perhaps too much maligned the image by speculatively modeling it along the lines of likeness. It is only just to not be a victim of its speculative sectarianisms.

1. Of a child who is hardly like the idea one forms of children—"a little animal never at rest"—a mama will readily say that he is as good [*sage*] as an image.[5] These words of the common people have a profundity that we would be wrong to neglect. How would the child who supposedly has this wisdom [*sagesse*] of the image be an image? One remembers, perhaps, the little Samuel that an English painting, formerly widely circulated, offered as a model to young clerks. Hearkening to the voice that calls him thrice, Samuel with his hands clasped is the perfect image of the image. Like him, the image holds itself before that of which it is the image, a bird fascinated by the serpent in the fixity of military attention that forbids all movement. This is the immobility of an eye that can no longer close, absorbed by the openness that it inhabits. It is an obstinate vigil that defines the Absolute, from which it can no longer detach itself, like *Energy* in the ancient sense, that is, like Waking, thus refuting a god who would no longer be anything but the spirit's dormitive principle. The image, in the tension that afflicts and beatifies it, holds itself in the place that belongs to it as an original foundation. It is there that it rests. Any veritable image, when it is not, in the order of the sacred, this mediocrity that saddens us, would be like a transit [*transit*], transfixed [*transi*] by the attraction that wounds it by making it what it is. But that, I acknowledge, is a conception that feels the effects of theological presuppositions. It is not sure that the history of art can ratify them. I prefer, in consequence, when I speak of images in a poetics of the sensible, to leave to the artist the path of figuration and to deliver him of the image in its most pregnant religious meaning.

In its religious use, I would define the image, in what poetic content it has, as a similitude that senses its difference too much to be conflated with its original but that knows what it is in its *being-toward* too much to not sink into precisely that which breathes it in. It is this ambiguity that always caused the difficulty in iconoclastic controversies. What worship should be vowed to it? If one valorizes the distance, it is no longer anything but a bit of wood or canvas: it in-itself collapses it into insignificance. If, inversely, it is the movement that holds our attention, it is identified with the model and calls for the same veneration, at the risk of a more or less camouflaged idolatry. And what is said of the sacred image applies more generally to our manner of inhabiting the sensible: either we linger in its carnal immediacy at the risk of sinking into it, or else we refer it to its indefinite other at the risk of dissipating it in the system of its relations. These are old questions that have never been well resolved or that irritation dissolves into pseudo-problems. For some, it is reference that is essential; for others, suspected of substantialism, it is the coordinates of the relation that matter most. No dialectic succeeds at masking the reality of a difference of opinion. The poet, with reason, disregards these obstacles. "But passing through their midst, he went away."[6] To the degree that his sensibility lightens things to give them wings, in a certain manner he fulfills in the unity of the image what our dichotomy divides. Without being an image-maker, and wholly unaware of our disputes, he projects on the world an *a priori* of respect and love that makes it the Ark [*Arche*] of the Covenant or the rainbow [*arc-en-ciel*] of our joy.

2. Nevertheless, when the terminology of the image appears in discourse, one most often thinks of something else. The myth of Narcissus has forever fixed this discourse within the mirror's illusions. Narcissus' error, mirror stage. Let us leave aside the problems of self-recognition in the ego's genesis. What poetic genius could it be that fascinates us in this double that floats on the waters or that the mirror sends back to us? Philosophers have discoursed much on this in their theories of knowledge, and one could refine them unto infinity. We are told that "images are naturally delightful to us." How do the old adults that we are experience in them a child's happiness? What pleasure is there in seeing oneself in a mirror, immobile or fluid, balanced on the waters or fixed in the glass? For these two modalities must be distinguished. The waves, barely troubled, that double me in their movement rock a childhood that is more or less suppressed but that at bottom never disappeared and that is perhaps that freshness of soul by which we recognize in each thing, when we name it or truly encounter it in its existing, the gift and the unforeseenness of a birth. But seeing oneself in a glass comes from a wholly other manner of being and acting. The fixed mirror puts us

on the path of the object and of reflection. And yet, to not malign it too much, as if it were a matter of a too-quotidian prose, it would be useful to look at it well. I will pass over what is best known: seeing oneself in order to arrange appearances according to the necessities or the proprieties of the moment. I will neglect the more or less feminine hour of seduction. There still remains the objectivity of a rudimentary knowing that attempts to detect the illusion by comparing what I believe to what is said on that cold surface.

But all this, however obvious it may be, is perhaps not what makes the mirror and the double the surprising thing that captivates in us the gaze of a certain childhood. In our archaic memory, which has doubtless forgotten it, the double throws as a lightning-flash the happiness of over-existing. By doubling us, it does not perpetuate the Biblical "go forth and multiply." It is not a question of propagating the species, which indeed does quite well without any mirror. It is a mode of being that is without equal in what is called the domain of the real; it is an unreal that is already, on the fluidity of the waters, a beyond need and beyond necessity, something that nothing awaited and that is come. It is a sort of surplus or excess that enlarges but without adding, properly speaking, a determination of the same order. The image and the mirror are already, toward the imaginary, the announcement of the other kingdom. The world of images and of representation has been somewhat mistreated because one saw in it either the facile spectacle of the repetitive understudy [*doublure*] or, finally, the idea-portrait and impure reflection. What more? In short, all of Western metaphysics with its afterworlds, its specters, and its illusions. We have not seen what is essential, which the painter, for his part, has some reason to not neglect. Like language, of which it is the complement, the double in the mirror is not a simple repetition. Let us say this once more in terms that I like to borrow from an old friend: it is "the void of a distance taken."[7] Instead of being what one is by persevering in it, the image is the ruse that makes one escape what one is, a freedom with regard to being, and that is why philosophers have been so embarrassed by this quasi-nothing, which they knew not where to classify in their nomenclature. If it were a question only of fecundity, then yes, one could be grieved by this ridiculous surplus that offers us only its evanescence and that reminds lovers of the bonds of love and of death. But the poet watches over this nothing, over this "utopia" and this "uchronia" that delivers us. A moth that the Greek *psyché* remembers, it frees us without exiling us. It intimates that the world did not begin with gravity. That the weight of things is perhaps a fall. That it was better when there was nothing. Everything supposedly began in this *ex nihilo*. And this is perhaps the secret reason that pushes the artist toward those poor elements that do not exist according to the world and that characterize, for common sense, what are called madmen, who, as is known, live only on their images and are victims of their dreams, by a "perturbation of the function of the real." Explaining the unreal by the real then becomes a foregone conclusion that imposes itself and that each discipline adopts as an indispensable task. For religions and all that follows therefrom are, at bottom, qua image-reflections, only a reversal of the real. The scholar and the man of good sense put things right side out. But when they have supposedly done all that, they will have worked in vain. The image, the reflection, the mirror, the still waters that reflect, in the gardens of Kyoto, the temple sleeping in a dream from which the world was supposedly born will continue to speak and to be loved because they are absurd. The other part, which will not be taken from us, of a soul leaning on both its banks, perhaps poses the question: "Why is there something rather than nothing?" But all this is already too scholarly. The image, which the emotion of the nearby fountain agitates, is more and better than this classical question. More tenuous, as slight a thing as the shadow of the Cross in another place, the image-mirror is, over the world, the upsurging in the East of the question mark itself that was said, in a Hindu legend, to be Nature's firstborn.

Icon

From the image to the icon the passage and its reversibility seem assured by the simple Latin translation of the Greek term. The semantic equivalence would supposedly be only the transport to another place of a single intelligible quantity. One would have to be naïve to believe this. For it is a matter less of the relation of one word to another word than of one world to another world. The word then takes on its full sense only by the set of its relations to the universe. Let us suppose, however, that the presumed synonymy is granted. Let us suppose further that the image, in both cases, refers, beyond my preceding explanations, to a line-for-line reproduction of the original in the image or to a bijective application of a set of points onto the corresponding set-image. Even with this extreme hypothesis, we would not suspect the historical destiny of the icon. Should the icon be cloaked, moreover, with the theological context that remains inseparable from it, we would still have but a crude approach to what, in it, happens and is said. The icon was the "Pontus Euxinus" that, at a certain moment of religious poetics, connected the rising sun to the sun that sets, that happy interference where two universes sensed, on both sides, the possibility of an actual contact.

1. The Eastern icon and its Mediterranean sister have a number of common traits. Whether one contemplates, unable to weary of them, certain marvels of Buddhist art, at Kyoto or elsewhere, or whether one lingers over the works of a certain Christian east, circulated among us by more or less expert artisans and by their sometimes prestigious reproductions in our books of art, one is enveloped each time by a family atmosphere that inspires, for brothers separated by time, space, and culture, the recollection of a lost paradise. Community here becomes communion. It is based less on the repetition of a technique than on an impalpable ether that brings us together. The question of influences, without being secondary, here remains second. In the figures that very diverse traditions have modeled, where the Scriptures have played an essential role on both sides, what is striking first of all is the manner in which, here and there, humans carry out certain gestures. But beyond the gesture, or more exactly in it, what is essential is how the body is doing [*se porte*] and how one wears [*porte*] one's body. Our abstract *behavior* [*comportement*] of which psychology books speak would be but a distant approximation. Yet wearing [*porter*] is indeed bearing [*porter*] a certain heavy mass. What is important is the mode according to which one makes this mass or this weight exist. Among our contemporaries, when we encounter them either returning from work or in the banality of "public transport," the painful sensation of a yoke that overwhelms is imposed, as if the *load-bearing being* [*être porteur*] were identified with a law of gravity that it cannot master and that drags it where it does not want to go. The body thus becomes a blind necessity where the forces of the world pass, without any light settling on it, as in days of old the lightning-flash of a transfiguration settled on the falls of the Lord on his *via crucis*. The other example, more quotidian still, is that of a walk and gait [*marche et démarche*] of which one could say that it amounts to anything whatsoever. The interested one, girl or boy, sacrifices to a generalized negligence where the obvious heaviness is no longer a problem because it has become that general indifference, elevated to the normative dignity of an axiom of mediocrity.

2. The iconic body, in contrast, seems to me to be in a permanent act of invisible levitation. Everything is centered on the co-reference of the hand and the face. The elegance of the raising of fingers (as one speaks of the rising sun) lets a veritable East show through. The ring finger does not *take* the thumb. It does not flatten, it does not squeeze; it touches down, as though to land, on a bird's wing. On the discreet straight line it outlines a friendship that from all time has oriented the different one toward its cordial difference. Digital heterogeneity is significant in this regard. The different ones, in their lightness,

Figure, Image, Icon 121

and by it, can truly be united and make but one hand. This difference, as we see, is in no way static. One has, rather, the impression that movement here precedes alterity. But there is more. In a harmony that is in no way a dialectic, the fingers that are raised call to those that are lowered: *arsis* and *thesis*, East and West are tied together in a single "manual" footrace. If it were necessary at all costs to oppose "grace and gravity," we should add that the great art is to make this opposition be forgotten. One does not sense here, as in our cathedrals, whose analogies with the summa theologicas have been evoked, a learned organization of forces that balance their thrusts. Sometimes, I acknowledge, the artist, in certain icons, seeks harmonization too visibly: two fingers raised, two fingers lowered. The open and the half-closed fingers offset each other, but one would have wished, so that time would truly flow, for a less emphatic Ark of the Covenant. The author has not gazed long enough upon the rainbow. In another image, I observe another gesture, another way of holding the hand. It is a Virgin whose fingers taper inordinately and whose thumb moves aside as if to better see and imitate their upward thrust. The hand rests on a chest that seems to say to it: do not touch me. The crossing of the cloths confirms the modesty of a sensitive one who is averse to the slightest gentle touch. The theoretical possibilities for the arrangement are indefinite besides. The artists surely considered them. But that is not what directly matters to me. It is more instructive to envision the two extremes between which this art passes: the closed fist where the fingers fold under the watch of the thumb that grips them or that bends under their convergent pressure; inversely, the extension of all the fingers together that one moment outlines a rigid straight line and the next moment does not disdain a curve. The painter of these icons succeeded in avoiding both of these radicalisms that testify, each in their degree, to a stiffness foreign to the spirit. The speculative background is not, however, the same in East and West. Closure evokes, from a Christian point of view, the curved-back love (*amor curvus*)[8] that the spiritual rebuke and, by contrast, the ecstatic love that enchants them. Total openness would mimic the elevation of the praying woman if the rigidity of the movement were softened in the prayer of joined hands. The East, apparently more abstract, and without being ignorant of *Agapé*, accentuates in the lines' flexibility the ease of a freedom that is not caught up in anything, not even in its own independence. The two worlds unite in the refusal of a closed fist and of the grasp that seizes, in order to grip it, a totality that at last is supposedly at hand. Still it is necessary to hear well what is said in these gestures that are so stripped of themselves. They do not forbid alluding to all the world since, whoever we are, we cannot avoid glimpsing it at the horizon of every perception. But, and this is what is essential, if indeed it is necessary to rely on it in order that we exist, it is still more important to highlight, by this soaring of raised hands, that it is offered to us, in the form of power, only by a sovereign distance that renders it both possible and impotent. Never, doubtless, has the immortal word "You are in the world; you are not of it"[9] taken on a body so much as it has in these icons.

3. Certainly there are, in the history of men and of their innumerable writing systems, other portrayals of the human hand. There is that of the Egyptian scribe, so careful and fine, which holds the anonymity of a scriptural space under the attraction of a political power and a social position, confirmed by that bird's feather whose lightness inspires an aerial and spiritual aristocracy. I should mention also, because they are absent from our images, the knotty and lined hands that bear on their palms and backs the multiple proofs of a laboring experience whose harshness they exhibit like so many geological layers where the generous and aching earth establishes the memory of its past. Since I must be brief, in a nomenclature that imposes on me the partiality of choice, I would also like to point out the hand contracted into a raised fist that threatens in order to claim, against injustice, the proud affirmation of a wounded stature, where the right hand [*droite*] of an erect body proclaims the ought-to-be of rights [*droit*]. To this imperious figure I will append the complement that is those shaking hands that wave, like the palm branches on Palm Sunday, to acclaim the humble or imperial triumphant victor in whom, for his fortune or misfortune, a people seem to recognize themselves, as if they found in him the depth of their abode or the thinking clarity of a life that has so much difficulty thinking itself.

4. I evoke these figures only to better situate, in the field of possibles, the virtualities that have arranged a rendezvous in our icons. And without again coming back to it, but while always assuming it, I will meditate one last time on the illustrious Thinker that Rodin's chisel celebrates. The hand, in this play of power, concludes the quivering of a musculature that is there gloriously completed, like the sea's flow on the promontory where it expires without breaking. Few monuments of sculpture manifest such an impressive unity. The lines that, at each point of the body, crisscross its mass form a network, a well-ordered totality from which all dissonance appears absent. It is a totality that rests on itself, in itself, and by itself. The waves that swell the veins conspire in a single fundamental certainty: "I am what I can do"; "I can do what I am." This *acquiescence in oneself* exudes a happiness of being that before the mastery of the world consists in the mastery of oneself, in the tranquil possession and the tenacious vigor of a *virtù* that conjugates the world's ebbing back to its center and the total reflection in oneself of a being [*être*] finally returned to its essence.

Ebb and flow are composed in an organic silence, in a clear equilibrium where the thinking head settles on the upward-turned hand that bears, under the chin's thrust, the hegemonic imperative of a capital authority. For this body manifestly has a thinking capital, an idea that traverses all its limbs in the round trip of an Odysseus, forgetful of its storms and calm like a tempest that has subsided. The *Fiat* of the origin is there pronounced without words, sure of its truth in its first and efficacious totality. Being is indeed here the trace of an efficient unity and of a hidden light that illuminates, without residue, its illusory depth. Matter is not transfigured into light. It illuminates itself in its dominated heaviness. The idea is not dissociated from the will, any more than movement is from its sense. In the extreme point of its existence, the statue of essence says the victorious fusion of being, acting, the idea, form, and the will in the resting autarchy of a figure that is joined together from all sides because a single center animates, extends, and retains its rays around itself, as if the density of this idea-will imposed on all its straight lines the curve that fastens them to themselves. Such an eloquent sculpture is the best commentary on the philosophies that have played out, in its most varied modulations, the "causality of self by self" that posits itself, determines itself, realizes itself, justifies itself. In this Word that links man and the world, the thought that thinks itself and the thought that does not think itself, a magnificent universe has said its last word, the joy of resting in itself. And it is there that, even today, our Western and fragile liberty abides.

5. We must perhaps depart from this thought that is so strongly embodied in order to understand what is said elsewhere, in no less decisive a manner. We must depart from it in order to allow ourselves to be surprised by the other of this thought, its other qua other, this wholly other that comes to us from the East, from the Far or Near East, the cradle of religions, that teaches us another abode, the burning flower of its soul, that so-rare flower that the Greek *Ave, Xairé*, greets to say *Xaris*, grace. What does this old East, taken up and transformed by the Christian Near East, say to us?

I will meditate anew on this *Eastern* marvel that, for lack of anything better, I have baptized the *thinking Buddha*. Of all icons, it is perhaps the one that says the most with the greatest economy of means. Here again the hand and the face form an indissoluble couple. Whatever the order of the factors may be, the round-trip movement establishes no hierarchy. The hand inhabits the face and the face abides in the hand. Whether the hand is raised toward the face that bends down or whether the gaze inverts the route, a single arc, in the virtual straight line that traverses them while dying there, prolongs the immemorial feast of silence. And it is the same word that comes to our lips: *contemplation* [*recueillement*], an infirm term because of the repetitive suffix that, for us, is at once translated into reflection. Here everything conspires in the apparent void of an absent spiration, in a reciprocal opening inhaled by a superhuman Nothing. As in the sculpture of the essence, the thought is made body and the body thought. But it is no longer the thinking thought that is posited [*se pose*], is opposed [*s'oppose*], and is composed [*se compose*] through the resistances it gives itself and on which, victorious, its empire is affirmed. Below or beyond the world, a sublime imperfect[10] comes forth that spreads out over things before things are. Serenity, more than silence or night, precedes the landscape that it anticipates without inviting to it. If I had to risk, at the whim of my recollections, one or another of our paradigms, I would evoke the Gospel verse, "Passing through their midst, he *was going away*," or Goethe's well-known line, "Over all summits is rest."[11] At this height, on this summit, the understanding is not yet attentive to the murmur where things are troubled. "He was being," "He was going": in the play of assonant imperfects, the "immobile movement" of the ancients finds, without having sought it, the plastic miracle of its advent. I do not know how to translate Meister Eckhart's *Gelassenheit*. But *there*, perhaps, by virtue of the subterranean current that binds it to its older East, is the magic star that signals to us. From all time, it is in that Nothing that being rests.

6. The commentary that one could give on this risks making us fall into the vicissitudes of dialogue. If I venture into it, it would be to render homage to those who, in the temples of Kyoto, in times past invited me to discover the novelty of the most ancient world. To tell the truth, in this colloquium in which I was involved, on the poetics of the sensible, I would have lacked probity had I not, by the limits of my difference, notified those who heard me of the vanity of all apologetics. For there is a more or less subtle Eastern art of making one sense, by an effect of contrast, the glorious superiority of a simple alterity. I have never believed that the West would be healed in the waters of the Ganges or that Westernized Yoga would suffice to save us. Zen Buddhism is also legion. And it would be an error to think it supreme. Irremediably "legion," its essence, even supposing it has one, is no more sheltered than our own from existence and its vicissitudes. It is only in its perpetual reinvention. Any comparison is therefore disobliging when it has goals other than seeking together that in which we are one and of which we are not worthy. Initially, nevertheless, it was difficult for our respective diversities to not clash. Inevitably the garden of Versailles, with its well-domesticated nature, trimmed according to the straight reason that puts order into its frolics, had to introduce our debates. The Japanese garden, so consonant with the temple that it surrounds, that it borders with its moss,

its foliage, and its fountains (which do not sing so much as murmur), unfolded another world. What did we have to learn from this first contact? The West seemed to be summed up in two texts that figure at the beginning and almost at the end of our Judeo-Christian Scriptures. To the Genesis imperative, "Fill the earth and subdue it, and have dominion over the fish of the sea and over the birds of the heavens and over every living thing that moves on the earth" (Gen. 1:28) replies, in an equally sonorous echo, the imperative of Matthew's Gospel, "All authority [*puissance*] in heaven and on earth has been given to me. Go therefore and make disciples of all nations" (Matt. 28:18-19).[12] The complementarity of these two verses pointed to a single dominant chord. Throughout was the exaltation of power [*puissance*]. Could the Judeo-Christian world be summed up in the will to power, in a world as will and as representation of the will? At this level, which I find quite generic, the supposed antagonism between reason and faith disappeared. Politics and philosophy, technique and religion are intoxicated with the same impulsion of conquest. Prolonging the destructive drives of life in the refinements of an innumerable ruse, Western intelligence supposedly gives itself as a mission an ideal that makes nature into a battlefield and the prey of a paroxystic desire. Certainly, and our friends admitted it, it was possible to oppose another refrain and the glimpse of another way to this average image that they rapidly drew. Francis of Assisi, a poet of the sensible, spoke of my sister water, "chaste and pure," and of my brother sun. He preached to fish but did not eat them. In the same Gospel of Matthew, "the lilies of the field [that] neither toil nor spin" cause to fade, in a floral without care, the splendor of Solomon in all his glory, who was "never arrayed like one of these."[13] Could these be simple accidents, enclaves that deny the context, or indicators that quietly revive an immemorial heritage that is buried in an immemorial forgetting?

7. One could discuss this all day long. I will not lengthen a noble dispute in which metaphysics and spirituality clashed. The shortcuts that are the rule in these encounters sometimes exasperate, by their simplification, the sensibilities that they risk wounding. It is impossible to avoid them. Only a reciprocal generosity limits their pretentions by granting them the unconditional givenness of forgiveness. But the shock that they provoke, if it is not aggravated into an offense, remains to everyone's advantage. The very nearby icon signals to us. It does not resolve the question. But it invites another look. Whether it be from over there or from *here in our home* [*chez nous*], it reiterates, below any imperative, the lesson that the lilies of the field implied. Perhaps there is something other than power. In this beyond that unites us, will we find the place where our joy abides?

Face

From the icon, why come back to the face? Would this not be to fall anew, by this insistence, into anthropocentrism? Retracing my steps and binding the sheaf, I will observe anew, to conclude, that the classical image and the icon obey two divergent movements. The first emphasizes likeness, the second dissimilarity. The one reassures us, the other disorients us in an elsewhere that no longer has words to say itself. Should we, by too conspicuous an artifice, tune their dissonances in the formula of an analogy?

1. It would be ridiculous to want to reconcile East and West in a beyond of the image and the icon. We would gain nothing by those eclectic diplomacies. But it is permissible to go into more depth, in the very interest of a poetics, concerning the status of the Western icon. The little iconoclastic war could be, in this last stage, the occasion of a later reflection. By maximally simplifying a story with multiple twists, sometimes dramatic unto the shedding of blood, one could sum up the controversy in two antithetical propositions:

— thou shalt not make thyself any graven images. For the invisible that inhabits man's heart and the depth of things cannot, without sacrilege and blasphemy, lend itself to the play of representation;
— thou shalt make thyself an image of the invisible itself because if it did not appear, in one way or another, on our earth, where the God-Man set his tent, we would refuse him this terrestrial abode that he did not scorn. The invisible must make itself seen, as the ineffable must make itself spoken.

These two contrary positions assert, each in its order, an equal necessity. The icon, in its difficult existence, is a manner of satisfying this double postulate. It fulfills the very human need to "make oneself images." The idol that is denounced has always thwarted the rigor of the prohibitions. For all one drives it off, it is reborn in another form. One effectively denies it only by sublimating it by a detour. Philosophies and theologies, as well as art, however purified they may be, have made a place for it in their theories and their productions. If we cannot do without it, that is, as I attempted to explain, because the human is condemned to producing himself by producing. He realizes himself only by projecting into the world, upon contact with things and with their resistances, a work in which he recognizes himself and which, in this sense, is in his image and likeness. The very intensity of acting requires, to verify itself, this *formative movement* that was spoken of long ago and that outlines, by the figuration of an expanse, the body's dancing mobility or the will's energy.

With this first movement of man's inscription in his environment a second movement that I will call one of emergence is affirmed, in symmetry and contrast. However necessary it may be, every image is indeed partial, in both senses of the word. And, what is more, deceptive. For the danger of an immersion in the sensible is not chimerical. And it is to thwart this temptation that a critical jolt, identifiable over the course of the centuries in the most heterogeneous disciplines, periodically opposes to it a corrective that is sometimes inflamed to the point of pure and simple suppression.

2. This critical reduction has left its trace in diverse sectors of culture by the play of certain oppositions, the most obvious of which is that between myth, or the image-making tradition, and methodical reflection. I will readily add other dualities, which it is easy to harden: law of the mother and law of the father; figurative art, abstract art; descriptive music, music with a mathematical dominant chord; science and ideology; formal or floral imagination, imagination of matter. It is not a matter of indifference to point out, in passing, that contemporary physics has increasingly mortified our representative notion of the *object*, situatable and determinable by the customary coordinates of place, time, movement, figure. But it is in theology that iconoclastic rigor has at times been imposed with the least restraint in the conflict between the dogmatic tendency, supported by an ontology, and the reminder of the ineffable, based on and inspired by the more or less speculative mystics of Eastern origin. Yet for several decades, we have witnessed an inversion of the movement that is translated by the rehabilitation of the imaginary and the mythic, by a more solicitous attention to natural languages against the imperialism of technical languages, and most especially by a claiming of the positive values of the feminine against the simplifications that most often associate it with wandering or with the impurity of matter and with a sort of fundamental pathology that was invoked to justify the oppressive practices of which we know. Moreover, and above all, we note a calling into question of the massive dichotomy sensible-intelligible, sense and understanding. We even suspect at times that sense and understanding are rooted, as certain philosophies have boldly maintained, in a creative imagination of which the world itself is the product. I will leave this hypothesis to the side in order to confine myself to what can be read on the face as image-icon. Yet in this regard a reflection on the signification of Biblical iconoclasm could permit, so it seems, a rather novel approach to the subject.

3. The ban on graven images is indeed more complex than it appears. It first separates a people from the other peoples who are declared to be idolators. By mortifying a natural predilection, it awakens a sharper consciousness of difference, of the other qua other. Monotheism, instead of being stiffened in a unicity of excellence, is thus oriented no longer toward the exception (reinforced by the terminology of election) but toward an exceeding of the very condition of the object and of representation, in the most common sense of a "reproduction" of an original. The originary, on the basis of which we speak, could not be an original of which one could expect a copy. Such would be the signification of the great commandment that constitutes, at the dawn of its history, Israel's specificity.

It could be that pagan infiltrations softened the rigor of the initial prohibition. But that is not the most remarkable characteristic of the ban's evolution. On the contrary, Israel accomplishes its most improbable truth by the continual deepening of the ban that, by making it hold together in its vocation, grounds its history. We could formulate it in these terms: an ever-more faithful conformity to the categorical imperative that mortifies him reveals man (or the human) in his least questionable authenticity: that which, in his face, makes him "in the image and likeness of God." The paradox here borders on contradiction. How can one be like precisely that which defies all likeness? By changing graven images, would we not be subjugated anew to the same regime of idolatry? For at first sight, the relation of likeness can appear reversible. If x is like unto y, it is difficult to not add: y is like unto x. It matters little that the coordinates of the relation are not on the same level. The priority of the archetype indicates the distance but does not erase the qualitative unity of the things that differ. Consequently it would suffice to clarify, each time, the ground of the similarity to obtain the series of correlative images. Man will be an image by the knowledge, by the power, etc., of a knowledgeable, powerful, etc., god. The incommensurable vanishes in a mere difference that separates more and less from an ideal maximum.

4. And yet—and this is the sensitive point and the key moment of the reversal—it is not said that man is an "image" but that he is *in [à]*[14] *the image and likeness*. The preposition here marks not a state, which would be a precondition, but a movement that integrates us, that makes us walk toward the God who is beyond our most common ways of rendering him present to us. This is to say that the human does not copy, does not have to copy, but must tend toward that supreme freedom of a God who is beyond our determinations. By training in the practice of the first commandment that determined its existence, Israel is raised above the all-too-humanness of our anthropomorphisms. It is freed from

Figure, Image, Icon

the fallacious similarities that are ready to hand in order that it be fulfilled in a *None [Rien] of all that* that carries it, in the image of its God, tending toward sovereign independence. In the ban-indicator that shows it the other country, it finds again, in another form, that Exodus that made it leave the "region of likeness." It is true that it is a promised land, never conquered, that is seen from afar and toward which one goes, straight ahead before one. The halts or the stops, far from submerging it in the finitude of the elements or in their universal concatenation, invite the gaze to rest on the heights, in the nameless place where one "sees [*voit*] only the voice [*voix*]" of a constant call to abide *over there*.

5. Iconoclasm consequently has a double signification: on the one hand, it removes from the divine the reproductions that weigh it down and compromise it; on the other hand, it arouses in man a power of distance that, without making him the *image of* his God, perpetually creates him *in his image*. Negative theologies, from which we would gladly solicit analogies, constitute in this regard neither a precedent nor a model. Their discursive subtleties are entirely foreign to this desert people. In fact, it is less a question of discoursing than of doing. Doing [*Faire*] what? Making [*Faire*] the kingdom of God come [*advenir*] onto a man's face. But this human face of God on a man's face is never a given that it would suffice to read in its descriptive traits in order to observe its reality. It must become. In this becoming consists the advent [*advenir*] of a god who is foreign to our categories of essence and existence, of a god who is absent from nature's marvels in order to come toward us from the depths of an always-future future, even and especially when he would seem to be *already there*. The initial commandment that forbids graven images is thus inflected in the active service of an uncertain fulfillment. Everything happens as if God's descent coincided with man's ascent. What we will later name the Incarnation designates, in the abstraction of conciliar formulas about the two natures, the efficacy of a theandric process. History is this immense movement that unfailingly binds, in a "reciprocal genesis," the human and the divine. And what is most surprising is, if I may say so, its apparently prosaic character. Against a ritualism that renders homage to the Absolute by an overabundance of sacrifices or by the liturgical magnificence of the temple, the prophets recall, with an ever-more emphatic insistence, the unrefusable commandment that, faced with every form of exploitation, raises as an absolute the necessity of giving the poor, the widows, the orphans their due. Israel's faith truly serves the god that one cannot see without dying only by attaching itself to the quasi-nothing of what does not exist to make it accede to the dignity of an existence. Israel's faith turns us away from an ideal of contemplation to give us over, unconditionally, to the practice

of the everyday. Love of the neighbor and the love of God that is affirmed in it are what they are only in the accomplishing of a justice—a justice without pity for the tergiversations that tend to evade it by one or another of the good reasons that sometimes justify themselves by the holiest references. But the scandal that culminates in the last judgment of Matthew's Gospel remains no less earthshattering: "I was naked and you clothed me, I was hungry and you gave me food, I was a prisoner and you visited me" (Matt 25:35-36). It is not a question, in this last judgment of the world and of men, of what their religion or their belief was; it is not even, so it seems, a question of their immediate relation to the Most High. Could the enigmatic "I" that slips its mystery into the hearts of those who have nothing and who are nothing signify only that the most divine operations are also the most banal—eating, drinking, clothing, inhabiting—and that making God come to the earth of men is, at bottom, giving him a body in which and by which he can stand [*se tenir*] and gather on his face the light of heaven? The incarnation would no longer be a dogma but the audacity of an act that, in the same movement, makes an existence arise that takes form from all the forces of the universe assembled in a microcosm but that also lets us hear, beyond form, something, the name of which escapes us because the luminous cloud where the image shows through inserts in this image the dimension of an elsewhere. The strange power of this "I" that is more than the ego without being exterior to it is that which, in the image, transfigures it into an icon of the face. And if it remains to think, when we speak of a poetics of the sensible, something novel of which the history of art has nothing to tell us, it is precisely this other sort of poem and this other sort of poetry. This is the final point about which, to complete this sketch, I will formulate a few propositions.

6. First of all, and at the risk of breaking down an open door, I will state a few preliminaries about the poem and poetry:

— poetry and the poem are in relation to each other as is the operation [*opération*] to what it brings about [*opère*];
— the operated and the operating are not, however, exterior to each other like the sum in relation to addition or like the effect in relation to the cause;
— the operation is realized in its apparent result, such that both are the two movements of a single becoming-advent;
— writing, in the narrow sense that we give to the written, and in the broad sense that we give to the graphic, is situated in a vaster space that I have elsewhere named "scriptural" or figural space;

Figure, Image, Icon

— this figural space consists of two closely joined movements: *inscription* that fixes a "written" in a more or less resistant matter, and *ex-cription* (from which we have made *é-criture* [writing]) that permits, in an act of emergence, the forgetting of what was done or written;
— immersion and emergence thus constitute the two sides of a single page, of a single poetry, and of a single poem;
— this extension of the poem and of poetry is in no way a rhetorical figure. It corresponds to that *Meta* function whose constitutive elements I have described: meta-stasis, meta-phor, meta-morphosis.
— for a poetics to be possible as a poetics of the sensible, it is necessary and it suffices that its two moments be verified in it;
— the alpinist who has scaled the K2 knows what it is to inscribe one's steps on the rock and what the emergence is that, at the summit, rewards the effort and forgets the past in a free breathing;
— likewise, the generosity that makes a face come to that which does not have one inscribes an *image* on the *place* that awaits it and forgets itself in the joy that something is that will henceforth have a human name;
— image and icon are the two sides of a single realization: the first related to inscription, the second to emergence;
— the *I*, mysterious and from the Gospel in the expression "I was naked and you clothed me" (or "I was hungry and you gave me food"), gathers the two aspects of the image-inscription and the icon-emergence, as well as the two moments of the poem and of poetry;
— but, on both sides, the *I* of the enigma and the mystery guarantees the continuity of the movement;
— the *I* signifies, when we try—painfully—to explicate it, that our acting and its work come from farther than our poor egos and go much farther: there is a poem and poetry only if the one who inscribes and writes inscribes himself in that here below and that beyond;
— if I call it *enigmatic* it is because the little word that designates it, which we have made into a personal pronoun, poses an enigma to the logician who has much difficulty making a place for it, as much in his syntax as in his semantics. Recent studies have shown this fairly well;
— the enigma consists in this: "I" is an empty word, a bit like, but in a wholly other genre than, the deictics this, here, now;
— the *I* who speaks refers neither to a concept nor to an object, as critical idealism has already pointed out so well;

— nonetheless, the *I* that plays within the image and the icon is not the *I think* of old that accompanies all representations;
— neither is it, in a poetics of the sensible that is attentive to the image and the icon, a mere speaker addressing himself to a listener, even to speak to him of a third person.

What is it then? A voice that overturns our world and our manner of flaunting frenzy and insouciance in it; a voice that the artist gives us to see without reducing it to the figuration that renders it sensible to us. But if it says to us, "I was naked and you clothed me, I was hungry and you gave me food, I was in prison and you visited me, I was thirsty and you gave me drink," how would these calls that some would deem prosaic interest art, which is always presented to us as essentially "uninterested" in the quotidian routine of work and of days?

7. Perhaps this last question poses the true question to which an authentic poetics of the sensible responds or should respond. For it is here, in this culmination of the empty face, where the most profound postulates of what the dogma of the incarnation meant long ago are fulfilled, that the artist finds himself truly at home [*chez lui*] and in the poem that suits him. Certainly the distinctions that helped me think poetics are and remain precious. I have nothing to withdraw from what was said of *being-toward* and *being-in*. Their unity remains unbreakable. Every work of art, whatever it may be, tries to realize them. The powers of the *Meta* function, meta-stasis, meta-phor, metamorphosis, in their respective schematizations in the mask, the angel's wing, the unfoldings of fire, must animate every realization. But that said, and it was necessary to say it again, it is indeed, finally, toward the iconic face that every figuration of the poetic tends in the sensible quotidian routine of our woes and our joys. *Being-toward* marks the progress of this groping search that comes to light through the twists and turns of life that the great frescoes of evolution recounted to us long ago and even yesterday.

The *Meta* function is not restricted to poetry in its narrowest sense. The instability of impatience and exuberance that pushes every being [*être*] toward its most unforeseen turns asks only to ascend and to be metamorphosed in order to spread out, in metamorphosis, over the transversal branches of its turbulence. In all its twists and turns, it is the same passion that is masked and that shakes its wings to throw the branchings of the original fire to its own highest point. All this movement cannot be reduced to the enchantment of its own fervor. It is necessary that, abiding in itself, it does not cease to extend itself and to entwine itself in the contours of a home, of an image, in the serenity of an atmosphere and of a face. The iconic is thus, through its Eastern and Western expressions that murmur the sovereign peace of a Song of Songs, the destiny of being and of the world. One would be wrong to see in it only a new form of the West's optical tradition.

8. In this feast of the sensible, the senses of representation and the senses of intimacy are not dissociated. Each one, in its rank, is irreplaceable and royal. None of them suffices unto itself. And it is their beyond, in the icon of the face, that invites us to transit toward an elsewhere. I cannot forget that it is there, on the fragile stalk of a human and divine face, that the divine word resounds which gushes in return over the shadows of the past and present.

In the horror of the condemned neighborhoods of Calcutta, where I would have sought in vain the face of a man, a woman, or a child, on those paths that "lead nowhere" where distress drives the right to existence into impossibility, I saw arise, from that nothing that signaled to me in the shadows of another Good Friday, a voice that I had not yet heard and that urged me to hear it while forgiving me for being too happy. I will no longer forget the spectacle of abandonment that revealed to me, in a lightning-flash, the task of another poem that would no longer be written in words, even were they finely wrought like the fires of a precious stone or the colors of a writing system. The poet, I was saying to myself, has to disown none of his ancient nobility: raising language to the festivity of an incantation. But the icon that he pursues with his dream is also made of living and wounded flesh. Giving a face to that which never had one or which has lost it, in order that the being of what is might come from what is not; making sure that an intrepid acting frees the anonymous "I" that retains, in its open wounds, the innumerable chain of its torments so that this chain will be broken: this would be, if the word has not grown too old, the poem of a poetry enlarged to the dimensions of a world of the icon.

9. By evoking the iconic stage that should transfigure the sensible, I do not claim to convert anyone to the worship of the image or to the legitimacy of a theology. It is a matter of something wholly other, even if religious belonging has permitted me to see things otherwise. The Eastern icons do not plead for any form of religiosity. They are beautiful enough to merit existence and spare us from any justification. Inspiring myself by another East, I wish for them to exist anew in a less ethereal flesh, until now resigned to the ineluctable. It seems to me that poetry itself, if its most beautiful care is the joy of making a world [*monde*], cannot disregard this extension of the poem that makes it complicit in a birth [*mise au monde*] that is less bound to the scribe's blank page and to the resistances of an anonymous matter. It does not suffice, or it

no longer suffices, to hold forth on the "play of the world" or the gold ring that celebrates the wedding of earth and heaven, of gods and mortals. I fear at times that we are too quickly consoled from tragedy. And if one objects that I mix with poetry preoccupations that do not belong to it, I will answer that this partitioning comes from a theory of genres that one would have supposed long gone. It is not necessary to tease out the etymology of the verb *poiein* to surprise there a transgression of common boundaries and to read in it a broader destiny. "Engendering in beauty," according to the Platonic formula, is neutral and precise enough to let us hear in the "poem" a power of metastasis and metaphor that ensures, beneath differences, the unicity of a vection. Nor do we fall again into an ancient illusion when we link to the human face the very possibility of a world. It is from the same impulsion that the human and the cosmos must exist in the happiness of being, of living, and of thinking.

Must we consequently unite in a single call the poets of inscription and those who operate on the living flesh of the man of sorrows? I leave the question, thus posed, and which has not ceased to obsess me, without a decisive response. I prefer to conclude, if a conclusion is possible, with a memory that gathers a few elements of a poetics that is perhaps too obedient to the spirit of system.

The Ballad of Nadine

In Khaznadar, near Tunis and the Sahel, the orange garden that the nuns cultivate is a paradise for children. It is there that Nadine, scarcely three years old, from an unknown father, found a home whose nooks and crannies she knows. Two very black eyes whose pupils, when I take her in the evening to look at the sky, seem to flame in the night. She loves the stars so much that I must take her for walks to calm her stellar appetite. I hoist her onto my shoulders to offer immensity to her improvised observatory. The little hands wave at once to rejoin that constellation she loves so much: Orion's shield. I do not know if she seeks in it her name or the mirror of her face. It is indeed there that her heart abides. The quivering that at that age is in no way feigned warns me of a complicity that harmonizes her with things above. The upward thrust that obliges me to hold her back from a possible fall transforms her into a pure "being-toward" whose fervor I control poorly. The miniscule index finger then outlines a vertical line that seems to chant, in a song of ascents, the powers of an anonymous metaphor whose metamorphoses, from right to left and from left to right, follow the swaying of the little hands. In the calm of the orange trees, I follow the transformations [*avatars*] of a metastasis that endlessly traces on the world the childish enigma of a sign of the cross. Marvelous child who suggested to me, while changing a word, the poet's exclamation, "Little girl, I loved you as an old man can love only his childhood."[15] I have not seen Nadine again. She did not know how to count the stars but she was three years old. It seemed to me that this play of the world in a child's hand could be the clear symbol of a never-finished poetics that would come back indefinitely toward that first gaze that, one summer evening, had revealed to me the dawn of things. Nadine, my first and last overseas love.

With this ballad of Nadine, I will complete a journey that she invites me to begin again.

Notes

Preface

1. Erwin Straus, *Vom Sinn der Sinne: Ein Beitrag zur Grundlegung der Psychologie*. Translated into English as Erwin Straus, *The Primary World of Senses: A Vindication of Sensory Experience*.
2. Georges Didi-Huberman, *Génie du non-lieu: Air, poussière, empreinte, hantise (Claude Parmiggiani)*, 144, commenting on Straus. [My translation.—Trans.]
3. See Maurice Merleau-Ponty, *The Visible and the Invisible*, 57, note 10.
4. "[I]f the body constantly expresses the modalities of existence […] this is not in the same manner as the stripes signify an officer's rank or as a number designates a house. The sign here does not only indicate its signification; it is inhabited by it; it is, in a way, what it signifies" (Maurice Merleau-Ponty, *Phenomenology of Perception*, 164). [Translation modified.—Trans.]
5. "Or do you not know that your body is a temple of the Holy Spirit within you, whom you have from God? You are not your own, for you were bought with a price" (1 Cor. 6:19-20, English Standard Version).
6. David Abram, *The Spell of the Sensuous: Perception and Language in a More-Than-Human World*.
7. Richard Kearney, *Poetics of Imagining: From Husserl to Lyotard*.
8. Richard Kearney, *Poétique du possible: Phénoménologie herméneutique de la figuration*.
9. One will recall Heidegger's thesis in § 31 of *Being and Time*, where he presents comprehension as one of the three co-originary structures of Dasein's being-in-the-world: "Because of the kind of being which is constituted by the existential of projecting, Da-sein is constantly 'more' than it actually is […]. But it is never more than it factically is because its potentiality of being belongs essentially to its facticity. But, as being-possible, Da-sein is also never less. It is existentially that which it is *not yet* in its potentiality of being" (*Being and Time*, 136). ("*Auf dem Grunde der Seinsart, die durch das Existential des Entwurfs konstituiert wird, ist das Dasein ständig "mehr," als es tatsächlich ist […]. Es ist aber nie mehr, als es faktisch ist, weil zu seiner Faktizität das Seinkönnen wesenhaft gehört. Das Dasein ist aber als Möglichsein auch nie weniger, das heißt das, was es in seinem Seinkönnen noch nicht ist, ist es existenzial*" [*Sein und Zeit*, 145].)
10. Stanislas Breton, *De Rome à Paris: Itinéraire philosophique*.

11 *Le Verbe et la Croix* appeared in English as Stanislas Breton, *The Word and the Cross*. As yet there is no English translation of *Du Principe* or *Être, Monde et Imaginaire*. [—Trans.]
12 *Poetics of the Sensible*, 4.
13 Hans Blumenberg, *Höhlenausgänge*.
14 Breton, *Du Principe*, 12.
15 Ibid., 24.
16 Breton, *Philosophie buissonnière*, 144.
17 Plato, *Sophist*, 224a4-7. [Translation modified to follow the French more closely.—Trans.]
18 *Vouloir-dire* is one of several French words that can be translated as "meaning," and it is composed of the infinitives "to want" and "to say." To preserve its resonances, I employ a more literal translation here and throughout Breton's text. [—Trans.]
19 As the distinction between being and beings is generally clear from context, I have preferred not to capitalize the former; within this particular quotation, however, I make an exception to this rule because capitalization is the most straightforward way to make clear which word indicates the former and which the latter. [—Trans.]
20 Psalm 36:9. [—Trans.]
21 Plato, *Republic*, 509b.
22 Emmanuel Levinas, *Otherwise than Being or Beyond Essence*, 63-4, as well as, more generally, the entirety of chapters 2-3 of the work.
23 Shakespeare, *Hamlet*, Act I, Scene 5. The same motif is evoked at the beginning of Sonnet 107: "*Not mine own fears, nor the prophetic soul / Of the wide world dreaming on things to come, / Can yet the lease of my true love control, / Suppos'd as forfeit to a confin'd doom.*"
24 Aristotle, *Peri psychès* III, 8, 431b21. [Unless otherwise specified, all translations of quotations from Greek texts are my own and are based on Greisch's French.—Trans.]
25 *Faire feu de tout bois*, a French idiom that I have translated literally for lack of a sufficiently exact English equivalent and because Greisch's commentary immediately makes its meaning clear. [—Trans.]
26 Rémi Brague, *Aristote et la question du monde*, 214-15. [My translation.—Trans.]
27 Anaxagoras, DK 59A102; B21B.
28 Aristotle, *De Partibus Animalium* [PA] IV, 10, 687a8-10.
29 Ibid., IV, 10, 687a21.
30 Ibid., IV, 10, 687a4s.
31 Aristotle, *Peri psychès* III, 8, 432a1s.
32 Rémi Brague, *Aristote et la question du monde*, 257. [My translation.—Trans.]
33 Ibid., p. 258, with reference to PA, II, 16, 660a11s; III, 10 673a7s. [My translation.—Trans.]
34 Aristotle, PA, II, 16, 660a12s PA, II, 16, 660a12s.

35 Touch is not linked only to intelligence but to its condition of possibility, to the degree that it is touch that puts us in *contact* with the world: "Without touch, there is no presence to the world" (Rémi Brague, *Aristote et la question du monde*, 259). [My translation.—Trans.]
36 Aristotle, *Peri psychès* II, 9, 421a19-26.
37 *L'écorché vif*, an idiom that figuratively means "the hypersensitive one"; literally the words mean "the one flayed alive." [—Trans.]
38 Friedrich Hölderlin, *Sämtliche Werke*. Band I.2, Stuttgart, F. Beissner, 1951, p. 372. See Martin Heidegger, "*Dichterisch wohnet der Mensch* ...." in *Vorträge und Aufsätze*. Pfullingen, Neske Verlag, 1990, pp. 181-98.
39 *Poetics of the Sensible*, 10.
40 Jean-Pierre Vernant, "Hestia-Hermès. Sur l'expression religieuse de l'espace et du mouvement chez les Grecs," in *Mythe et pensée chez les Grecs: Etudes de psychologie historique*; Jean Greisch, *Hermeneutik und Metaphysik: Eine Problemgeschichte*, 29-49.
41 *Habitation à loyer modéré*, "reduced-rent housing." HLMs are rent-controlled public or private housing and are generally associated with a low quality of life. [—Trans.]
42 Stanislas Breton, "Réflexions sur la fonction méta."
43 Paul Ricœur, "De la métaphysique à la morale."
44 Jean Greisch, *Le cogito herméneutique: L'herméneutique philosophique et l'héritage cartésien*; Jean Greisch, *Transcender: Libres meditations sur la fonction méta*, dedicated to the memory of Stanislas Breton, "Master of living and of thinking."
45 Hans-Georg Gadamer, *Truth and Method*, 341; *Wahrheit und Methode*, G.S. 1, 329, 352.
46 Concerning the semantic field of the English term "experience," see J.M. Hinton, *Experience. An Inquiry into Some Ambiguities*, 13-21. For the use of the term in contemporary philosophy, see *Der Begriff der Erfahrung in der Philosophie des 20. Jahrhunderts*, ed. J. Freudiger, A. Graeser, and K. Petrus.
47 In French the word *expérience* in fact means both "experience" and "experiment." [—Trans.]
48 *Poetics of the Sensible*, 33.
49 Ibid., 34.
50 Jacques Derrida, "White Mythology."
51 Paul Ricœur, *The Rule of Metaphor*.
52 Hans Blumenberg, *Paradigmen zu einer Metaphorologie*; translated into English as *Paradigms for a Metaphorlogy*.
53 *Poetics of the Sensible*, 42.
54 *Nous nous sentons bien ou mal dans notre peau*, "we feel comfortable or uncomfortable with ourselves." I have translated this idiom literally to preserve the word "sense" and the reference to embodiment. [—Trans.]

55 Ibid., 89.
56 Jean Greisch, *Le cogito herméneutique*, 186–8.
57 Rainer Maria Rilke, *Sonnete an Orpheus* in *Gedichte*, II, 1 Leipzig, Insel, 1923, [trans. J. Greisch].
58 On the terms "home" and "at-home," see chapter 2, note 1. [—Trans.]
59 See Emmanuel Levinas, *Totality and Infinity*, 152–8. [*Demeure*, which I translate here as "abode," is the same word Lingis renders as "dwelling" in his translation of *Totality and Infinity*. On the choice of "abode" to translate *demeure*, see the Translator's Introduction.—Trans.]
60 Ibid., 157. [Translation modified.—Trans.]
61 See Georges Didi-Huberman, *L'homme qui marchait dans la couleur*.
62 Georges Didi-Huberman, *Devant l'image: Questions posées aux fins d'une histoire de l'art*.
63 Georges Didi-Huberman, *Ce que nous voyons, ce qui nous regarde*.
64 John 20:8. [—Trans.]
65 *Poetics of the Sensible*, 132.

Introduction

1 Plato, *Parmenides*, trans. Mary Louise Gill and Paul Ryan (Indianapolis: Hackett, 1996), 166c4–7, translation modified to follow the French more closely. [—Trans.]
2 The point in the east at which the horizon and the celestial equator intersect (there is also such a point of intersection in the west). This point is due east everywhere on earth. [—Trans.]
3 La Palice is associated with truisms because the inscription on his gravestone, "*S'il n'était pas mort, il ferait encore envie* [If he were not dead, he would still arouse envy]," could be misread as "*S'il n'était pas mort, il serait encore en vie* [If he were not dead, he would still be alive]." [—Trans.]
4 *L'école buissonnière*, "the school of the bushes" or "bush school," comes from the phrase *faire l'école buissonnière*, which means "to skip school," "to play hooky." [—Trans.]

Chapter 1

1 The term *intérité* [interity] was coined by the French logician, linguist, and philosopher Louis Couturat. Neither identity nor alterity, it can be understood as a sort of in-betweenness. [—Trans.]
2 See John 17:14-18. Unless otherwise noted, all Scriptural quotations are my translations from the French. [—Trans.]

3   *Être-au-monde*, the usual French translation of *In-der-Welt-sein* (*being-in-the-world*), translates literally as "being-at-the-world" or "being-to-the-world." [—Trans.]
4   General nouns, such as "being," "metaphysics," and "history," all take definite articles in French. Note also that in the logical statements that follow, I have retained the definite article in my translation, even when this requires the awkward phrasing "the automobile of Claude," rather than "Claude's automobile," in order to make Breton's point clear. [—Trans.]
5   The "etc." refers to the various forms of the definite article that exist in French. [—Trans.]
6   See Acts 17:28. [—Trans.]
7   This is a reference to John 3:8, which reads in full: "The wind blows where it wishes, and you hear its sound, but you do not know where it comes from or where it goes. So it is with everyone who is born of the Spirit" (English Standard Version [ESV]). [—Trans.]
8   Matthew 6:21, ESV. [—Trans.]
9   *Fondement* can mean "ground," as in "x grounds y" or "x is the ground of y," or "foundation." So that the reference to architecture makes sense, I have here translated it as "foundation"; in chapter 7, however, I translated it as "ground" in order to distinguish it from *fondation*, which also means "foundation." [—Trans.]
10 *Se trouver bien* means "to feel a sense of well-being" or "to be in good health"; *se trouver mal* means "to be in ill health" or "to faint." *Se trouver*, however, literally means "to find oneself," and given the context and the importance of this word in chapter 6, I have chosen a literal translation here. See also chapter 6, note 8. [—Trans.]
11 *Sentir* means "to smell," "to sense," or "to feel" in the sense of feeling something external. *Se sentir*, literally "to sense oneself" or "to feel oneself," means "to feel" in the sense of feeling an internal sensation. One would use *se sentir*, for example, to say "I feel well" or "I feel ill." The middle voice is neither active nor passive: languages that have the middle voice use it to indicate the subject acting on herself or for her own sake. Strictly speaking, French does not have a middle voice, but reflexive pronominal verbs, including *se sentir*, do indicate that the subject is acting on herself. See also chapter 4, note 2. [—Trans.]
12 *Dépayser*, translated here and elsewhere as "disorient," more literally means "to take out of the country." It is usually no longer used in this sense, but the literal and figurative meanings are both relevant here and throughout the text. [—Trans.]
13 *Être* in French, when used as a noun, can refer to being (as opposed to beings) or to an individual being. When Breton employs it in the latter sense, I have placed the French in parentheses to make clear that there it is not a matter of the ontological difference. The one exception to this is that "human being" always translates *être*

humain, and in this case I do not include *être* in parentheses. Note that in cases where *être* does refer to being but this is not clear in English from context alone, I have also placed the French in parenthesis. [—Trans.]

14 See Preface, note 18. [—Trans.]
15 Note that *reposoir* is also an archaic word for *resting place*. [—Trans.]
16 God says this to the prophet Ezekiel in Ezekiel 37:3. [—Trans.]
17 *Querelle de clochers*, literally "quarrel of bell towers" or "quarrel of church towers," a play on words that it is unfortunately impossible to render in English without losing the sense of the phrase. [—Trans.]

Chapter 2

1 *Chez soi* is a prepositional phrase meaning "at home," "at one's home," or "at one's place." As a noun it would generally be translated as "home," but to emphasize its prepositional character I have translated it as "at-home." When *chez soi* appears as a prepositional phrase, I have rendered it as "at home." *Maison* means both "house" and "home," and with a few exceptions, I have translated it as "home" to avoid giving the incorrect impression that *maison* and *chez soi* correspond to the house/home distinction. This distinction is in fact not easily translatable into French. [—Trans.]
2 Paraphrased from Proclus, *A Commentary on the First Book of Euclid's Elements*, 16.8–13.
3 Martin Heidegger, "Letter on Humanism," in *Pathmarks*, 252.
4 The common herd; the common people; the ignorant. [—Trans.]
5 A repoussoir is an object in the left or right foreground of a painting that guides the viewer's eye into the painting and that gives an enhanced sense of depth. [—Trans.]
6 See chapter 1, note 7. [—Trans.]
7 The phrase is from G.W.F. Hegel, *Phenomenology of Spirit*, 96. [—Trans.]
8 "Transformism" is one term that was used, pre-Darwin, to refer to the idea that species had evolved from other species. [—Trans.]
9 *Vouloir dire*, as a verb, means "to mean," but it literally means "to want to say." I have translated it literally here in order to more fully bring out its resonances. [—Trans.]
10 The word *infant* derives from the Latin *infans*, which literally means "without speech." [—Trans.]
11 New American Standard Bible (NASB), translation considerably modified to follow the French more closely. [—Trans.]
12 Literally "with-breathing," in French [*conspiration*] as in English. [—Trans.]
13 Song of Songs 4:14. My translation. [—Trans.]

14 A part of the olfactory system, located in the brain, that is underdeveloped in humans as compared to animals and hence "archaic" in that it diminished significantly over the course of human evolution. [—Trans.]
15 See Genesis 1:10, 12, 18, 21, and 25. [—Trans.]

Chapter 3

1 *Prosopon* is a Greek word that originally meant "face" or "mask" and that came to refer to the manifestation of the person. In Christian theology it refers to the aspect of God turned toward the world. [—Trans.]
2 See Chapter 2, note 10. [—Trans.]
3 Plato, *Parmenides*, trans. Mary Louise Gill and Paul Ryan (Indianapolis: Hackett, 1996), 166c4–7. Translation modified. [—Trans.]
4 As a noun the French *personne* means "person," and as an indefinite pronoun it means "nobody," the name Odysseus gave to the Cyclops in Homer's *Odyssey*, a story to which Breton here alludes. As English has no equivalent word, I have retained the French one, except when context requires one or the other. In the latter cases, within this section, I have placed the French word in parentheses. [—Trans.]
5 At the Battle of Waterloo, the general Pierre Cambronne allegedly answered the British demand that he surrender with a single defiant word: "*Merde!*" Merde [shit] is thus "Cambronne's word." Cambronne himself denied having said it, but Victor Hugo popularized the story in his account of the battle in *Les Misérables*. [—Trans.]
6 The phrase "mouth of shadow" comes from the title of a poem by Victor Hugo, "Ce que dit la bouche d'ombre" ["What the Mouth of Shadow Says"], *Les Contemplations*, in *Œuvres poétiques*, vol. 2, 801–22, which considers the nature of the universe, man, and God. [—Trans.]
7 Latin for "nothing further beyond." [—Trans.]
8 *The Cloud of Unknowing* is an important English mystical text of the fourteenth century. [—Trans.]

Chapter 4

1 *Esprits non frappeurs*, or "spirits who are not poltergeists." *Esprit frappeur* is the French for "poltergeist." [—Trans.]
2 For an explanation of this verb and of the middle voice, see chapter 1, note 11. Strictly speaking, *se sentir* is transitive, with *se* as the object, but it cannot take an object other than this pronoun that is in fact part of the verb and that refers to the subject. Note, however, that Breton goes on to say that *se sentir* should not be

understood as a reflexive verb, although it is classified as such, and that it does not in fact point to the subject. Unfortunately no English translation can properly indicate that the pronoun is an integral part of the verb. [—Trans.]

3   On the verb *se tenir*, see chapter 7, note 2. Given its importance in chapters 7 and 8, I have included the French within brackets when it has not made sense to employ the more literal rendering "to hold oneself." [—Trans.]

4   A *hapax*, or *hapax legomenon*, is a word that occurs only once in a text, in an author's works, or in all written records of a given language. [—Trans.]

5   Plato, *Parmenides*, 166c4-7, translation modified. [—Trans.]

6   Given the reference to "listening," note that *entendement*, "understanding," is derived from the verb *entendre*, "to hear." [—Trans.]

7   This is the English translation of the French translation of Ludwig Wittgenstein's statement, "The world is everything that is the case," in *Tractatus Logico-Philosophicus*, 5. [—Trans.]

8   See Matthew 28:6, Mark 16:6, or Luke 24:6. [—Trans.]

9   ESV. [—Trans.]

Chapter 5

1   Literally, "carbonic snow." [—Trans.]

2   *Mont cinère*. *Mont-cinère* is the title of a novel by the Catholic author Julien Green in which fire, or the lack of it, plays a crucial role. [—Trans.]

3   *De par soi*, literally "of by itself." The phrase thus includes two prepositions. [—Trans.]

4   *Buissonner*, derived from *buisson* (bush). This word can mean "to go through bushy terrain," particularly with reference to hunting; "to set out at random"; or "to skip school." [—Trans.]

5   The phrase is a quotation from Pierre Duhem, who, paraphrasing Blaise Pascal, applied this description to nature in his work *The Aim and Structure of Physical Theory*, 23. [—Trans.]

6   See chapter 1, note 16. [—Trans.]

Chapter 6

1   The reference is to the plant *Impatiens noli-tangere*, or "touch-me-not balsam." [—Trans.]

2   *Accordance* ("accord" or "accordance"; here translated as "accordance") is an old French word with the same meaning as the more modern *accord* (here translated

as "accord"); the *-ance* ending generally indicates the result of an action, and it is perhaps for this reason that Breton uses the word here. [—Trans.]

3   On this point see Luce Giard's admirable study, intended for the use of contemporary philosophers, *Habiter, cuisiner: L'Invention du quotidien* [*Inhabiting, Cooking: The Invention of the Everyday*], vol. 2.

4   The reference is to Aristotle, *Meteorology*, 388a2-3. [—Trans.]

5   See Preface, note 18. [—Trans.]

6   The ordinary meaning of the German *Gelassenheit* is "calm," "serenity," or "composure." Meister Eckhart used it to mean something like "letting go" or "abandonment"; Heidegger then took up the term, and in a Heideggerian context it is often translated as "releasement." [—Trans.]

7   *Se trouver* literally means "to find oneself" and can sometimes be translated this way; it also means "to be located" or "to be." Here and in the next sentence I have rendered *se trouver* as "finding oneself, being located" in order to preserve as wide a range of meanings as possible. On the middle voice, see chapter 1, note 11. [—Trans.]

8   *Se trouver, c'est toujours se trouver bien ou se trouver mal. Se trouver bien* means "to feel a sense of well-being" or "to be in good health"; *se trouver mal* means "to be in ill health" or "to faint." [—Trans.]

9   Louis Veuillot, who published *Le Parfum de Rome* in 1851 and *Les Odeurs de Paris* in 1866. [—Trans.]

10 Breton here alludes to a famous line from Marcel Carné's film *Hôtel du nord*, spoken by Arletty (the stage name of Léonie Bathiat), who plays the character Madame Raymonde. The line from the film is "*Atmosphère! Atmosphère! Est-ce que j'ai une gueule d'atmosphère?* [Atmosphere! Atmosphere! Do I look like some kind of atmosphere?]" See also Greisch's Preface, xxi. [—Trans.]

Chapter 7

1   Sarcellitis, named for the *banlieue* Sarcelles, refers to a malaise supposedly caused by impersonal urban life in large, concrete apartment buildings. It was much discussed in the 1960s. *Sarcelle* is the French word for "teal," a type of duck. There is no exact English equivalent to *banlieue*; the word refers to roughly the area that would in English be called "the suburbs," but "suburb" fails to capture the connotations of the French term, as the *banlieues* are often associated with crime and poverty. [—Trans.]

2   Depending on context, the reflexive verb *se tenir* can have various meanings, including "to stand," "to stay," and "to remain." Breton insists on it enough in the final two chapters that it is useful to have a single translation that suits the contexts

in which he uses it. I have therefore chosen, in most cases, the comparatively literal rendering "to hold oneself." This translation also has the advantage of preserving the reflexivity as much as is possible in English. When this rendering has sounded too strange and I have used a different one, I have placed *se tenir* in brackets. [—Trans.]

3   In French, *là*, meaning "there," is pronounced the same way as *la*, meaning the sixth note of a solfeggio scale. [—Trans.]

4   The phrase "calm of the gods [*calme des dieux*]" is from the first verse of Paul Valéry's poem "Le cimetière marin," in *Charmes*, in *Œuvres*, vol. 1, 147–51. The poem concludes by rejoicing in the disruption of this calm. For an English translation, see "The Graveyard by the Sea," in *Charms and Other Pieces*, 133–41. [—Trans.]

5   "Tells" is here to be understood in the sense of telling rosary beads. [—Trans.]

6   This phrase comes from Paul Valéry, *Idée Fixe*, 31. [—Trans.]

7   *La Cathédrale engloutie* [*The Sunken Cathedral*] is a piano prelude by Claude Debussy. [—Trans.]

8   "Ispahan" is a type of rose named for the city of Isfahan. [—Trans.]

9   The imperfect, in French, is the past tense used to express continuous or habitual past action as well as past actions, states of being, or conditions with unspecified ending points. [—Trans.]

Chapter 8

1   See chapter 4, note 4. [—Trans.]

2   The French here is *natures mortes*, "still lifes." Here and throughout I employ the literal translation "dead natures," as Breton insists so much on the term "dead" that "still lifes" would be unintelligible in context. [—Trans.]

3   See Mark 5:41. [—Trans.]

4   French has both singular and plural forms of the definite article, which must agree with the noun it modifies. *Le* is the masculine singular form of "the"; *autres*, plural, means "others." *Le autres* is thus as clearly wrong in French as "an others" is in English. I have retained the French in the text, rather than writing "an others," because of the importance of the definite article. [—Trans.]

5   The French expression *sage comme une image*, literally "as good (or well-behaved) as an image," corresponds roughly to our expression "as good as gold." Note that *sage* can also mean "wise," hence the reference, two sentences later, to *sagesse* (wisdom). [—Trans.]

6   Luke 4:30. [—Trans.]

7   The phrase is from Louis Althusser, "Lenin and Philosophy," in *Lenin and Philosophy and Other Essays*, trans. Ben Brewster (New York: Monthly Review Press, 2001), 38, translation modified. [—Trans.]

8   Cupidity, or selfish love. [—Trans.]
9   See chapter 1, footnote 2. [—Trans.]
10 On the imperfect, see chapter 7, note 9. The imperfects in the following sentences are translated as "he was going away," "he was being," and "he was going," a construction that in English serves to suggest a continuous action with no reference to its completion. The phrase "assonant imperfects" later in this paragraph refers to the fact that any verb, conjugated in a certain person in the imperfect, will have the same final vowel sound as any other verb conjugated in that person in the imperfect. [—Trans.]
11 From "Ein Gleiches" ["Wanderer's Nightsong II"]. See Johann Wolfgang von Goethe, "Ein Gleiches," in *Goethes Werke*, vol. 1, 142. For an English translation, see "Another Night Song," in *Johann Wolfgang von Goethe: Selected Poems*, 59. [—Trans.]
12 The translation of both these verses is from the ESV. [—Trans.]
13 Matthew 28-29. ESV. [—Trans.]
14 The preposition *à* often corresponds to *at* or *to*. Breton has this latter sense in mind here. [—Trans.]
15 The reference is to a line from Paul Éluard's poem "Dominique aujourd'hui présente" ["Dominique present today"], in *Le phénix*, in *Œuvres*, vol. 2, 422–4. The original line is "Petite fille je t'aimais comme un garçon / Ne peut aimer que son enfance" (Ibid., 423). ["Little girl, I loved you as a boy / Can love only his childhood."] [—Trans.]

Bibliography

Abram, David. *The Spell of the Sensuous: Perception and Language in a More-Than-Human World*. New York: Random House, 1997.
Blumenberg, Hans. *Paradigmen zu einer Metaphorologie*. Bonn: Suhrkamp, 1960. [*Paradigms for a Metaphorlogy*. Translated by Robert Savage. Ithaca: Cornell University Press, 2010].
Blumenberg, Hans. *Höhlenausgänge*. Frankfurt: Suhrkamp, 1979.
Brague, Rémi. *Aristote et la question du monde*. Paris: Éditions du Cerf, 2009.
Breton, Stanislas. *Du Principe*. Paris: Éditions du Cerf, 1971.
Breton, Stanislas. "Réflexions sur la fonction méta." *Phi zéro: Revue d'études philosophiques de la Faculté de philosophie de l'Université de Montréal* 9, no. 3 (1981). Reprinted in *Dialogue* 21 (1982), 5–56.
Breton, Stanislas. *Philosophie buissonnière*. Grenoble, Jérôme Millon, 1989.
Breton, Stanislas. *De Rome à Paris: Itinéraire philosophique*. Paris: Desclée de Brouwer, 1992.
Breton, Stanislas. *The Word and the Cross*. Translated by Jacquelyn Porter. New York: Fordham University Press, 2002.
Derrida, Jacques. "White Mythology." In *Margins of Philosophy*, translated by Alan Bass. Chicago: University of Chicago Press, 1982.
Der Begriff der Erfahrung in der Philosophie des 20. Jahrhunderts. Edited by J. Freudiger, A. Graeser, and K. Petrus. München: Beck, 1996.
Didi-Huberman, Georges. *Devant l'image: Questions posées aux fins d'une histoire de l'art*. Paris: Ed. Minuit, 1990.
Didi-Huberman, Georges. *Génie du non-lieu: Air, poussière, empreinte, hantise (Claude Parmiggiani*. Paris: Ed. Minuit, 2001.
Didi-Huberman, Georges. *L'homme qui marchait dans la couleur*. Paris: Editions Minuit, 2001.
Didi-Huberman, Georges. *Ce que nous voyons, ce qui nous regarde*. Paris: Ed. Minuit, 1992.
Duhem, Pierre. *The Aim and Structure of Physical Theory*. Translated by Philip P. Wiener. Princeton: Princeton University Press, 1991.
Éluard, Paul. "Le phénix." In *Œuvres*, vol. 2, edited by Marcelle Dumas and Lucien Scheler. Paris: Pléiade, 1968.
Gadamer, Hans-Georg. *Wahrheit und Methode*, G.S. 1. Tübingen: Mohr Siebeck, 1990.
Gadamer, Hans-Georg. *Truth and Method*. 2nd ed. rev. Translated by Joel Weinsheimer and Donald G. Marshall. New York: Continuum, 2004.

Giard, Luce. *Habiter, cuisiner: L'Invention du quotidien*, vol. 2. Paris: U.G.E., collection 10-18, 1980.
Goethe, Johann Wolfgang von. *Goethes Werke*, vol. 1, Edited by Erich Trunz. Hamburg: Christian Wegner Verlag, 1949.
Goethe, Johann Wolfgang von. *Johann Wolfgang von Goethe: Selected Poems*. Edited by Christopher Middleton. Boston: Insel Publishers, 1983.
Greisch, Jean. *Hermeneutik und Metaphysik: Eine Problemgeschichte*. München: W. Fink, 1993.
Greisch, Jean. *Le cogito herméneutique: L'herméneutique philosophique et l'héritage cartésien*. Paris: Vrin, 2000.
Greisch, Jean. "Das Spiel der Transzendenz: 'Trans-Aszendenz', 'Trans-Deszendenz', 'Trans-Passibilität', 'Trans-Possibilität.'" In *Hermeneutik der Transzendenz*, edited by Ingolf U. Dalferth, Pierre Bühler, and Andreas Hunziker. Tübingen: Mohr-Siebeck, 2015.
Hegel, G.W.F. *Phenomenology of Spirit*. Translated by A.V. Miller. New York: Oxford University Press, 1977.
Heidegger, Martin. "*Dichterisch wohnet der Mensch* ...." In *Vorträge und Aufsätze* II. Pfullingen: Neske, 1967.
Heidegger, Martin. *Sein und Zeit*. 7th ed. Tübingen: Max Niemeyer Verlag, 1993.
Heidegger, Martin. *Being and Time*. Translated by Joan Stambaugh. New York: SUNY Press, 1996.
Heidegger, Martin. "Letter on Humanism." Translated by Frank A. Capuzzi. In *Pathmarks*, edited by William McNeill, 239-76. Cambridge: Cambridge University Press, 1998.
Hinton, J.M. *Experience. An Inquiry into Some Ambiguities*. Oxford: Clarendon Press, 1973.
Hugo, Victor. "Les Contemplations." In *Œuvres poétiques*, vol. 2, edited by Pierre Albouy. Paris: Pléiade, 1967.
Kearney, Richard. *Poétique du possible: Phénoménologie herméneutique de la figuration*. Paris: Beauchêne, 1984.
Kearney, Richard. *Poetics of Imagining: From Husserl to Lyotard*. Hammersmith: HarperCollins, 1991.
Levinas, Emmanuel. *Totality and Infinity*. Translated by Alphonso Lingis. Pittsburgh: Duquesne University Press, 1969.
Levinas, Emmanuel. *Otherwise than Being or Beyond Essence*. Translated by Alphonso Lingis. Pittsburgh: Duquesne University Press, 1998.
Merleau-Ponty, Maurice. *The Visible and the Invisible*. Edited by Claude Lefort. Translated by Alphonso Lingis. Evanston: Northwestern University Press, 1968.
Merleau-Ponty, Maurice. *Phenomenology of Perception*. Translated by Donald A. Landes. New York: Routledge, 2012.
Plato. *Parmenides*. Translated by Mary Louise Gill and Paul Ryan. Indianapolis: Hackett, 1996.

Plato, "Sophist." In *Theaetetus and Sophist*, translated by Christopher Rowe. Cambridge: Cambridge University Press, 2015.

Ricœur, Paul. *The Rule of Metaphor*. Translated by Robert Czerny with Kathleen McLaughlin and John Costell, S.J. New York: Routledge, 2003.

Ricœur, Paul. "De la métaphysique à la morale." In *Revue de Métaphysique et de Morale* 98, no. 4 (October-December 1993). Reprinted in *Réflexion faite*, 85–115. Paris: Esprit, 1995.

Rilke, Rainer Maria. *Die Sonnete an Orpheus*. Frankfurt: Surkampf, 1955.

Straus, Erwin. *Vom Sinn der Sinne: Ein Beitrag zur Grundlegung der Psychologie*. Berlin: Springer, 1935.

Straus, Erwin. *The Primary World of Senses: A Vindication of Sensory Experience*. Translated by Jacob Needleman. New York: Free Press of Glencoe, 1963.

Valéry, Paul. "Charmes." In *Œuvres*, vol. 1, edited by Jean Hytier. Paris: Pléiade, 1957.

Valéry, Paul. *Idée Fixe*. Translated by David Paul. Princeton: Princeton University Press, 1971.

Valéry, Paul. *Charms and Other Pieces*. Translated by Peter Dale. London: Anvil Press Poetry, 2007.

Vernant, Jean-Pierre. "Hestia-Hermès. Sur l'expression religieuse de l'espace et du mouvement chez les Grecs." In *Mythe et pensée chez les Grecs: Etudes de psychologie historique*. Paris: Maspéro, 1965.

Wittgenstein, Ludwig. *Tractatus Logico-Philosophicus*. Translated by D.F. Pears and B.F. McGuinness. New York: Routledge Classics, 2001.

Index

abiding 8–10, 15, 20–22, 30, 44, 50, 81, 93–95, 97, 100–1, 105, 107–8, 110, 114, 132
abode 7–9, 18, 21, 24, 30, 50, 53, 55, 70, 84–85, 90, 92, 97–105, 108, 112, 122–23, 126
alterity 26, 32, 68, 114, 121, 124
angel 1, 4, 42, 53–55, 57, 59, 63, 68–70, 72–73, 75, 94, 132
at-home 26, 101, 105, 108

being 1, 3–8, 10, 15–18, 20–27, 29–30, 32–33, 40, 44, 47–50, 54, 57–58, 60, 62–69, 71–72, 76, 81–82, 84, 89–91, 95–96, 98–102, 104–5, 108, 110–15, 117–18, 120, 122–24, 132–34
being-in 4, 6–9, 11, 14–15, 19, 22–24, 26, 40, 82, 84, 87–89, 92–93, 95–96, 99–100, 108, 114, 132
being-there 21, 25, 67
being-toward 6–8, 10–11, 14–16, 19–20, 22–24, 26, 28–29, 31–32, 40, 42, 72, 75–76, 80–82, 84, 99, 107, 117, 132, 134
body 18, 38, 40, 43, 54–57, 59, 61, 71–73, 89, 91–92, 97, 105, 120, 122–24, 130
burning bush 78, 81–83, 102

Cézanne, Paul 44
Chaldean Oracles 78, 82
Christ 51, 66, 72, 89 (*see also* Jesus)
Christian 3, 20, 47, 49, 56, 66–67, 87–88, 94, 103, 105, 120–21, 123, 125
Christianity 30, 50, 66
circumincession 16, 21
color 21, 24, 31, 35, 39–40, 61, 70, 84–85, 87, 92, 94–97, 100, 111, 133
cosmological 12–13

diversity 3–4, 9, 21, 42, 54, 63, 70, 84, 101, 110, 114–15

East 1, 28, 44, 55–56, 58, 67, 72, 76, 87, 91–92, 94, 103, 107, 110, 119–21, 123–24, 126, 133
Eckhart, Meister 20, 81, 124
essence 13, 18–19, 27, 30, 32, 35, 38–39, 41, 44–45, 48–49, 56, 58–59, 81, 91–92, 94, 96–97, 112–13, 115–16, 122–24, 129
Eucharist 88–90
exotropism 11, 13

fable 78
flowers of fire 78, 82
Francis of Assisi 40, 125
freedom 17–18, 20, 24, 26–27, 29, 31, 47–48, 50–51, 55–56, 59, 65, 78, 91, 95, 98, 108–09, 111, 118, 121, 128

God 17, 20–21, 41, 47, 50, 65–67, 73, 88, 105, 126, 128–30
Goethe, Johann Wolfgang von 124
Gospel 4, 8, 30, 78, 83, 87–88, 112, 124–25, 130–31

hapax 61, 67, 110
henological 113–14
henology 62
heterological 115
Holy Spirit 9, 30

iconoclasm 127, 129
idealism 7, 18, 43, 131
idolatry 117, 128
imaginary 14, 32, 58, 63, 80–81, 115, 118, 127
immanence 79, 81
in-itself 81, 108
inhabiting 6–8, 10, 13–14, 19, 22–23, 50, 90, 97–98, 108, 117, 130

Jacob's ladder 21, 57, 59–60, 63, 70, 73
Jesus 66, 87 (*see also* Christ)

Index

knowledge 1, 5, 7, 12, 14, 16, 19–20, 24, 31, 34, 59, 61, 77, 79, 98, 100, 103, 109, 114, 117, 128
Kyoto 44, 119–120, 124

logos 3, 37, 47

mask 42–43, 46–51, 108, 132
meta function 25, 33–34, 37–38, 40–42, 57, 84, 107, 131–32
metaphor 9, 12–13, 25–29, 31, 38–39, 53–55, 57, 59, 68–69, 71–73, 75, 134
metaphoral law 35–37
metamorphosis 31–33, 37–39, 41, 78, 80, 82, 84, 132
metaphysical 57, 82, 98

nothing 1, 8, 16, 27–28, 33, 39, 44, 46–48, 62–63, 66, 70, 76–79, 92–93, 104, 108, 118–19, 124, 129, 133

ontological 4, 12–13, 32, 58, 65–66, 69, 71, 91, 99, 115
ontology 48, 62, 81, 107, 127
origin 9, 16–21, 24, 29, 43, 45, 50, 56, 60, 62, 65–66, 72, 76, 79, 81, 83, 98, 102, 105, 110, 123, 127
Our Lady 21 (*see also* Virgin Mother)

perception 5, 11, 14–15, 61, 89, 110, 121
perspective 7, 67, 69, 76
Plato 1, 46, 62, 76, 114
Platonic 3, 20, 22, 34, 62, 71, 81, 93, 134
Platonism 30, 66
Plotinian 115
Plotinus 62
position 31–32, 54, 58, 60, 65–66, 69, 79, 94, 112, 122

prepositional 6–7, 10, 16–17, 25, 29, 81, 107
propositional 19, 33

Rabelais, François 33
reflection 9, 32, 43, 47, 55, 71, 82, 89, 94, 98, 115, 118–19, 122, 124, 126–27
religion 9, 10, 13, 18–22, 24, 30, 79, 119, 123, 125, 130
religious 8–9, 19, 21–22, 55, 57, 70, 76, 88, 100, 107, 109, 116–17, 119, 133
Rodin, Auguste 55–56, 122

Sabbath 94, 107
Saint-Sulpice 113
self 9, 100–01, 108, 123
singularity 5, 34, 37, 63–64, 83, 101–02
Song of Songs 38–39, 70, 133
synthesis 46, 54, 59, 62, 96

touch 13–14, 58, 87, 95–96, 110, 121
transcendence 29, 49, 88, 108

uchronia 118
unity 15–17, 21–22, 24, 30, 35, 39, 42, 50, 59, 75, 82, 96, 105, 114–15, 117, 122–23, 128, 132
utopia 55, 118

Van Gogh, Vincent 35, 84
Virgin Mother 21 (*see also* Our Lady)

West 14, 55, 76, 78, 87, 91, 101, 107, 121, 124–26, 133
write 1, 26–29, 64, 131
writing 19, 25–29, 40, 44–45, 93, 122, 130–31, 133

Zen Buddhism 44, 124

Made in United States
North Haven, CT
19 August 2025